T0250691

Lecture Notes in Artificial Intelligence 766

Subseries of Lecture Notes in Computer Science
Edited by J. G. Carbonell and J. Siekmann

Lecture Notes in Computer Science
Edited by G. Goos and J. Hartmanis

Philip R. Van Loocke

The Dynamics
of Concepts

A Connectionist Model

Springer-Verlag

Berlin Heidelberg New York
London Paris Tokyo
Hong Kong Barcelona
Budapest

Series Editors

Jaime G. Carbonell
School of Computer Science, Carnegie Mellon University
Schenley Park, Pittsburgh, PA 15213-3890, USA

Jörg Siekmann
University of Saarland
German Research Center for Artificial Intelligence (DFKI)
Stuhlsatzenhausweg 3, D-66123 Saarbrücken, Germany

Author

Philip R. Van Loocke
Lab for Applied Epistemology, University of Ghent
Blandijnberg 2, B-9000 Ghent, Belgium

CR Subject Classification (1991): I.2.4, I.2.6, I.2.11, K.3

ISBN 3-540-57647-9 Springer-Verlag Berlin Heidelberg New York
ISBN 0-387-57647-9 Springer-Verlag New York Berlin Heidelberg

© Springer-Verlag Berlin Heidelberg 1994
Printed in Germany

Typesetting: Camera ready by author
45/3140-543210 - Printed on acid-free paper

PREFACE

This book offers a model for concepts and their dynamics. Since one of our basic assumptions is that concepts are composed by components, we start with some specifications about the nature of these components. In our model, they are represented by large binary patterns; the psychological meaning of these patterns is governed by the interaction between the conceptual modules and other functional modules. The components of a concept do not define the concept in terms of necessary and sufficient conditions. Although this view has been dominant for quite some time, it has been abandoned during the last two decades. Indeed, concepts are sometimes quite flexible, and their membership function usually is not discrete but has different gradations instead.

Connectionist models repeatedly have been put forward to describe these properties of concepts. Especially recurrent networks have an interesting descriptive power in this respect, because of the fact that they include the notion "attractor". Some inputs are attracted faster than others by an attractor, and convergence times can be interpreted as decision latencies. Since decision latencies are central variables in the experimental psychology of conceptual organization, a direct comparison between relative decision latencies from both sources is fairly relevant. In the present book, a recurrent connectionist model is developed that adds some substantial points to other connectionist models. We argue that psychological evidence strongly suggests that the components of a non-familiar concept interact multiplicatively, whereas additive interactions become important as the concept becomes familiar. This fact determines the form of the learning rule of our model. In this way, we obtain correct relative decision latencies as concerns, for instance, properties of prototypes, typicalities, and contextual influences on typicalities.

The learning rule that is proposed is extracted from psychological experiments that concern inner-conceptual organization. However, when it is embedded in our model, it allows to predict a number of central features of inter-conceptual processes. A prominent property in this respect is that, when a context becomes more familiar, then the associations between the concepts of this context spontaneously evolve from loose associations to a more taxonomic organization. A significant part of our simulations illustrates this process. The dynamical properties of our model follow in part from the fact that concepts are represented, just like their components, by large binary patterns. These patterns do not belong to a vector space; rather, they are "vote mixtures". In order to enhance the readability of the text, we give the mathematical details concerning these entities in appendix I.

I am glad that this preface gives me the occasion to express some words of thank. The software for the simulations in this book was developed in BIKIT (in special by F. De Brabander). The work that is described in this book has been carried out at the lab for Applied Epistemology (University of Ghent), and has been supported by the Belgian Fund for Scientific Research. Although comments by numerous colleagues were vital for the final formulation of this text, I would like to mention in special Prof. Vandamme (BIKIT/Lab for Applied Epistemology) and dr. Dalenoort (Chairman of the European Society for the Study of Cognitive Systems). Most of all, I would like to thank Cathérine for her continuous support.

THE DYNAMICS OF CONCEPTS
A CONNECTIONIST MODEL

TABLE OF CONTENTS

I. INTRODUCTION

1 The dynamics of concepts

Concepts have a number of profoundly documented properties. The present book gives an exact model that shows how some of these properties are a natural consequence of other ones and how these properties are related to one another. The model belongs to the connectionist family. More specifically, we construct a recurrent attractor model, but with dynamical capacities which are richer than the ones provided by most other connectionist models. This is necessary, since an adequate description of the dynamics of concepts requires that, for instance, the following six properties have to be described:

i. Concepts are content addressable. This means that a partial activation of a concept may lead to its retrieval. For instance, a concept may be activated partially when one or more cues are provided. Also, a concept can be retrieved when an input contains noise or when it contains irrelevant characteristics. These points can be described in a straightforward way if one makes use of a model in which concepts are represented as attractors.

ii. Concepts have components. When a component of a concept is active, it may act as a cue for the concept. When two concepts share some components, they may show a tendency to follow each other in an associative search process. The components that are manifest in a concept may vary as the context varies. For instance, in the context of a store, "dark rind" and "moist substance" may be prominent components of "potato". In the context of a restaurant, components like "hot" and "floury" may be active. The components of a concept do not form necessary and sufficient conditions that must be fulfilled by an input in order to retrieve the concept. This follows from point i: if a concept is an attractor, it may be retrieved from a variety of inputs.

iii. The components of a concept interact with each other. As we will see, there are two models that make different predictions concerning these interactions. According to the prototype model, the interactions are additive: the chance that a concept is retrieved is proportional to the sum of the activations of its components. The exemplar model predicts multiplicative interactions: the chance that a concept becomes active is proportional to the product of the activations of its components. Actually, it appeared that these models correspond to different stages of familiarity. The exemplar model describes new and unfamiliar concepts; the prototype model describes concepts that belong to familiar contexts.

iv. Concept membership is not an all or nothing issue: an item may be a central or a less central member of a concept. The extent to which an item is typical can be measured with help of decision latencies: the more typical an item is for its category, the more quickly it is classified as one of its members. Concepts may have one or more prototypes, around which less typical instances are centered. Typicalities are context dependent. For instance, in the context created by the sentence: "The bird sits on the branch", "robin" is a more typical instance of "bird" than "chicken". In the context created by "The bird is roasted on the grill", the relative typicalities are reversed. Some contexts have a weak influence on typicality distributions, whereas others may have a more profound influence.

v. Taxonomies of concepts contain a basic level. This is not the most concrete, nor the most abstract, but an intermediate level. Most communication is situated on the basic level of abstraction. The basic level has a number of convergent empirical properties. For instance, it is the level of concepts that is accessed most frequently in free naming conditions. Objects are classified most quickly as members of basic level concepts. The basic level is the highest level of abstraction at which it is still possible to associate a form with a concept. Also, it is the highest level of abstraction at which a substantial number of motor-movements can be associated with concepts. The number of attributes that can be attributed to a subordinate concept is slightly higher than the number of attributes that can be associated with a basic level concept, but the number of properties that correspond to a subordinate concept is significantly lower than the number of properties of a basic level concept.

vi. The organization of concepts evolves. Non-familiar concepts are organized in a complexive way: they show loose and unstructured mutual associations. As a subject becomes more familiar with a domain, the associations between concepts show a tendency to become organized taxonomically: clusters and subclusters of concepts may emerge. This theme has been addressed frequently in ontogenetic psychology.

In the chapters that follow, we consider these constraints with more detail, and we will construct an exact model that describes these properties. The activations of concepts and their components are important variables of this model. However, we do not confine ourselves to such "macroscopic" variables. If we would try to formulate a model in terms of these variables only, for instance if we would try to write down a set of differential equations that describes properties i-vi, we would encounter rather tough problems. For small knowledge bases and for particular interactions between the components of concepts, such equations can readily be found. However, in case of a larger knowledge base with concepts of different degrees of familiarity, a search for adequate differential equations would require a hopelessly complex task of fine-tuning numerous parameters that couple the terms of the differential equations (Van Loocke 1991a,1993). The task becomes much easier if a number of supplementary variables are introduced. These variables have a "microscopic" interpretation in terms of the activations of formal neural units and in terms of connections between these units.

2 The components of concepts

We will differentiate between different levels at which the components of concepts can be studied.

a. At the lowest level, one may study "single modality microfeatures". This type of microfeature is analyzed in a quite early stage of pre-processing. It refers to local properties. For example, "line-segment", "angle" and "curve" are single modality microfeatures.

b. At the next level, we encounter "single modality features". They are detected at a later stage in pre-processing and they may involve less local properties. Their detection may require that different microfeatures and "emergent features" are integrated. A single modality feature may also refer to a simple motion of an external object. We use the term "single modality feature" in a quite broad way: it may refer to particular patterns of a modalities which are not directly concerned with the analysis of inputs. For instance, it may refer to a kinesthetic movement by the subject, or to an emotion.

c. At the third level, we consider "attentively integrated feature packages". Such packages integrate different single modality features. When an input is processed, this integration requires an intervention of mechanisms of attention. For each modality, at most one single modality feature participates in a particular package.

An integrated feature package may correspond to a "skeleton" or a main part of an object or a scene: it may express on a relatively coarse level a global spatial configuration. Further, an integrated feature package may correspond to an "image schema" that has been recognized in a scene or in an object. An image schema can express several kinds of relations that may be detected only after substantial abstraction; it gives structure to mental images.

d. At the next level, different feature packages may be integrated into a "multi-component concept". If a multi-component concept represents an object or a scene, it may contain feature packages that refer to a skeleton or a main part of the object or of the scene. It may also include feature packages that correspond to the skeletons of its parts.

e. Finally, different multi-component concepts may be integrated by a verbal label. Such a set of multi-component concepts is called a "complex".

In the next two chapters, we will be more specific about these aspects of concepts. The main part of this monograph will concern the integration of feature packages in multi-component concepts. It is mainly at this level that the phenomena mentioned in the previous paragraph can be described. Throughout this monograph, we will use the following abbreviations:

smf: single modality microfeature
sf: single modality feature
P: attentively integrated feature package
M: multi-component concept
C: complex

3 Concepts

We can differentiate between different types of concepts. A concept corresponds to a multi-component concept *M* or to a complex *C*.

If a concept is represented by an *M*, two possibilities apply. First, the concept may be a category of which this *M* is the only instance. Second, the concept represented by *M* may have instances $M^1,..,M^n$. These instances may be obtained from *M* by addition of supplementary components. In the latter case, two kinds of terminology are possible: one may say that the more abstract category is represented by *M* or that it is represented by the set defined by $[M,M^1,M^2,...,M^n]$. The former terminology corresponds to an "intrinsic definition"; the latter one defines categories with reference to their extension. According to the terminology that we will adopt, the more abstract category is defined by the core M instead of by the set of its instances (see figure 1).

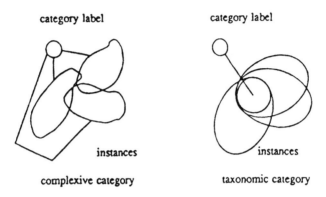

Figure I.1

If a category has instances which contain a common core, the verbal label may be attached to this core instead of to all instances separately. Concepts which can be defined by a common core are called "taxonomic concepts". Taxonomic concepts may have taxonomic sub-concepts. Then, all instances which belong to the same sub-concept share a number of components which are characteristic for it.

However, it is not always the case that the instances of a complex C can be characterized by a common core of attributes. A concept for which no such common core exists is called a "complexive concept". In case of such a concept, all instances have to be linked to the verbal label. A concept may be partially complexive and partially taxonomic. For instance, the typical instances of a concept may share a core of components which are characteristic for the concept. The exceptional instances, on the other hand, may share only a part of this core. It is fairly well documented in classical genetic psychology that a child's concepts evolve from complexive to taxonomic.

4 Specifications concerning the representation of *P*'s and *M*'s

Integrated feature packages *P* as well as multi-component concepts *M* are represented by very large binary patterns with values +1 and -1 (note 1). These values can be interpreted as activation values of formal neurons of a large network. If the i-th value of a pattern equals +1, we say that the i-th formal neuron of the network is active for this pattern. Value -1 corresponds to a non-active neuron. An integrated feature package *P* must be generated according to a random schema that has probability 1/2 to generate activation +1 or activation -1 in a particular unit. In case of very large patterns, such a random schema ensures that two different *P*'s are orthogonal, and that each *P* has a mean activation equal to zero. Suppose that the i-th activation value of P^μ, respectively V^ν, is denoted P_i^μ, respectively P_i^ν. Then, orthogonality means:

$$\frac{1}{N}\sum_{i=1}^{N} P_i^\mu P_i^\nu = 0$$

for each couple (μ,ν) with $\mu \neq \nu$. The mean activation value of the μ-th pattern is equal to zero if:

$$\frac{1}{N}\sum_{i=1}^{N} P_i^\mu = 0$$

A crucial point of our model is the insight that the set-operation for sets of *P*'s with an odd number of elements can be represented by a non-linear local vote operation. In case of an odd number of *P*'s, the pattern that results from such an operation can be decomposed unequivocally in its components. The significant advantages of such a non-linear operation over a linear one will become apparent in the course of the book. The number of *P*'s contained in an *M* is denoted "n". It is called sometimes the "level" or the "order" of the multi-component concept *M*. In order to define the vote operation, we differentiate between multi-component concepts with an odd number of components and multi-component concepts of an even number of components.

a. The case of odd n.

Consider n binary patterns $P^1,...,P^n$ and suppose their components can have values +1 and -1. The i-th component of the μ-th pattern is denoted P_i^μ.

Then, the i-th activation M_i of the "vote-pattern" $M(P^1,...,P^n)$ is defined by:

$$M_i = +1 \ \text{if} \ \sum_{\mu=1}^{N} P_i^{\mu} > 0$$

$$M_i = -1 \ \text{if} \ \sum_{\mu=1}^{N} P_i^{\mu} < 0$$

This rule expresses a vote-procedure in each neuron: if more than half of the components which participate in a vote-pattern M are active in a particular neuron, then M is active in it. Conversely, if more than half of them are inactive, M is inactive. The number of "active" votes never equals the number of "inactive" votes since n is odd.

b. The case of even n.

Next, suppose that n is even. Consider a set of n patterns $P^1,...,P^n$. With the same notational conventions as in case of odd n, we define:

$$M_i = +1 \ \text{if} \ \sum_{\mu=1}^{N} P_i^{\mu} > 0$$

$$M_i = +1 \ \text{if} \ \sum_{\mu=1}^{N} P_i^{\mu} < 0$$

$$M_i = C(rand(-1,+1)) \ \text{if} \ \sum_{\mu=1}^{N} P_i^{\mu} = 0$$

$C(rand(-1,+1))$ is a random choice between -1 and +1. In case of even n, also the third case may occur. Hence, the vote-operation does not lead to an unequivocally defined pattern. As we will see, the asymmetry between even and odd that raises in the present context is a quite fundamental one (Appendix I). In practice, the point that the even multi-component states are not unequivocally defined entails that the odd vote-patterns are more suited to represent concepts or scenes. This point will be reflected in the learning rule of the model that we construct.

5 Topological properties of mixture states

The vote-patterns that we introduced in the previous paragraph have appropriate topological and metric properties. A technical discussion is given in Appendix I; here we mention some properties that illustrate this fact. Consider two multi-component concepts M^1 and M^2 ; suppose that M^1 contains p components and that M^2 contains q components (p and q are odd). If M^1 and M^2 share r components, then their correlation Q is given by:

$$Q = -1 + \frac{1}{2^{p+q-r-2}} \sum_{s=0}^{r} \binom{r}{s} \sum_{\substack{x+s>\frac{p}{2} \\ x=0,\ldots,p-r}} \binom{p-r}{x} \sum_{\substack{y+s>\frac{q}{2} \\ y=0,\ldots,q-r}} \binom{q-r}{y} \qquad \text{(eq.I.1)}$$

and their Hamming distance can be obtained from:

$$H = \frac{1}{2}(1-Q)$$

The correlation between two M's is called sometimes the "overlap" between them, because it is a measure for the number of units in which the M's have the same activation. In general, correlations between multi-component concepts have the following properties:

a. Consider three multi-component concepts M^1 , M^2 and M^3 ; suppose that M^1 and M^2 are of order p and that M^3 is of order q (p and q are odd). Further, suppose that M^1 and M^3 share r components and that M^2 and M^3 share r' components. If r is larger than r', then the correlation between M^1 and M^3 is larger than the correlation between M^2 and M^3 .

b. Consider three multi-component concepts M^1 , M^2 and M^3 ; suppose that their respective orders are p, q and r. Further, suppose that all components which participate in M^3 participate also in M^1 and M^2 . If q is larger than p, then the correlation between M^1 and M^3 is larger than the correlation between M^2 and M^3 .

Property b. can be extended:

c. Consider three multi-component concepts M^1 , M^2 and M^3 ; suppose that their respective orders are p, q and r. Further, suppose that r components of M^3 participate in M^1 and that r components of M^3 participate in M^2 . Then, if q is larger than p, then the correlation between M^1 and M^3 is larger than the correlation between M^2 and M^3 .

Consider an n-th order mixture M (n is supposed to be an odd number). Then, the correlation Q between M and each of its components V^i can be obtained as a special case of expression (eq.I.1):

$$Q = m^*(n) = \frac{1}{2^n} \begin{bmatrix} n-1 \\ \frac{n-1}{2} \end{bmatrix}$$

(eq.I.2)

This expression is a decreasing function of n.

6 The threshold overlap required to trigger a multi-component concept

In the model that we will construct, the degree to which a multi-component concept is activated can be defined as the correlation between the actual state of the system and the representation of the concept. It follows from this definition that the degree of activation of a concept can vary between -1 and +1. In the limit of an infinitely large network, such a degree of activation can take all intermediate rational values. If it is equal to +1, the state of the system coincides exactly with the multi-component concept. If it is equal to zero, the network state and the multi-component concept are not related. If it is equal to -1, the network state coincides with the "mirror-image" of the multi-component concept (note 3).

Suppose that the system retrieves a memorized multi-component concept M. It may take quite some time before the correlation between the state of the system and M has become one. For instance, consider an input pattern that has a correlation of 0.695 with a memorized concept M. The evolution of the state of the system to a pattern B that has a correlation of 0.9 with M takes significantly less time than the evolution of the network state to M itself. Therefore, it is useful to associate a threshold value for the activation of M, and to stipulate that M is active as soon as the correlation between the state of the system and M is higher than this threshold value. Our simulations (see chapters VI-X) suggest to choose the threshold at about 0.9. This point is illustrated in the following figure.

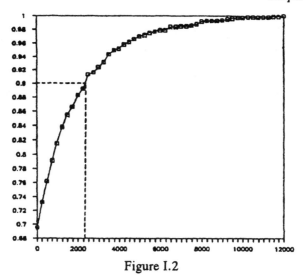

Figure I.2

7 The contents of the next chapters

In chapter II, we differentiate between pre-semantic and semantic representations. It is useful to discuss some properties of pre-processing mechanisms, since they constrain the type of representations used in semantic processing. More specifically, we pay attention to the microfeature hypothesis and to theory of Marr concerning levels of processing. Our discussions allow to define the concepts *smf*, *sf*, *P* and *M* in a way that is more specific than older feature-approaches. In chapter III, we point out that mental images are quite relevant as concerns human mental functioning. We propose that the modularity of mental images is reflected in the components *P* that participate in the representations of concepts. Images offer an economic way to store information in the sense that they may allow to derive a lot of implicit information. In order to extract such information, they must be analyzed with help of image schema's. Some of these schema's may allow to extract quite abstract information. We propose that it is possible to associate a *P* with the patterns which are detected by image schema's. Hence, such patterns can integrated in a concept *M*. Chapter IV considers if a representation of concepts in terms of *M*'s and *P*'s is reconcilable with the fact that functional knowledge contributes to the meaning of a concept. Although feature approaches and functional approaches are sometimes opposed to each other, our frame allows to define *P*'s in such a way that central elements of function can be grasped by our type of representation.

Chapter V examines the interactions between the components of concepts. Prototype models propose that components interact additively, whereas exemplar models argue that they interact multiplicatively. We point out that exemplar models are suited to describe non-familiar concepts, whereas prototype models are more appropriate for familiar contexts of concepts. In chapter VI, we propose our connectionist model, and we specify its learning rule. The learning rule includes sub-rules that refer to the connectionist model only, and sub-rules that refer to the more general frame in which it is embedded. Different examples are considered in order to explain the properties of the model.

Chapter VII is concerned with prototypes and more general typicality effects. The typicality of an item can be estimated by our model by the time that is required to classify the item as a member of its category. Typicality arrangements which are obtained in this way can be directly compared with psychological typicality arrangements. We show that both arrangements coincide, and that different properties of typicalities can be explained by our model. In chapter VIII, we point out that typicalities are context dependent. The fact that typicality distributions restructure gradually under the influence of contexts can be straightforwardly described by our model. In chapter XI, we consider the fact that there is a basic level in conceptual taxonomies and that the basic level has a number of remarkable convergent properties. These properties are discussed from the point of view of our model. Finally, chapter X addresses the evolution of conceptual structures. When a child gets older or when an adult becomes more familiar with a particular domain, the structure of his concepts of this domain evolves from complexive to taxonomic. This fact is discussed in classical ontogenetic psychology as well as in more recent studies. We show that our model predicts this evolution.

The monograph closes with three appendices. In Appendix I, we give an introduction to the mathematical properties of vote-mixtures. Appendix II links the discussions of chapters II and III to some recent discussions concerning hemispheric lateralization. We point out that the conceptual database of the right hemisphere is one of the candidate modules to be described by our model. Finally, Appendix III contains some specifications with respect to the simulations which have been made to sustain our argument.

NOTES

Note 1. We point out in next chapter that the differentiation between sf's and smf's is mainly a theoretical one: present neuro-psychological research does not offer a conclusive list of sf's and smf's.

Note 2. Usually, one calls these patterns "vectors". However, in case of our model, this terminology would be misleading: the network states of our model do not form a vector space, since multi-component vectors are obtained from their components by a non-linear operation.

Note 3. Notwithstanding the fact it may be useful for certain ends that the "negation" or the "mirror image" of a pattern is represented, we will not study the possible semantic applications of such mirror images.

II. SEMANTIC AND PRE-SEMANTIC REPRESENTATIONS

1 Introduction

Inputs are pre-processed by a number of complex neural operations before they are integrated in high-level semantic processes. Pre-processing can be divided in different stages. In a first stage, local properties are detected. In a later stage, more global information can be obtained (paragraph 2). According to the microfeature-hypothesis, an input is segmented into features during pre-processing. In order to recombine these features correctly, attention is required. Integrated packages of features are send serially to semantic modules. Although a definitive list of the microfeatures that the brain uses can not be given yet, this view can be supported with quite some evidence (paragraph 3). We discuss the relation between this view and the theory of Marr concerning the different stages in visual processing (paragraph 4). We propose that semantic non-verbal representations are continuous with the code that results at the end of pre-processing. This leads us to the introduction of our concepts *smf*, *sf*, *P* and *M* (paragraph 5). In comparison with older feature approaches, this approach is more specific (paragraph 6).

2 Pre-processing and semantic processing

2.1 Introduction

During the last decades, neuropsychologists have made significant progresses as concerns the identification of the brain circuitry that processes sensory information. Although present neural knowledge is far from complete yet, it is possible to extract some points from this area which are relevant for our concerns. Lissauer (1889) anticipated an important point. He differentiated between two stages. In the apperceptive stage of perception, a sensory impression is perceived. In the second stage, called the "associative stage", the content of perception is connected with a meaning. In a more specific form, this differentiation has received support from two approaches in recent physio-psychological research. The first approach studies subjects with brain-lesions. The second one makes recourse to psychological experiments in order to test and to specify the microfeature hypothesis. This kind of surveys is discussed in paragraph 3. In the present paragraph, we focus on the first kind of studies.

2.2 Two pre-processing stages

2.2.1 The first pre-processing stage

In the first phase of processing, an input is analyzed in "single-modality" systems. For instance, in this phase, sound-information does not yet interfere with visual information. Also within the visual system, form-, location-, texture- and color-information appear in first instance to be processed relatively independent from each other (e.g. Ungerleider and Mishkin, 1982; De Renzi, 1982; Sagi and Julesz, 1985). Physiological records suggest the existence of specialized populations of neurons, selectively tuned to particular colors, disparities, orientations and spatial frequencies (Treisman and Paterson, 1984, p. 12). However, many details in this domain are still unknown (note 1). Therefore, arguments of calculational plausibility often guide speculations and models, in special as concerns the way in which information from different modalities is combined (e.g. Marr, 1976; Marr and Hildreth, 1980; Marr, 1982; Biederman, 1987; also the work of Grossberg on this subject is well known, e.g. Grossberg, 1976, 1978 and Grossberg and Mingolla, 1985).

In order to illustrate the main characteristics of the first processing phase, we consider the example of texture information. In first instance, texture information is present implicitly in the pattern that falls on the retina. Retinal neurons transmit the activation to areas at the back of the brain. There, the areas responsible for texture-recognition receive a massive amount of input. During this processing stage, the coarse aspects of the texture are detected. For instance, a surface of an orange can be differentiated from a smooth surface, but more refined differentiations are not noticed yet. For instance, the texture of a snake, a honeycomb or a pineapple are not yet differentiated from each other. Both brain-hemispheres appear to be equally involved in this task (e.g. Vaina, 1987). At this stage, the brain operates in parallel (Treisman and Paterson, 1984, see paragraph 3). Seriality comes into play at a further stage, when mechanisms of attention scan spatial areas one after another.

Hence, the first pre-processing is called a "pre-attentive" or "perceptual" phase, in contrast to later semantic phases. This distinction was drawn first by Neisser (1967) who differentiated between an early pre-attentive level of "automatic" processing and a later serial stage that requires focussed attention. In the same vein, Treisman and Gelade (1980) suggested that the flow of neural activation first passes a level at which the features that form the primitive elements of the perceptual language are analyzed by specialized populations of detectors. At a second level, these features are recombined to form the complex objects and events that we perceive (see also Treisman and Paterson, 1984).

2.2.2 The second pre-processing stage

After coarse texture information has been extracted, more fine-grained differentiations are made. They may involve the integration of different pieces of information that stem from the first pre-processing phase. Then, non-local spatial properties can be detected. For instance, it becomes possible to differentiate between the texture of a snake and of a honeycomb. In contradistinction with the texture of an orange, the recognition of these textures depends on the detection of non-local spatial symmetries. The neural areas involved in this task appear to be situated in the left hemisphere. Textures with the same coarse-grained structure are often confused by patients with brain-lesions at particular area's at the back of this hemisphere. For example, such patients may confuse the texture of a sheep with the texture of a cauliflower, and the texture of a snake, fishnet or honeycomb with the texture of a pineapple (Vaina, 1987, p.101-102). Also in studies that concern pre-processing issues in the context of shape-recognition (e.g. Marr and Vaina, 1982; Marr 1982), the assumption that the detection of global properties is preceded by the detection of local ones has been put forward (see paragraph 4).

2.3 Semantic processing stages

2.3.1 The integration of packages of information

The information extracted in the pre-processing phases is transmitted to semantic areas. With help of mechanisms of attention, this information is "integrated": shape, texture, color, location and motion are coupled to each other. As a consequence, a normal subject has no difficulty to decide, for instance, which of the colors present in his visual field corresponds to a particular form. Also, visual patterns are integrated with information from other modalities such as touch, smell, taste and sound. We will see that "integrated packages of features", which integrate single modality features that concern a relatively simple part of an object, may be transmitted quickly one after another to the semantic area's. Recognition at a semantic level differs in some significant aspects from recognition at a pre-processing level:

a. Semantic processing depends in part on serial processes.

b. Semantic pattern recognition often involves the mental rotation of an input to a canonical orientation.

c. At the semantic level, properties may be inferred which have no trace in the visual field (or in another input modality). For example, when a subject sees a green apple, he may infer that it has white pulp. Also, the function of an object may be inferred, its relation to other objects can be determined, its appearance in memorized scenes can be inspected, and so on.

d. Semantic representations have a profound influence on the coarse of thought processes. As we will see, the semantic patterns which are associated with objects determine how they are situated within the knowledge-base of a subject.

2.3.2 The differentiation between verbal and non-verbal semantic stages

It is quite generally agreed that one can differentiate between a non-verbal and a verbal semantic stage. Different observations of subjects with brain lesions bear evidence of this point. Ratcliff and Newcombe (1982) studied patients with visual agnosia. Such patients are unable to name the forms that they can recognize. They offer an illustration of the fact that objects can be identified on the basis of their visual characteristics alone, and that other modalities, for instance the modality that contains the names of objects, correspond to independent processing stages. Vaina (1987) made a similar point. In one experiment, the capacity to recognize textures was examined for subjects with particular left hemisphere lesions. Some subjects claimed to see the fur of a tiger when shown the texture of a bear, the texture of a pineapple instead of the texture of a cauliflower, the surface of a saddle instead of the texture of a horse, and so on. When their visual recognition capacities were checked by asking them to point to the shape of the object corresponding to a particular texture, they sometimes pointed to the right picture but they still attached the wrong name to it.

There is also evidence for the stance that the function of an object is represented independent of its name. Goodglass and Kaplan (1963) observed that aphasics frequently used their hands or their fingers to represent an intended object, as in hammering with the fist as the hammer (see also Vaina, 1983, p.18). Thus, a deficiency in naming ability does not inhibit the recognition of the function of objects. Similar phenomena can be observed in (normal) pre-school children. These observations suggest the existence of a non-verbal functional representation of objects and actions.

The differentiation between verbal and non-verbal semantic processes is a central stance of advocates of the "dual-code" theory (Paivio, 1971, 1978 and 1986; Paivio and Lambert, 1981). The verbal system works with its specific code. The elements of this code are called "logogens" after Morton (1969, 1970). Similarly, an "imagegen" is the central representational element of the non-verbal system. The dual code theory proposes that the structure of the non-verbal system differs from the structure of the verbal system. The organization of logogens is sequential and diachronic. A reversal of the order of the words of a sentence usually leads to a nonsensical result. Imagegens, on the other hand, are processed synchronously and in non-fixed order. For instance, a mental image of a living room can be described starting from any part of the image. Instead of being organized in a temporal way, imagegens are structured by part-whole-relations (Denis, 1982; Hoffman, Denis and Ziessler, 1983; Tversky and Hemmenway, 1984). Actually, this view is too schematic. In Appendix II, it is pointed out that there are different kinds of mental images with different kinds of structures. Categorical and schematic images indeed have a structure that is reminiscent of the imagegens of the dual code theory. Metric images, on the other hand, have a different structure (Kosslyn, 1987). This differentiation is tightly related with the discussion concerning the lateralization of imagery (see Appendix II).

3 Pre-processing and the microfeature hypothesis

3.1 Atomistic and holistic feature-detection

We mentioned higher that local features are detected in an earlier stage than global ones. This, in a sense, is an "atomistic" view on pre-processing: the input is partitioned in small atoms and eventually, the representation of an object can be obtained by particular combinations of the atoms. However, it is also possible to adduce some arguments in favor of a holistic view, according to which a decomposition into atomic parts does not occur during the first processing phases. Different studies demonstrated that a whole is identified faster than its parts (Navon, 1977; Savin and Bever, 1970). Also, the presentation of a whole object can facilitate the detection of its parts (Weisstein and Harris, 1974). Hence, there is a set of psychological results that seems to be more compatible with the intuition behind Gestalt-psychology than with the idea that an input is decomposed into atomic elements.

In all these studies, subjects were asked to assert something about some phenomenon. Then, the experimenter evaluated these assertions or the reaction speed with which they were produced. Such an approach suffers from an important drawback: the experiments rely on conscious judgements of the subjects. The processes which were investigated, however, were unconscious. For example, small horizontal binocular disparities can not be accessed directly by consciousness; rather, they appear in consciousness as stereoscopic depth. The question raises to which extent conscious judgements allow for inferences concerning pre-conscious processes. It can be imagined that a conscious judgement reflects the semantic stage of processing and that it is not suited to assess preparatory phases. Hence, it may be argued that the studies at issue are not in contradiction with the microfeature-hypothesis, since the microfeature hypothesis with respect to preprocessing concerns a phase that is not assessed by these studies (Treisman and Paterson, 1984). Actually, psychological tests that use other methods give substantial evidence for the atomistic stance.

3.2 Psychological evidence for microfeatures in pre-processing

In the past decade, Treisman and colleagues (e.g. Treisman and Gelade, 1980; Treisman and Schmidt, 1982; Treisman and Paterson, 1984; Treisman, 1988) collected substantial evidence for the microfeature hypothesis. Their basic assumptions can be summarized in two points:

1. Inputs are decomposed in features. Some of these features are "microfeatures": they do not result from combinations of other features.
2. Microfeatures are detected without intervention of attention: they are activated automatically and in parallel. Patterns that depend on their combination, on the other hand, require attention in order to ensure an adequate integration of different microfeatures.

These hypothesises were confirmed by three kinds of experiments.

a. Since microfeatures are processed in parallel, they require no serial search. Consequently, if a screen is filled with one microfeature and with several distractors, the microfeature is detected faster than objects which do not correspond to microfeatures. For instance, in Treisman and Gelade (1980), subjects were asked to search for targets which were defined by the single feature "pink" and which were embedded in brown and purple distractors. Next, they were asked to search the pink O's in a screen filled with green O's and pink N's. Apparently, the latter condition involved the detection of a combination of features. The curve which related search time to display size was constructed for both conditions. When the target was defined by a single feature, this curve turned out to be flat or non-monotonic. When a conjunction of features was required, the curve increased linearly. This agrees with the assumption that the first task could be carried out in parallel, whereas the second one required attention and serial scanning.

b. A second test made use of the supplementary hypothesis that texture segregation occurs early and pre-attentively in input-processing. The rationale behind this assumption is that texture-segregation is necessary for figure-ground separation, and that figure-ground separation occurs pre-attentively, since attention does not focus on random-parts of the visual field, but fixates on figures which are demarcated from the background. According to this assumption, texture-segregation depends on microfeatures: otherwise it would require attention. Treisman and Gelade (1980) showed that texture segregation is difficult or impossible when elements in different areas differ by conjunctions of microfeatures. For example, when red curved shapes and blue straight lines figured in one area and red straight lines and blue curved shapes in another area, it appeared to be hard to separate both areas from each other. Areas defined by a single feature, on the other hand, were easily and quickly demarcated. Hence, conjunctions of microfeatures which refer respectively to color and shape are not detected pre-attentively. Only at the expense of a sufficient amount of attention, the participating microfeatures are integrated and associated with a certain place in the visual field. Thus, if one has to test if an element is a microfeature or not, one may test if it mediates texture-segregation or not.

c. A third test follows from the consideration that, if attention is not strong or diverted, it may lead to wrong combinations of microfeatures and thus give raise to illusory conjunctions. Features involved in such illusions correspond to microfeatures, since they are detected pre-attentively. Different sources report evidence for such phenomena. Treisman (1977) gave his subjects a list with couples of items and asked them to decide whether the two items of each couple were the same or not. When the shape and color of the two target-items were interchanged, the subjects made a quite large number of errors. Lawrence (1971) observed that subjects sometimes wrongly recombine the case and the content of visual words presented successively in the same location. As concerns auditive phenomena, it has been reported that the pitch and the loudness of dichotic tones are sometimes heard in the wrong combinations (Effron and Yund, 1974).

3.3 Microfeatures within a single modality

The experiments considered in the previous sub-paragraph concerned combinations of features from different modalities (such as color and form). Treisman and Paterson (1984) argued that similar methods could bear interesting results for stimuli which belonged to the same stimulus-dimension. More specifically, they considered different features of the form-modality. Stimuli such as lines, angles, curves and other components of form have the remarkable characteristic that their combinations may give raise to "new" properties which are not present in the components. For example, two lines in different orientations may combine to form an angle or an intersection. After Pomerantz, Sager and Stoever (1977), such properties are usually called "emergent features". In the context of the present discussion, one may wonder if emergent features are picked as microfeatures or if they are encoded as the combination of their constituents. Another question of relevance is if the simultaneous activation of microfeatures can give raise psychologically to emergent features. For example, suppose that a subject is confronted with the following image:

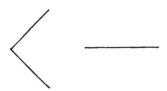

Figure II.1

The question raises if, under conditions of distracted attention, the activation of the features corresponding to the right angle and to the diagonal can give raise to the illusion of a triangle. If not, a triangle would be either a microfeature itself or it would be build from more microfeatures than the two ones which are shown. One may suspect that a physically composite image is psychologically often not constituted by its parts only. Otherwise, the occurrence of these parts in configurations which do not correspond with the image would evoke too often the illusion of the image (Treisman and Paterson, 1984, p.14). Experiments indeed allow to conclude that the representation of a triangle involves more than just the microfeatures corresponding to the elements of figure II.1. The supplementary feature required for its activation is "closure". This can be inferred from the fact that subjects formed illusory triangles from the features of figure II.1 when circles were added (Treisman and Paterson, 1984). Such a hypothesis is continuous with research of Caelli, Julesz and Gilbert (1978), who proposed that closure is a primitive perceptual element that mediates easy texture segregation.

These results allow to conclude that triangles are not processed holistically. A further argument for this stance can be found in the fact that triangles yield their sides to form illusory dollar signs when they are spread in a display filled with S'es. They do so with as little reluctance as single lines (Treisman and Paterson, 1984). Another example, also studied in Treisman and Paterson (1984), is the arrow. In close analogy with a triangle, it is formed physically from a combination of the components of the following figure:

Figure II.2

However, unlike in case of a triangle, closure is not an emergent feature for an arrow. Consequently, arrows do not behave as if they possess a simple, pre-attentively available feature in addition to the components shown in the picture (note 2). Suppose that a display is filled with triangles and with distractors which lack the feature "closure". We call it "display A". Since closure is an elementary microfeature, it can be detected in parallel. Consequently, in case of display A, also the triangles can be detected in parallel and they may help to segregate textures. Arrow junctions, on the other hand, do not contain the microfeature "closure". Hence, if a display B contains arrows as well as distractors consisting of the elements of figure II.2, arrows can not be detected in parallel and they can not mediate easy texture segregation. Treisman and Paterson indeed showed that triangles are detected in screen A with higher speed than arrows in screen B. Further, as concerns texture segregation, triangles which are embedded in screen A lead to better performance than arrows which are displayed in B.

3.4 The problem of attention

These points suggest that attention comes into play when different microfeatures have to be combined (Treisman and Paterson, 1984, p.14):

"Our results suggest that early processing of features is independent of attention but that later stages of object- identification require focussed attention to each potential object in turn in order to ensure the correct allocation of features and to prevent the formation of illusory conjunctions from random recombinations of the features of different objects."

We notice, however, that the following two questions are left without answer:

a. One may wonder if attention operates at different levels. Some of the experiments of Treisman et al. show that attention integrates microfeatures which belong to the same modality. At other instances, it is argued that attention integrates stimuli which belong to different modalities. The relation between the attention that integrates features of different modalities and the attention that integrates features of the same modality is unclear. It is tempting to assume some or other hierarchical structure, but this question has not been addressed experimentally.

b. Second, one may wonder how many microfeatures can be integrated at a single attentive moment. Further, what exactly is an "attentive moment"? In paragraph 4, we will use some plausibility arguments from a slightly different context in order to try to be more specific about the "attentively integrated feature packages" which are send serially to the semantic area's.

3.5 Textons and other hypothetical elementary microfeatures

It would be psychologically and epistemologically highly relevant if someone could give a complete list of the microfeatures by which the brain analyzes its inputs. Some authors combined plausibility arguments with empirical data and arrived at preliminary proposals. For instance, in paragraph 4, we consider Marr's theory. It contains suggestions concerning candidates of microfeatures, but as concerns this issue, the approach remains on a tentative level. For instance, nor the methods of 3.2, nor related methods have been used in the context of this theory to test if hypothetical microfeatures are elementary or not. As far as concerns the features involved in texture-recognition, Julesz' "texton"-model has been fairly influential (e.g. Julesz, 1981, 1984). The model introduces three kinds of elementary features, called "textons". The first kind consists of elongated blobs with particular orientations, lengths, widths and intensities. The second kind consists of the terminators of these blobs. Finally, the third class of textons contains crossings of line-segments. However, the empirical basis of texton-theory is not without problems, and the evidence that is adduced in favor of the theory can be interpreted in different ways (Gursney and Browse, 1988).

It is fair to say that current research in this field revealed several facts of high significance, but the definitive collection of microfeatures can not be given yet. In fact, Treisman (1988) points out that rather few elements can be considered to be microfeatures on a solid empirical basis. In a sense, however, this is encouraging, since (Treisman, 1988, p. 376):

"we would not want to assume that there are hundreds of visual primitives, each of which is separately represented in a map in the brain".

The idea behind this assumption is that the brain operates in an economic way, without invoking a host of redundant primitives. A similar point can be found in Biederman (1987). Future physio-psychological research has to find out if this assumption is justified.

4 Marr's theory and the relation between pre-processing and semantic patterns

4.1 Processing stages for visual stimuli

Marr's work on vision pervasively influenced the pre-processing debate during the last ten years. Marr (1982) differentiates between four stages when visual stimuli are processed:

a. In the first stage, retinal input leads to the formation of an "image". An image is a set of intensities defined for each point on a gray-level array. This representation is not suited for the recognition of three-dimensional shapes: first, three other phases have to be passed.

b. In the next stage, a gray-level array is transformed into a "primal sketch". It provides explicit information about the directions, the magnitudes and the spatial extents of the intensity changes which are present in the image. The motivation for the introduction of the concept "primal sketch" is twofold. First, from a computational point of view, it is a useful intermediate stage towards a representation suited for shape-recognition. Second, it is possible to adduce some physiological evidence for it. The X- and Y-cells of the retina and the simple cells discovered in the visual cortex carry out a kind of differential- and detection-analysis on intensity-values (Hubel and Wiesel, 1962, 1968). This analysis appears to be the one that is required to make the transition from the intensity array to the primal sketch. The mathematical side of this contention has been worked out in Marr and Hildreth (1980).

c. The local information which is contained in the primal sketch is analyzed in such a way that more global information is obtained. The representation thus acquired is called the 2-1/2 D-sketch. It makes explicit the orientation and the rough depth of the visible surfaces in a viewer-centered frame of reference. Discontinuities in depth and in orientation are detected.

d. Next, the 3D-representation is constructed (note 3). In this stage, shapes and their spatial organization are described in an object centered frame of reference. The description relies on volumetric primitives (i.e. primitives which represent simple volumes). In the 3D-representation elaborated by Marr and colleagues, these primitives are cylinders (see also Vaina, 1983). The volumetric primitives have a modular hierarchical organization. This means that an object is in first instance approximated by one volumetric primitive. On the next level of detail, this volume is replaced by different smaller volumetric primitives. On the subsequent level of detail, each of these volumes is again replaced by smaller ones, and so on. The volume at the coarsest level of precision may be considered as an anchor to which volumes at subsequent levels of detail are attached. However, Marr suggests that a "skeleton" may offer a more flexible anchor on which parts can be attached. A skeleton is a *"spatial configuration of a few sticks or axes"* (Marr, 1982, p.37). Hence, along with its volume elements, a 3D-representation may include such a skeleton.

We saw in paragraph 3 that different authors propose that "microfeatures" are primitives which emerge in the early processing-stages of visual input. Also Marr proposes such features (e.g. Marr, 1982, p.37). They can be classified according to the processing-stage in which they appear. In the primal sketch, these features consist of zero-crossings, blobs, terminations and discontinuities, edge segments, virtual lines, groups, curvilinear organization and boundaries. Next, in the 2-1/2 D-sketch, the features which are detected are: local surface orientation, distance from the viewer, discontinuities in depth and discontinuities in surface-orientation. Finally, in the 3-D-sketch, the features correspond to hierarchically organized volumetric primitives.

4.2 Simple volumetric elements and attentively integrated packages of features

We saw higher that the level at which attention comes into play is not well defined in the Treisman's theory: it seems that both the combination of microfeatures of the same modality (e.g. line-elements) as well as the combination of microfeatures belonging to different modalities (e.g. the combination of letters with colors) depend on mechanisms of attention. Also the theory of Marr does not give a satisfactory answer to this problem. For instance, Marr does not point out to which extent attention is involved to arrive at a 2-1/2 D- or a 3D-representation of a complex object. According to the theory of Treisman, such representations would be impossible without attention since they require that several microfeatures are combined. However, the extension of a package of features that can be integrated in a single attentive moment is relatively unspecified.

We notice that the results of Treisman et al. suggest that the extension of such a package is not quite large. In some experiments considered in paragraph 3, subjects are asked to search for an object that integrates a combination of microfeatures. The object is embedded in a display filled with distractors which also integrate more than one microfeature (e.g. Treisman and Gelade, 1980). It appears that subjects scan serially in such conditions: the scanning time is proportional to the size of the display. Treisman and Gelade conclude that each of the depicted objects requires serial attention. At closer look, one observes that the objects used in these experiments are composed of two or three microfeatures. Notwithstanding this fact, Treisman et al. suggest that attention focusses on a single object at a every instance. This suggests that, in general, the number of microfeatures which are integrated by a single moment of attention is not very large. Then, the question raises how a complex scene or object is processed. In some or other way, its complexity must be broken down into simple "packages" or "slices" of features which can be treated in a single moment of attention.

We suggest that a simple volumetric primitive of the kind considered by Marr are candidates for such packages of features. On the one hand, since the number of features that are integrated in a single attentive moment is not very large, it is plausible that attentively integrated feature-packages do not exceed significantly the sets of features that are integrated in a simple volumetric element. On the other hand, it a natural assumption that the features which participate in such a volume element are transmitted in an integrated way. After all, in a 3D representation, these features are adequately combined. Hence, we propose that packages of microfeatures which correspond to a simple volumetric element are integrated at a single attentive moment (as an extrapolation of this schema, one might suggest that also a simple skeleton may be integrated at a single moment of attention). As some of the experiments of Treisman et al. illustrate, not only features referring to form or location are integrated, but also features that refer, for instance, to texture or to color may be coupled in an attentive moment. In order not to overload the terminology, we will use the term "simple volume element" also to refer to an attentively integrated feature package that contains, along with features that specify shape-information, features referring to color, texture, and motion.

The connection between attentively integrated feature packages and volumetric primitives suggests that attention operates in a modular, hierarchical way. It may focus first on the coarse, global volumetric organization of objects; subsequently, it may focus on more specific aspects on successive levels of detail. This scenario has an advantage of economy. If, in a particular problem situation, the problem can be solved after transmission of volumetric elements which correspond to a high level in the modular organization, then more detailed volumetric elements do not need to be transmitted, and it is not necessary to scan the input any further. If attention would transmit volumetric elements in a random arrangement, this scenario would be impossible.

4.3 The 3D-representation and semantic representations

We saw that a 3D-representation is organized in a modular, hierarchical way. Kosslyn (e.g. 1980; see next chapter) proposed that this fact is reflected in the semantic long term representations of images. More specifically, he suggested that these representations have the following four characteristics. First, they contain a "skeleton"-file or a file that corresponds to a main part of the object or scene at issue. This file contains coarse information about the overall configuration of the scene or the object. Second, the parts of the object are stored in separate files. Third, in case of detailed representations, also the parts of these parts are stored in different files, and so on. Finally, all files contain relatively "coarse" information: when a file is displayed mentally, the resulting image has a quite limited resolution.

If the components of the long term representations would correspond to volumetric elements, there would be a striking continuity between the mechanisms of attention, the structure of 3D-representations and of non-verbal semantic representations. The mechanisms of attention integrate microfeatures which correspond to a simple volumetric element. These elements build up a 3D-representation. When the latter sends its information to the semantic areas, then 3D-volumetric elements would be mapped on patterns (or component patterns) which represent the same simple volumes. Again, as an extrapolation, we suggest that a component of a long term semantic memory trace may correspond to a skeleton (note 4).

5 Semantic features

A feature package that is integrated by one instance of attention is called an "attentively integrated feature package". We abbreviate this term by "*P*". According to the previous paragraph, such a package corresponds to a simple volume element. We have seen that the notion *P* can be introduced at the 3D-level as well as at the semantic level. In order not to overload the terminology, we use the same term to refer to both cases. In case of the present text, this will not lead to confusion: from chapter the next chapter on, we are concerned with semantic patterns only.

We assume that the features which participate in an integrated feature package have a trace in the semantic areas. For instance, a subject may judge that the boarder of a simple object is a straight line, or that its color is red, and so on. We will call this semantic trace a "single modality feature", and we abbreviate this term by "*sf*". A feature package *P* must contain at most one *sf* of each modality. Else, a variable binding problem would appear. For instance, if a *P* would contain one simple form but two textures, then it would be unspecified how these textures are distributed over the form. In order to specify this point, two form-*sf*'s have to be associated with the form at issue, so that a single texture-*sf* can be associated with each form-*sf*.

In principle, one may try to differentiate between semantic features and semantic microfeatures. More particular, the semantic traces of elementary microfeatures in the sense of Treisman et al. (paragraph 3) could be called "semantic microfeatures", whereas the semantic traces of composite features could be called "semantic features". A semantic microfeature is given the notation "*smf*". We notice that this is only a tentative definition, since, as we have pointed out, a complete list of preprocessing microfeatures is lacking.

In accordance with the previous chapter, we assume that the semantic components which correspond to attentively integrated feature packages can be integrated in multi-component concepts M. For instance, the P's which represent the parts and the skeleton of an object may be integrated into an M. In the course of our discussions of the present and the next chapter, the concepts sf, P and M will be extended in two ways:

a. In order to be able to deal with the role of emotions in associative reasoning, we allow that an emotion is represented formally as an sf or as a P. In the former case, it is integrated first in a P and subsequently in an M. In the latter case, it is integrated directly in an M.

b. We allow that P's refer to image schema's which have been detected in an image. Basically, an image schema expresses schematic information that is implicit in an image. We anticipate that image schema's play an important role in the generation of abstractions and in the representation of function.

6 Older approaches which invoke semantic microfeatures

In older approaches, several authors suggested the existence of biologically determined semantic atoms. However, these theories did not dispose of the evidence that we considered in the previous paragraphs. Hence, they remained on a quite general and speculative level. The "universal-primitives" hypothesis of Bierwisch is a fairly well known example (Bierwisch, 1970). According to this assumption, humans automatically and unconsciously decompose their inputs into a code determined by the structure of the brain. The atoms of this code are "universal primitives" (Bierwisch, 1970, p. 181-182):

"It seems natural to assume that these components represent categories or principles according to which real and fictitious, perceived and imagined situations and objects are structured and classified. The semantic features do not represent, however, external physical properties, but rather the psychological conditions according to which human beings process their physical and their social environment. Thus they are not symbols for physical properties and relations outside the human organism, but rather for the internal mechanisms by means of which such phenomena are perceived and conceptualized. This then leads to the extremely far-reaching, but plausible, hypothesis that all semantic structures might finally be reduced to components representing the basic dispositions of the cognitive and perceptual structure of the human organism. According to this hypothesis, semantic features can

not be different from language to language, but are rather part of the general human capacity for language, forming a universal inventory used on particular ways by individual languages. "

Katz and Fodor (1963) uttered similar ideas in terms of "semantic markers". Postal (1966, p.179) stressed on the innateness of the atoms of semantics:

"... the relation between the semantic primitives ... and the world is not learned but innate. What must be learned is only the relations between fixed sets of semantic primitives and sets of phonological and syntactic properties. "

The obvious problem with these proposals is that the elementary features which they propose are unspecified and entirely hypothetical. Further, the concept of "feature" has been used in this context in rather diverging ways. One might expect that features would have been defined as non-complex entities, but for instance Anglin (1970, p.95) proposes:

"... a feature is a complex verbal concept rich in properties just as a word is".

Hence, we conclude that, although our perspective still contains some tentative elements, it is a step forward relative to these older approaches.

NOTES

Note 1. See for instance the discussions that follow the target paper of Ballard (1986) in Behavioral and Brain Sciences.

Note 2. One may notice that a point of incidence for three lines might also be an emergent feature; however, the results of Treisman and Paterson (1984) suggest that this is not the case, at least not as apparently as closure is an emergent feature for "triangle".

Note 3. We notice that in Marr and Vaina (1982), the 3-D representation serves as the basis for a further representational stage in which motion is included. This representation is called the state-motion-state representation. The name reflects the inspiration that motion should be modeled as a succession of static images. This stance, however, is not trivial. In early processing, some neurons are specialized in the detection of motion (e.g. Allman, Miezin et al. 1985; Ballard, 1986). It may be that at higher processing stages, motion is still represented by specific patterns rather than just by a succession of patterns. We will not discuss this point here.

Note 4. We notice that the present argument is not dependent on the specific type of volumetric elements that is used by a 3D-sketch. The primitive volume elements proposed by Marr are chosen on the basis of plausibility arguments only. In principle, our argument might be repeated with other volumetric elements. For instance, one might suggest that it is more plausible that a simple volume element would contain a simple configuration of cylinders, or that a volume element would correspond to "geons" (Biederman, 1987).

III. DEMARCATION OF A MODULE FOR NON-VERBAL REPRESENTATIONS

1 Introduction

Present insights in the modularity of the brain suggest that there are different modules in which non-verbal information is stored. The module that we will describe is one of them. In the first paragraphs of the present chapter, we consider psychological criteria that allow to demarcate between different non-verbal modules. To start with, we point out that the module that we will describe is suited for non-temporal associations (paragraph 2). Next, we differentiate between modules that generate non-specific associations and modules that control specific relations. The model that we will consider is of the former type (paragraph 3). In paragraph 4, we consider modules that control mental imagery. We argue that operations with mental images are important to cognitive functioning. Images allow to extract implicit information. As a consequence, they are an economic way to store spatial types of information. Images can be inspected and analyzed with help of image schema's. We propose that patterns which are detected with help of image schema's can be encoded as P's. This way, information about configurations and about relatively abstract schema's can be included in M's that represent concepts or scenens (paragraph 5). Another approach to demarcate the module that we describe can be found in Appendix II, where this topic is addressed from the point of view of hemispheric lateralization.

2 Representations of temporal associations and representations of non-temporal associations

Temporal and non-temporal semantic associations are both important for human knowledge. Temporal order is important, for instance, in event schemata. One first enters a restaurant and next sits down at a table. One sits at a table before one starts to eat, and so on. Other associations are non-temporal. For instance, one can make an association between the concept "orange" and the concept "lemon", but one can make the reverse association as well. This symmetry is often absent in event-schemata. A particular concept can be associated with many other concepts if an appropriate hint is given. For instance, an apple can be associated with all things that are round, with an apple tree, with different kinds of cakes, and so on. There are two basically different possibilities to store all these associations:

i. According to the first one, one stores explicitly all links between a concept and the concepts to which it is related.
ii. According to the second possibility, these links are represented implicitly. They are generated by the representaitons of the concepts themselves.

The model that we will propose is in accordance with the second possibility. The representations of concepts or scenes consist of sets of feature packagess. As a first approximation, the associative link between two memorized items can be determined if one counts the number of feature packages that they share (note 1). We will see that this kind of representations has some important advantages. If it is supplemented with an appropriate set of learning rules, it allows to explain some crucial psychological processes. Further, such representations allow for an economic storage of the non-temporal relations. The number of possible non-temporal associations between concepts is that large that an explicit representation of all these links would demand a rather large storage-capacity; implicit representations avoid this problem. Temporal associations can not be stored implicitly in this way, since the relation " M^1 shares k components with M^2 " is symmetric.

3 Specific relations and non-specific associations

3.1 Two kinds of semantic relations

On a general level, one can make the point that a semantic association process may be constrained or unconstrained, with a whole bunch of intermediate possibilities. Two classes of constraints can be differentiated. First, the constraints may entail that a concept B that is associated with A has some specific relation with A. For instance, a search process may search for concepts related with "horse" by the relation "can". Valid outcomes are, for example, "eat" and "neigh", since a horse can eat and neigh. A second kind of constraints can be formulated in terms of the components that must occur in concept B. For instance, a constraint may express that B has components that are compatible with a given context, or it may entail that B shares components with A, or that a concept C exists with which both A and B share components, and so on. Associations guided by the second type of constraints may relate concepts related by a variety of specific relations, especially if the constraints are weak. Therefore, they will be called non-specific associations. We argue that the module that carries out such non-specific associations differs from the module that controls specific relations (note 2).

To start with, we notice that the associative relations provided by the module or modules that store specific relations often do not change. The non-specific associative links supported by the second kind of module are more sensitive to the succession of incoming information. To make this point more clear, consider the following two sentences:

i. A young man walking at the coast wondered who he would request to tend his horse.
ii. His friend suggested to ask a farmer to tend the horse.

The reader keeps a large number of relations between concepts constant while reading the second sentence after the first one. For instance, he keeps on believing that a horse "is an" animal, or that a young man "is a" man. Similarly, he does not have to change the pairs of concepts related by the relations "has" or "can": he remains convinced that a horse normally "has" four legs, that a horse "can" neigh and that young man "can" eat. In the present context, relations like "is a", "has" or "can" are called "specific relations". The information that two concepts are related by such a relation is more specific than the statement that the first concept may follow the second one in an association process. Sometimes, a sentence may aim at a modification of such relations. For instance, a child may be taught that a whale "is a" mammal. However, in every day communication, this kind of semantic relations does not change constantly as a new sentence is processed.

Non-specific associations change more constantly. Suppose that a concept is mentioned a couple of times during a conversation. Then, the strength of the associative link between this concept and another concept depends on the context that is active at that moment. In case of the example, the context that is activated by the first sentence may include elements that remind of a vacation, of beach activities, of sports, and so on. The second sentence creates a somewhat different context, and for some persons it may contain elements reminding of a holiday on a farm, of goats and sheep, of corn, and so on. Hence, when the concept "horse" is activated while hearing sentence i., its context is different from the one it that has when sentence ii is processed. As a consequence, the strength of the associative link between "horse" and other concepts varies as sentence i is followed by sentence ii. For instance, the associative link between "chicken" and "horse" may be weak while processing sentence i, and may be stronger after hearing sentence ii. Conversely, the strength of the associative link between "horse" and "sports" may be strong in case of sentence i, but may become weaker as sentence ii follows (see e.g. Roth and Shoben, 1983 for a related point).

In the present context, the strength of the associative link between two concepts refers to the extent to which these concepts prime one another. Priming experiments have been used, for instance, to assess the context dependency of the associative links between concepts. A context may vary subtly or it may vary more substantially as subsequent words and sentences are processed. However, the context dependency of the associative link between two concepts is not absolute. It may be possible to determine a number of typical contexts in which both concepts occur. The association strengths for these contexts may be called the "typical association strengths" for these concepts. The less typical a context, the stronger the strength of association between two concepts may deviate from the typical association strengths.

Quite often, unspecific associations, like the ones involved in priming processes, are described by one or other variant of a semantic network or of a neural network. A semantic network is not an interesting way to describe a set of specific relations. To see this, suppose that two concepts x and y would be related by two links, one corresponding to the specific relation R and the other to the specific relation S. Then, if x and y would be active, it would be impossible to decide if the state of the system would correspond to "x&y", "xRy" or "xSy". Some kinds of neural networks are more interesting in this respect (e.g. Hinton, 1990; Smolensky, 1990). However, a network that consists of a single module, that describes the phenomenon of spread of activation and that allows to manipulate specific relations has not been constructed. In effect, this is no coincidence. The point that specific and non-specific associations have to be represented in a different module can be made on a more general level.

For instance, consider a driver who is distracted by a conversation. At a given moment, he may be warned by his passenger: "Look out, that boy will try to catch the ball that rolls over the street!" As a result of this utterance, the driver's attention may be drawn to this scene. His module that stores unspecific associations may start a number of association processes. The boy may remind him of other children, of his own child years, and so on. The ball may remind him of the results that his favorite soccer team obtained last weekend, of the goal he made himself during his last play, and so on. If a reaction would have to be based on such a whole cluster of more or less activated concepts and scenes, the reaction might be rather confused and slow. Obviously, there are instances in which such a confusion or state of distraction may be undesirable or even dangerous. Some of the modules that represent relational information call for patterns that are suited as a basis for well defined subsequent reactions or for perspicuous and directed cognitive operations. As concerns such processes, the capacity to focus on a specific relation may be crucial. Other processes depend on less focal patterns of activity. Since the constraints to be fulfilled by the different kinds of processes are opposite, it is not plausible that they are realized in a single module.

The model that we will construct is a model for a module that generates unspecific associations. In the previous chapters, we gave specifications concerning the components of the concepts which we will describe. In 3.2, we argue that a module that stores concepts and that generates non-specific associatons must include the representations of the components of concepts. In 3.3, we point out some other constraints for a module that stores non-specific associations.

3.2 Modules that store unspecific associations include the representations of the components of concepts

It is plausible that a module for non-specific associations does not only include the representations of concepts, but also the representations of the components of these concepts. This is suggested by the fact that unspecific association processes may be guided by constraints that are expressed in terms of components that have to be present (or that have to be avoided) in the endpoint of the process. For instance, a context may stimulate particular components, and this may affect which concepts and scenes are primed by the spread of activation. For instance, the sight of a green jersey with small knobs may remind someone of the jersey of his grandfather. As a consequence, a partial activation of a cluster of patterns connected with "grandfather" may result. A green jersey with a zip-fastener may remind the same person of a jersey that he saw in a store yesterday, and this may result in another cluster of partial activations. This process can take place the other way round as well: the scenes which are present in a context may determine which components of a concept receive emphasis. For instance, if the concept "potato" is activated in the context of a restaurant, this may activate components like "hot", "yellow", "floury", and so on. If "potato" is activated in the context of a store, this may activate components like "dark rind", "moist substance", and so on (note 3).

In this elementary sense, the module at issue has to rely on distributed representations: a concept is represented together with its properties (note 4). One familiar possibility to realize this constraint is to specify that the representation of a concept can be obtained in some way from the representation of its components.

In the most simple case, a pattern representing a concept is build up by the units or patterns that correspond to its components. We notice that, if this kind of representation is used, priming effects occur inevitably: if a first concept that shares components with a second one is active, then the latter is also partially active. If the representation of a concept is not composed by the representation of its components, for instance if a local representation is used, then priming effects do not occur inevitably. In the latter case, priming effects may in principle occur at some instances, and may be inhibited at other moments.

3.3 Further general constraints

A module that stores non-specific associations must be able to learn new concepts. When a new concept is added, it must be localized appropriately in the complex web of associative relations. For instance, suppose that a child is taught a new breed of dogs, such as "fox terrier". Then, this new concept must become one of the concepts that are primed if "dog" is active. Conversely, the activation of "fox terrier" should lead to a partial activation of, for instance, the concept "pet". The associative link of the new concept with other pet-animals should be stronger than its associative link with most zoo-animals. This is not trivial, since it can not be read off from an instance of the new breed of dogs that they are pets, nor how strong the associative links with other concepts should be. In some or other way, there must be a mechanism that draws a new concept into its context or in the categories to which it belongs. If a concept is represented by its components, then new concepts may contain components that can be derived from perceptual input, but in addition they must be given components that put them at the appropriate place in the associative web.

Suppose that a person becomes familiar with a context. Scenes and concepts which belong to this context may accumulate. Then, it would be desirable not to arrive at an associative net that is like an unstructured mesh. Rather, it would be preferable to obtain a set of representations in which different clusters are present, possibly with more general clusters embedding more specific ones. It would also be interesting to have representations which allow that concepts can be more or less central in such a cluster. These points would enhance the expressivity of the net. It is not trivial that more or less hierarchically organized clusters emerge as contexts become more familiar. However, there is an extensive literature dealing with this issue, and this literature indeed documents such a process: as a context becomes more familiar, the associations present in it tend to evolve from loose associations to more taxonomically organized ones (e.g. Chi and Koeske 1983; this theme is frequently encountered in ontogenetically oriented studies, e.g. Ornstein and

Corsale, 1979; Lucariello and Nelson, 1985; Smiley and Brown, 1979; Vygotsky, 1962; Inhelder and Piaget, 1964; Annet, 1959; Anglin, 1970; Sigel, 1953). In view of the aim of the present text, it is of importance to notice that to a substantial extent, the studies referred to address relations which are, according to our terminology, non-specific (e.g.Chi and Koeske, 1983; Vygotsky, 1962; Inhelder and Piaget, 1964 and so on; see also chapter X). Hence, we suggest that the processes at issue may take place in at least some of the modules that store non-specific associations.

The model that we propose describes a module that stores non-specific associations. Hence, our model has to fulfill the constraints that we considered in the present paragraphs. We notice that these constraints form a subset of the constraints i-vi of chapter I. Since our model satisfies the latter constraints, it also satisfies the ones of the present paragraphs. In the next paragraphs, we consider non-verbal modules with which the non-verbal module that we consider has close interactions, in the sense that they help to specify the components that have to be included in the representations of concepts.

4 Non-verbal patterns and mental imagery

4.1 The dispute concerning the function of mental imagery

Among the non-verbal modules, the ones that control processes of mental imagery have been intensively discussed during the past two decades. We pay attention to this discussion because it allows us to situate the module that we describe in a more global frame, and because these discussions give us some further suggestions concering the nature of the components of the non-verbal representations of concepts. In discussions concerning mental imagery, two points of view can be opposed to each other. First, the "propositionalist" view puts forward that imagery is not quite important as concerns cognitive functioning. Furthermore, when processes of imagery have to be described, it is better to use propositional descriptions than descriptions in terms of "mental image", "mental image operation", and so on. Second, the "imagerist" stance argues that imagery has a significant cognitive function and that it has characteristics that are not easily described in propositionalist terms. The discussion can be summarized by an argument between Pylyshyn and Kosslyn. We mention the four most important criticisms of Pylyshyn (e.g. Pylyshyn 1973, 1980) and show how they are refuted by the imagerist stance. These criticisms are:

a. Imagerist theories often use a picture-metaphor. This metaphor wrongly suggests that mental images are experienced much as unstructured templates. Mental images, however, are structured by higher-level knowledge. This point can be easily evidenced. Suppose that someone does not retrieve an image for a long time and that he partially forgets it. Then, the part of the image that is forgotten is not a random part. If an image of a room is incomplete, it does not miss half a sofa or half a lamp-shade. The nature of the process by which images are forgotten suggests that they are encoded in terms of their semantically meaningful constituent parts rather than like a template.

b. The second argument is known as the "mind's eye" argument. The picture-metaphor introduces a host of inappropriate analogies between seeing and imaging. A mind's eye is often said to "see" images internally and the inner eye is endowed with the capacities of scanning and focussing just like real eyes. This metaphor bears two kinds of problems. First, suppose that the mind's eye sees internal images. Then, this eye would transmit its input to the "mind's eye's brain".

The latter "brain" would require in turn a "mind's eye's brain's eye" in order to see the images which are transmitted to it, and so on. An infinite regression results. Second, one may wonder how it may be conceived that a mind's eye "scans" and "focusses". In fact, there are no mind's eyeballs to do the scanning.

c. The third point is a storage-capacity argument. If pictures are stored in long term memory like templates and with a resolution that is comparable to the one of directly perceived pictures, then an enormous amount of storage capacity would be required to store all the images which people claim to remember.

d. Finally, Pylyshyn notices that it is problematic to address unstructured templates during a search procedure. If images would be stored in a more structured and decomposed form, on the other hand, the search space in case of a retrieval process could be restricted by the constraint that one or other component should be present in the retrieved image.

As an alternative for the imagerist stance, Pylyshyn proposes that all knowledge in the brain is encoded propositionally. Hence, he proposes to search for a propositional "third code" which can describe phenomena of imagery as well as thought processes which are guided by language (see also Clark and Chase, 1972). The existence of a common code for verbal phenomena and phenomena of imagery would furnish an explanation for the fact that images and language can be simultaneously integrated in thought-processes.

As to imagerists, this argument is not convincing (e.g. Kosslyn and Pomerantz, 1977; Kosslyn, Pinker, Smith and Schwartz, 1979; Kosslyn 1980, 1987). We consider their replies to the four points of Pylyshyn.

a. Pylyshyn's first reproach points out that images are not represented by the way of template-like pictures. However, imagerists readily agree with this. Images are stored after they have been pre-processed and interpreted. Hence, the long term representation of an image depends on the way in which these processes analyze and decompose it. In fact, we will see that Kosslyn's theory of imagery proposes that the parts of an image are stored in separate files. Hence, a theory of imagery may explain that image parts are not forgotten in a random way.

b. Although the second point is quite widespread, is easy to refute. According to this point, working with mental images presupposes an "internal eye". In a well known extrapolation of this point, this eye is ascribed to a "homunculus". However, as for instance Kosslyn and Pomerantz (1977) point out, one could make a similar objection against propositional accounts of cognition. Just as internal images have to be "seen", internal propositions have to be "scanned". Thus, according to a similar argument, propositional accounts would have to postulate a homunculus analyzing propositional structures. A propositionalist would reject this point. He would argue that propositions are embedded in mental systems which are functionally integrated in the overall behavior of a subject. This integration ensures that no "scanning" by a homunculus is required. However, such an argument can also be made in case of theories of imagery: mental images are functionally embedded in systems that govern the overall behavior of a subject. There is no reason to postulate a homunculus here when it is not postulated in the context of a propositionalist view.

c. Also the third reproach can be countered in a straightforward way. We noticed in reply a. that imagerist theories propose that images are memorized after they have been processed semantically. Now during the pre-processing, a lot of noise and irrelevant details may be filtered out of the input. Further, it is plausible that an object is stored in semantic memory in its canonical orientations only (see e.g. Rosch and Mervis 1976). Consequently, the images which are memorized may be considerably more simple than the noisy input patterns which are ranged over the retinal neurons. Thus, the storage-capacity required by images may be not as large as one may suspect at first sight. Further, images with a part-whole configuration are stored by the way of their components and a skeleton or a main part to which they are attached (see further). Hence, the representations of images which share parts share components. This bears a further reduction of the involved storage capacity. Remarkably, imagerists reverse the argument: as far as concerns the representation of spatial information, images are much more economic than propositions. In fact, images may contain a lot of implicit information. Imagerists propose that the brain includes mechanisms that allow to extract this information.

d. Fourth, Pylyshyn conjectures that images are addressed serially in search-processes. This conjecture can be answered in two ways. First, as we have noticed, in non-naive models of imagery, it is accepted that the memories of images are structured in terms of their part-whole organization. Hence, a search process may be guided by the constraint that a particular part should be present in an image that is searched. Second, if the discussion is seen from a connectionist point of view, it is easily accepted that images are content-addressable: several neural network models can recognize a stored pattern from an activation of some of its parts. Further, several connectionist models easily filter out substantial amounts of noise.

4.2 Mental imagery and experimental evidence

We consider three experiments which favor imagerist models (see Kosslyn (1980) for a more complete review). The experiments on mental rotation by Shepard and Metzler (1971) are well known. They assessed the time subjects needed to rotate mentally a first picture in a second one. The second picture was identical to the first one, except for its orientation. It appeared that the relationship between the time involved to rotate an image and the rotational disparity was linear: for every increment in amount of rotation, an equal increment in rotation time was observed. Other experiments confirmed this relation. For instance, Cooper and Shepard (1973) used letter stimuli and examined the time subjects required to rotate the same letters with different orientations in each other. They obtained again a linear relationship between angular disparity and time involved to carry out the rotation. These results show that mental images are rotated mentally in analogy with a uniform rotation of physical objects: it seems that each angular position between the initial and the final position is passed with uniform velocity. The explanation of Kosslyn (e.g. Kosslyn, Pinker et al., 1979; Kosslyn, 1980) invokes a "surface matrix" on which a mental image is rotated with uniform velocity.

The imagerist interpretation agrees with evidence of Shepard and Feng (1972) on mental paper-folding. In these experiments, subjects were shown unfolded cubes with arrows marked on two surfaces. The task was to determine if the arrows would meet when the cubes would be refolded. The time required to solve the problem mentally appeared to be linearly related with the number of folds which would be required when the problem would be solved with physical folding. The introspective reports of the subjects were continuous with this fact: they claimed to refold the cube mentally. Like in case of experiments on mental rotation, this point fits in an imagerist explanation if it is specified, first, that mental operations on mental objects reflect physical operations on physical objects and, second, that equal sub-operations take an equal amount of time. On the other hand, it is not obvious how a propositionalist theory of imagery might explain these observations.

Finally, we consider a mental scanning experiemnt. In Kosslyn, Ball and Reiser (1978), a map of a fictitious island was presented to a subject. Several objects were drawn on it: a cloud, a tree, a lake, and so on. The subject was asked to memorize the map. Next, he was asked to focus mentally on one of the objects on it. Then, the experimenter named a second object and he instructed the subject to search mentally for it. When the subject focussed on it, he pressed a button. A plot of the reaction times as a function of the distance between both objects showed that scanning time increased when larger mental distances had to be scanned. These results suggest that mental scanning can be interpreted as an interiorization of a simple physical operation, for instance a movement with uniform velocity of a pointer over a screen. Also here, it is not straightforward to give a propositional explanation of these facts (note 5).

The experiments considered in the present paragraph are explained more elegantly in terms of images and properties of operations on images than by a propositional description. Still, propositionalists continue to claim that their kind of representations can cope in principle with all these problems. However, such claims are never worked out (note 6). As a general point, we notice that, in principle, a propositionalist theory can compute all functions and operations that an imagerist theory proposes: it is well known that Turing machines can compute any computable problem (see e.g. Johnson-Laird, 1979). Hence, a propositionalist theory that formalizes Kosslyn's one would predict exactly the same things. However, this argument does not render the discussion meaningless. In fact, the point at issue is not a syntactic one, but is of a semantic nature. If the terms of a propositional theory would have a direct interpretation in terms of images that are ranged over a surface matrix, of mental scanning operations, of mental rotations, and so on, then one would have an imagerist theory of imagery rather than a propositionalist one. The point that matters in the present discussion are properties that a theory ascribes to the mental processes which are studied. In case of a computationalist theory, operations on mental images are explained in terms of structural properties of strings of symbols and in terms of formal deduction rules. In an imagerist model, on the other hand, imagerist terms dominate the explanation.

4.3 Kosslyn's surface matrix model of mental imagery

Kosslyn's theory of mental images can be summarized by the following quote
(Kosslyn (1978, p.243)):

*" Images are temporary spatial displays in active memory that are generated from
more abstract representations in long-term memory. Interpretative mechanisms ...
work over ... these internal displays and classify them in terms of semantic
categories. "*

The theory has two components. First, it provides specifications about the way in
which image information is represented. Second, it specifies the procedures that
operate on mental images. As concerns the representation of images, the theory
proposes two kinds of data structures. If images are retrieved, they are represented
on a "surface matrix". In long term memory, the images are represented by "long
term memory files". When an image is activated on the surface matrix, it is like a
template: it consists of intensity values which can be written in the form of a matrix.
The surface matrix has limited resolution, as follows form the fact that subjectively
smaller images are more difficult to inspect (Kosslyn and Alper, 1977). The most
activated region of the surface matrix is round in shape, and flattens into an ellipse
in the less activated regions: images gradually fall off toward the periphery
(Kosslyn, 1978). Further, the matrix is a short term memory structure: in order to
maintain a representation on it, effort is required.

The long term representations of images contain two kinds of information.

a. First, long term representations include information about the "literal" appearance
of the objects which are memorized. Kosslyn suggests that this information is stored
by the way of files of polar coordinates, because operations like "zoom" and
"rotate" are expressed most straightforwardly with help of such coordinates. The
model assumes that the main part or the skeleton of the image and its more detailed
parts are stored in different files in long term memory. We met this point in the
previous chapter. Kosslyn, Pinker et al. (1979, p. 541) put forward that:

*"A given object may be represented by more than a single image file in the model.
One such file represents a global shape or central part (this question is open at
present). Other files represent "second looks" that can be integrated into the global
or central shape to form a fully fleshed-out image. ... "*

b. The second kind of data stored in long term memory contains facts about the image. These data can be divided in five classes:

i. For each independently stored detail or part of an image, it must be stored where it has to be attached on the skeleton of the image.

ii. For each such part or detail, a set of procedures has to be stored that makes possible its detection in a mental image that has been loaded on the surface matrix.

iii. Each long term memory representation of a stored image or of a part must be associated with a name.

iv. The object's size must be specified.

v. Finally, also the name of the most frequently associated superordinate category has to stored (note 7).

4.4 Operations on images

A theory of mental images is complete only if operations are formulated according two which the images can be manipulated. Kosslyn proposes three classes of operations:

a. The first class of procedures controls the generation of an image from its long-term store. The central commands involved in this task are "picture", "put" and "find". "Picture" converts an memory-file in a pattern over the surface matrix. "Find" is used to know were a part has to be attached on an image. "Put" reads the results of the "find" procedure and then integrates the desired parts into an image.

b. The second class of procedures carries out search tasks on images. The primary procedure of this class is "find". It may search for a part of an image that satisfies a set of form-constraints. If the part is not readily detectable, "lookfor" may operate on the image in order to generate more detailed or more global representations.

c. The command "lookfor" has the commands "rotate", "zoom" and "pan" (i.e. the converse of "zoom": it contracts an image) at its disposal. The latter commands are typical members of the third class of image-operations: they generate image transformations. Kosslyn distinguishes between "field-general" and "region-bounded" transformations. The field-general ones transform the whole of the visual matrix in some way. Region-bounded ones delineate a particular region in the surface matrix and transform only the part of the image within this region.

4.5 Images and movements

An adequate theory of mental imagery should address how movements are represented. This point is not addressed in Kosslyn's studies. We suggest that the representation of simple movements in an approach like Kosslyn's one is possible in principle. The question of relevance for us is whether the aspect of movement of an object or of a part of an object may be represented by extension of the involved P's with sf's that refer to movement. This issue is different from the one of the image manipulations discussed by Kosslyn: the present point concerns the storage of movement in long term memory, not the mental manipulation of images on a surface matrix.

To start with, we consider how the movement of a simple object may be represented in long term memory. More specifically, consider an object that is represented by a single P only (we argue in chapter IV that initial child-concepts may be of this kind). For instance, suppose that a ball is represented by a single P; its static aspects may be represented by two sf's that express respectively "smooth surface" and "round shape". Then, "rolling" may be expressed by a third sf that is added to the P. For instance, the movement-sf may specify which parts of a mentally activated image are subject to a velocity flux (we are reminded of the existence of pre-semantic movement-sf's (see chapter II, note 3; Allman, Miezin et al. 1985; Ballard, 1986); hence, as is the case for other visual sf's, also in the case of a movement-sf it is meaningful to presume a correspondence between pre-semantic sf's and semantic sf's). In case of a more complex object (i.e. an object represented by an M that consists of more than a single P), an additional problem raises. For instance, consider the representation of a car and suppose that it embraces that the car can move. If a car moves, then all parts of the car move along with it: its windows, its steering wheel, and so on. One may wonder if the movement of the car is reflected in the P's that represent these parts, or whether the aspect of movement is integrated in the P that refers to the car-skeleton. We give two plausibility arguments in favor of the second possibility:

a. Probably, the mental coordination between the movement of an object and the movement of its parts does not take place automatically. As has been argued in classical developmental psychology (Piaget and Inhelder, 1956), children acquire the spatial insights of adults (as concerns the coordination of perspectives) only about the age of 9 or 10. Before this age, children have difficulty to coordinate different perspectives. Hence, if the parts of a complex moving object may themselves make relative movements, one may suspect that young children have severe difficulty to show the spatial insight required to integrate the moving parts and the moving object in a spatially consistent whole. Consequently, it is plausible to suppose that the movement of a complex object is reflected in first instance in the P which refers to its skeleton or to its main part, since subjects may lack the ability to attach the correct movements to parts.

b. Second, if the movement of an object is expressed in the *P* that corresponds to its skeleton or to its main part, then the movements that are expressed in the *P*'s corresponding to the parts may express their specific function.

Although we will not work out these considerations in detail, they give some plausibility to the stance that some aspects of the memorization of movements (in long term memory) may be described by *sf*'s. We adopt this stance as a working hypothesis. The present point only concerns relatively simple movements. Complex or profound movements can not be expressed by a velocity field in a part of a mental image, since then the image itself changes drastically. In order to represent such movements, different images have to be linked by explicit temporal associations (see IV,8).

5 Images and image schema's

5.1 Implicit information and image schema's

If the number of inferences that can be drawn from representations that contain implicit information is high, they allow to memorize information in a quite economic way. In this sense, implicit representations have a potential advantage over explicit ones (e.g. Hayes-Roth 1979, p.553). Kosslyn, Pinker et al. (1979) argue that propositional models do not allow to represent configurational information implicitely, and that a surface matrix model, on the other hand, allows for this point. At closer inspection, this claim is substantiated only to a limited degree. The latter model includes a "find"-operation that allows to find objects or their parts (note 4). However, an adequate model must also be able to detect relations like "X is contained in Y" or " X is the second object on the left of Y", and on on. The issue is not considered by Kosslyn et al.

In an appraoch that he terms "cognitive semantics", Lakoff (1987) examines the problem which relations subjects may derive from their mental images, and he suggests that the answer is furnished by his theory on image schema's. Image schema's are elementary and relatively abstract schema's which can be used to analyze mental images. For example, one may examine if a container-schema is realized in a particular image: one may control if a particular object is contained in another one or not. As another example, the link-schema can be used to determine if two objects are connected in an image. The contact-schema can be used to find out if two parts of a mental image contact each other. The above-schema determines if something is above something else, and so on. Image schema's not only analyze static properties: some of them structure images which contain movement. For example, Lakoff suggests that the image schema that expresses the relation "over" in "the dog jumps over the fence" contains a dot moving over a line. Further, image schema's bear testimony of the "embodiment" of thought. According to this hypothesis, the way our bodies interact with the world determines the way we structure it. Each image schema is assumed to have a kinesthetic counterpart. The following quote (Johnson 1988, see also Lakoff 1987, p. 271) illustrates how many times we may use the container-schema to structure kinesthetic experiences within the three first minutes of a day:

"Consider just a small fraction of the orientational feats you perform constantly in your daily activities - consider, for example, only a few of the many 'in-out' orientations that might occur in the first few minutes of an ordinary day. You wake 'out' of a deep sleep and peer 'out' from beneath the covers 'into' your room. You gradually emerge 'out' of your stupor, pull yourself 'out' from under the covers, climb 'into' your robe, stretch 'out' your limbs, and walk 'in' a daze 'out' of your bedroom and 'into' the bathroom. You look 'in' the mirror and see your face staring 'out' at you. You reach 'into' the medicine cabinet, take 'out' the toothpaste, squeeze 'out' some toothpaste, put the tooth-brush 'into' your mouth, brush your teeth and rinse 'out' your mouth. At breakfast you perform a host of further 'in-out' moves - pouring 'out' the coffee, setting 'out' the dishes, putting the toast 'in' the toaster, spreading 'out' the jam on the toast, and so on. "

The kinesthetic aspects of image schema's can be evidenced experimentally. If congenetically blind people are asked to carry out cognitive tasks that involve, for instance, mental rotation, one obtains the same relations between the experimental variables as in case of non-blind people. This suggests that image schema's are tightly related to basic experiences of body-movements, irrespective of the fact whether body-movements are made sensitive by touch or by vision. In this sense, image-schemas are more than just simple image structures. Still, they usually contain a component that can be visualized straightforwadly by a simple schema that consists of simple elements like circles, lines, squares, and so on. In effect, in his applications of the theory of image schema's to concrete problems, Lakoff systematically uses simple images in order to explain what an image schema is about. In complex cases (e.g. in case of the image schema for "over"; see Lakoff, 1987), one may solve ambiguities if one associates more than one simple image with a word.

Also at other places in literature, quite some attention has been payed to the detection of relations and schema's in images. Such detection mechanisms allow to make inferences which would be much harder without image representations. In the sixtees, Huttenlocher (1968) and Elliot (1965) examined the performance of subjects on inferences based on statements like "Tom is smaller than Sam" and "John is larger than Sam". The evidence supported the hypothesis that subjects imagined tokens of Tom, John, and so on, translating heigth relations into spatial relations in a mental image. Later, in the literature about machine vision, different proposals were made to extract relations from images (Brady, 1982; Rosenfeld and Kak, 1976; Ullman, 1984). Also in cognitive science, different proposals have been formulated that allow to make deductions based on schematic images (e.g. Johnson-Liard, 1983; Funt, 1977,1981; Larkin and Simon, 1987; Lindslay, 1988).

At this instance, we are reminded of the fact that connectionism is reproached by several "computationalists" that it is not able to represent relations in any adequate way. For instance, Fodor and Pylyshyn (1988) argue that connectionist models can not deal with relations like "X is to the left of Y". In his direct reply, Smolensky (1988b,1990) proposed a connectionist tensor-product model that could graps some aspects of the representation of relations. Slightly later, different connectionist authors tried to develop models which aimed to represent aspects of relations (see Hinton, 1990). However, none of these models allows to infer relations like "X is to the left of Y" from images, and they are not capable to make elementary spatial inferences. According to the present view, a better reply to the computationailist criticism is to refer to the modularity of the brain. Some important semantic modules are not concerned with the representation of spatial relations; some of them are concerned with non-specific associations only. Hence, a connectionist model must not necessarily be able to manipulate specific relations or spatial relations in order to have psychological relevance. This argument gains force if one is able to localize the module that one describes in the global whole of cognitve modules. The present approach follows this direction.

5.2 The explicit storage of detected image schemas as components of a multi-component patterns

In paragraph 4, we pointed out that images have a long term representation in a format that is different from their representation on the surface matrix. The long term representation stores an image in terms of its components. This is reminsicent of the structure the of multi-component patterns that we considered in the previous chapter. Since we use these multi-component patterns to describe a module for non-specific associations, one may wonder if the long term memory for images coincides with the module in which non-specific associations are carried out.

This is not the case. First, the latter module does not include specifications concerning relative locations on skeletons or on main parts of a more global image. Second, the constraints imposed on a module for non-specific associatons entail that not all components of a multi-component concept M that corresponds to an object have a direct visual counterpart in the object. As we will see (chapter IV), in order to obtain apropriate topological relations between different M's, it is necessary to allow that an M has components of the following kinds:

i. A representation of an object may include a component that expresses the presence of the object in a particular scene. For instance, the M that corresponds to an object may include one or more P's that correspond to the skeletons of the scenes in which it frequently occurs.
ii. Second, if an image schema has been detected in an object or a scene, and if the structure revealed by the image schema is of high relevance, then a subject may benefit from a permanent, explicit storage of the information that the image schema can be detected in the image. We propose that this point can be represented by the fact that a component P that corresponds to the image schema is added to the multi-component state M that corresponds to the object or to the scene.

An image schema is not literary present in the visual representation of an object or a scene, but it must be inferred. However, an addition of components that correspond to image schema's to the representation of an M has important topological advantages. Such components may help to localize the representaiton of a scene or an object in the complex web of associative relationships between memorized patterns. According to the associative topology of the model that we construct, the associative relationship between two items is determined, among others, by the number of P's that they share. The larger this number, the tighter the associative link between the items. Hence, if the same image schema is recognized in two scenes (or objects), then these scenes (or objects) become associatively more close to each other. The fact that two items share an image schema may indicate that they share a function. This is an important principle for the formation of superordinate categories (see next chapter). Similarly, the fact that two objects occur in the same scene may express that these objects are functionally related.

Finaly, we notice that a P that corresponds to an image schema may include sf's which refer to movements. More specifically, we cna differentiate between movements of two kinds:

i. First, a movement-*sf* may refer to a bodily movement of the subject. Since an image schema often has a kinesthetic counterpart, such *sf*'s can be integrated in it in a meaningful way.

ii. Second, it may refer to a movement of an external object. For instance, the visual component of an image schema may contain a circle that moves over a line. This aspect can be included in the image schema by the way of an sf that expresses a velocity field in the points where circle is located.

NOTES

Note 1. This is a simplification, since we will see in the next chapter that also "indirect" links between concepts may be present in a knowledge base that stores non-temporal associatons.

Note 2. More concisely, we should formulate: we argue that at least one of the modules that stores specific relations differs from at least one of the modules that generates non-specific associations, since the argument that follows does not exclude that a multitude of modules for concepts exists. Along with the modules that can be differentiated according to the criterion that is considered, some modules might be present that have more hybrid properties.

Note 3. A similar point is made in Smolensky (1988) in the context of a discussion between connectionists and computationalists.

Note 4. In the context of the discussion concerning hemispheric lateralization (Appendix II), the issue of the distributedness of the representations is considered with more detail.

Note 5. Pylyshyn (1979), p. 563 notes that the scope of the scanning experiments is not quite wide since it does not entail that subjects necessarily make use of mental scanning in order to search for a particular place or object in a scene. He points out that it seems plausible that subjects can imagine a map and draw attention to lights going on simultaneously in different locations. Or, as another example, one can imagine that at one place in the visual field a light switches off and that, immediately afterwards, a light switches on at another, removed location. For this situation, one would not expect time delays which are dependent on distance. Hence, Pylyshyn argues that imagerists should take into account also other mental detection procedures than mental scanning Notwithstanding this point, the fact remains that mental scanning can be described straightforwardly by an imagerist model while it is less obvious to describe it by a propositionalist one.

Note 6. As Mandler (1983) points out: *"It is fair to say that although claims have been made that the complexities of imagery can be represented purely propositionally, no one has tried to do so in any detail."*

Note 7. If concepts are represented in an intrinsic way, then it suffices to associate the name of a superordinate concept with the representation of this concept only: it is not necessary to couple the superordinate name to the representations of all instances of this concept (see chapter I). Actually, the fifth specification is only necessary if abstractions are made within the module that stores the long term representations of images. This is not trivial: concepts are represented also in other modules, and these other modules may be better suited to implement operations like abstractions. For instance, the non-verbal module that we will describe allows in a straightforward way for operations like abstraction and instantiation.

IV. FEATURE PACKAGES AND THE REPRESENTATION OF FUNCTION

1 Introduction

The chapter starts with the debate between the stance that concepts are composed of features and the hypothesis that concepts are defined in terms of their function. We consider evidence that shows that young infants are able to use form-information to differentiate between different basic level concepts and, to some extent, between different subordinate concepts (paragraph 2). Then, we consider the view that concepts are composed of features. According to the feature-addition hypothesis, the number of features that is included in a concept increases during ontogenetic evolution (paragraph 3). The functionalist stance, on the other hand, proposes that a concept that corresponds to an object is generated only when a child becomes aware of its function. Gradually, perceptual features may be included in a concept. However, they are secondary relative to its "functional core" (paragraph 4). Our discussion suggests that form complements function, and that function complements form (paragraph 5).

We argue that there are crucial aspects of function that can be described by "generalized" sf's and P's (paragraph 6). Some aspects of function can be described partially by reference to needs and emotions. In order to include this possibility in our frame, we assume that "generalized" sf's can refer to emotions. Function can be represented by P's that correspond to image schema's which are recognized in memorized scenes. A P that is common to two or more concepts and that corresponds to an image schema may express that the concepts share a function. The perspective that is obtained suggests a particular version of the differentiation between intrinsic and extrinsic categories. Different types of concepts have different properties (paragraph 7). Finally, we comment on the fact that P's that correspond to image schema's may help to form abstract categories (paragraph 8).

2 The recognition of forms in infancy and in early childhood

2.1 The ability of infants to recognize forms

The ability of infants to recognize forms has been examined in numerous studies. In general, these studies use the habituation-dishabituation paradigm. The idea behind this method is that infants direct their visual attention to unfamiliar visual stimuli. When a stimulus becomes more familiar, it receives less attention. Hence, if a familiar stimulus appears together with a new object in the visual field of an infant, it will direct its attention to the latter one. Consequently, the familiarity of an object can be inferred from the absence of visual attention. Most studies which used this method agreed that infants are able to classify and to recognize forms. For example, it has been shown repeatedly that infants are able to form categories of faces (e.g. Cornell, 1974; Fagan, 1976; Sherman, 1985) and of facial expressions (Caron, Caron and Meyers, 1982). Infants can categorize also nonsense objects (Ruff, 1980; Younger, 1985) and dot patterns of geometric forms (Bomba and Siqueland, 1983). Further, they appear to be able to form categories involving motion (Gibson, Owsley and Johnson, 1978) and numerosity (Strauss and Curtis, 1981).

More recently, such experiments have been replicated for real-world objects such as "birds" (Roberts 1988). It appeared that infants could differentiate birds from non-birds immediately after the familiarization-phase, but also when the test-stimuli were presented with a five-minute delay. The latter fact suggests that infants are able to retrieve the stored form-category from memory. In principle, one might ascribe the fact that infants form a "bird" category to the fact that they would not be able to discriminate between the different instances of birds. Then, a genuine category formation would not have occurred: according to the common use of the term, "category formation" means that discriminable instances are grouped into a category. However, in a separate experiment, Roberts (1988) pointed out that infants are able to discriminate between different birds. Hence, children appear to be able to form a genuine "bird"-category on the basis of form-information corresponding to instances of birds. The concept "bird" is a category at the basic level of abstraction (chapter IX). We will see that the concepts corresponding to a child's first words refer in general to basic level categories. The present point suggests that verbal instruction may be facilitated by pre-verbal sensory-derived representations.

2.2 Infants and superordinate categories

There are a couple of remarkable studies in which it is argued that infants are able to form categories on a superordinate level (e.g. Ross, 1980; Golinkoff and Halperin, 1983). At the same time, these studies point to the limited use of form-information for category formation. For instance, in Ross (1980), infants between one and two years old were habituated to different pieces of furniture and to different kinds of food. As concerns the category "furniture", they were confronted with a couch, a bookcase and a table. The foods to which they were habituated were: bread, a hot dog and a slice of salami. The experiment contained two parts. The first one did not give evidence for superordinate categorization in infants, but the second one did.

First, it was tested if infants payed visual attention to a new piece of furniture. Since this appeared to be the case, the experiment suggested that infants do not create the "furniture"-category. Similar results were obtained for "food" (note 1). Hence, as concerns category formation, children appeared to depend on the presence of perceptual similarities. The second part of Ross' experiments, however, indicated that the opposite was true. A choice-task was added to the habituation-dishabituation paradigm. Instead of confronting an infant in the test-phase of the experiment with a single object, the infant was confronted with two objects and the experimenter noted which of them attracted his attention. For example, in the test phase, the infant was be confronted with both a chair and an apple. It was observed that the infant payed systematically attention to the object that did not belong to the superordinate category to which it was habituated. Hence, one may conclude that the infant was able to demarcate the superordinate category: in order to favor systematically objects that do not belong to a category, this category must have been constructed in some or other way. This is a remarkable point since it is in contradiction with the more classical conception (Ross 1980, p.395):

"In sum, the results of this study suggest a conclusion different from that made by classical grouping studies (Bruner et al., 1966; Inhelder and Piaget, 1964; Vygotsky, 1962). By using a procedure that relied on productive activity (i.e. sorting) and that required both consistency and completeness in category- groupings, they found that preschool children did not classify objects by category and concluded that young children do not from categories as do adults".

However, this contradiction does not entail that the "classical" results are wrong. Rather, they entail that experimental results have to be interpreted with care. In fact, the research by Bruner, Piaget and Vygotsky (to which Ross refers in the previous quote) relies on a different experimental methodology. Basically, these classical studies point out that, if children are asked to classify objects, they regularly and spontaneously switch their classification criterion in the course of the task. Adults, on the other hand, do not switch their criterion if a large set of items has to be classified. Clearly, these results concern something else than the facts which are revealed by the habituation-dishabituation paradigm. The necessity to pay attention to the specific experimental method that is used can also be illustrated by the different results obtained in the first and in the second experiment of Ross (1980). One may wonder why functional similarities are not revealed by the ordinary habituation-dishabituation paradigm. The answer must hide somewhere in the (incompletely known) mechanisms of visual attention. Perceptual similarities appear to be a sufficient ground to decrease visual attention. Functional similarities, on the other hand, have weaker or at least other effects on the mechanisms of visual attention.

Consider the question how infants may construct superordinate categories. It is improbable that the extract some common form: different pieces of furniture or different foods have very few (if any) form-aspects in common. Shared function seems to be the most straightforward alternative principle: foods all serve to eat, and furniture (in a child approximation) may be represented, for instance as something on which something can be put. This issue is considered in paragraph 4.

3 Feature-theories of concept-generation

3.1 The feature-addition hypothesis

The studies considered in the previous paragraph offer arguments in favor of the stance that form-information is of importance for concept formation. According to a related but more extreme position, perceptually derived information is at the heart of the concept formation process. This thesis has been put forward in a well-known paper of E. Clark (1973). It assumes that perceptually derived information is stored by "features" of the kind that Bierwisch (1970) had in mind (see the previous chapter; Clark (1973) also refers to the work on perception of Gibson, 1969). Clark (1973) added a hypothesis concerning the ontogenetic development of concepts. His view is generally known as the "feature-addition hypothesis". It asserts that, in the first stage of concept acquisition, a concept is typified by quite few features. Gradually, children add more such features to their representations of concepts and hence the latter become more complex.

The empirical arguments in favor of this hypothesis stem from the observation that young children overextend the meaning of their concepts. If a child associates only one or two features with a word, the extension of that word is considerably larger than if the concept would be defined by a larger conjunction of criteria: the more conditions to be fulfilled, the smaller the class of objects that satisfy these conditions. For example, suppose that a child has learned the word "dog" and that only the semantic feature "four-legged" is coupled to it. Then, the set of objects referred to as "dog" may include cows, zebra's, sheep and anything else that is four-legged. When other features are added, the child gradually narrows the meaning of "dog" until it coincides with the adult meaning. For instance, the child may add to the "dog"-concept features like "sound: barking" and "size: average" (in comparison, for instance, to a horse and a mouse). "Zebra" may receive in addition to "four-legged" the features "hoofs", "mane", "striped", and so on.

The overextensions which are predicted by this scenario can indeed be found in numerous diaries kept on the early speech of children. Diaries from different language backgrounds agree on this point (e.g. Ament (1899): German; Kenyeres (1926): Hungarian; Rasmussen (1922): Danish, Guillaume (1927): French; Luria and Yudovich (1959): Russian; Moore (1896): English, and so on). Four points appear to be common to all diaries:

i. The age ranges during which the overextensions can be observed are roughly similar for all diaries and they are situated between one year and one month and two years and six months. For every child, the overextension period lasts for about one year. The overextension of a single word, however, rarely lasts longer than eight months, and may occur only very briefly.

ii. The diaries seem to point out that there is a moment of sudden increase in the child's vocabulary. This moment is characterized by an intensive questioning activity of the "what is that?"- variety. It marks more or less the end of the overextension-period.

iii. Not all words appear to be overextended; some words appear to be used in a manner which is consistent with adult criteria from the moment of their introduction into the child's speech.

iv. The features which are used to define concepts in the overextension stage are of a perceptual nature. Similarities of visual, auditory, tactile or olfactory nature seem to guide the majority of the overextensions.

As an extrapolation of iv, Clark suggests that the principal concept criteria of infants and of young children are derived from perception, and that they consist of features that refer to elements of perception, such as movement, shape, sound, size, taste and texture. The feature addition hypothesis can be evidenced also in other ways. Suppose that two concepts are related in meaning and that they share some common features. In case of child-concepts, these common features may be the only ones that characterize these concepts. Hence, it is conceivable that a child is not able to differentiate between concepts which are different according to adults. This phenomenon can be observed indeed. Clark (1973) differentiates between two kinds of concept-confusion due to a lack of discriminating features:

a. It appears that the poles of antithetic concept-pairs such as more/less or same/different initially mean the same for a child. The explanation proposed by Clark is that, initially, children attach the feature "amount" to both "more" and "less". At this stage, it is not possible to differentiate between both concepts. In fact, both of them are used in the sense of "more". Clark (1970, p.91) suggests that this is due to the fact that the notion "having extent" is always best exemplified by the object that has most extent. Thus, "has amount" is accompanied by "+polarity". Only afterwards, the child learns that in case of "less", "has amount" has to be coupled to "-polarity" instead of to "+polarity". A similar scenario is proposed for the concept-pair same/different. This agrees with a study by Donaldson and Wales (1970), who show that young children tend to interpret both "same" and "different" as "same". Only after a certain period, they are able to attach the right feature-combinations to these antithetic concepts.

b. In case of verbs of a certain complexity, a child may not differentiate between two related verbs. For instance, consider the verbs "ask" and "tell". Chomsky (1969) argues that "ask" and "tell" initially are both used as "tell". Only after the addition of features, "ask" can be differentiated from "tell": "ask" involves that the "request-feature" and the allocation of roles are mastered. As a another example, but this time with nouns, consider the word-pairs brother/boy and sister/girl. Piaget (1928) found that, at the earliest stage, these words are treated as synonyms. The features that refer to the relational aspects of, for instance, "brother" are integrated in the concept only about the age of ten.

3.2 The limits of the feature-addition scenario

The feature addition hypothesis has some appealing aspects, but it leaves some issues unsolved. We differentiate between three weak points.

a. If perceptually derived features would form the basis of all conceptual knowledge, one might wonder how a concept like "furniture" would be acquired. Chairs, desks, beds, and so on, appear to share no common form-aspects nor other perceptually derived features. Hence, the formation of "furniture" has to be explained in another way, for example by reference to its function. In fact, as soon as more or less abstract concepts are considered, one arrives at the limits of the feature-addition scenario. As we will see in the following paragraph, this is one of the main arguments of the "functionalist" stance against Clark's position.

b. The second point of criticism concerns the way in which the feature addition scenario deals with the relational aspects of concepts. If relations would be encoded as features, a combinatorial storage capacity would be required. We saw in the previous chapter that, in order to account for relational information, different modules must be considered, such as modules that extract relations from mental images. An approach that reduces relations to features lacks a substantial pont.

c. The feature concept of the feature addition hypothesis can be criticized. In the previous chapter we commented on the concept "semantic feature". It appeared that the way in which this term is used by Bierwisch (1970) (and hence, by Clark) is quite vague and that our concepts sf, P and M allow for a more precise treatment.

One may wonder if the features considered by Clark correspond to our sf's, to P's, or to M's. They apprear to correspond to either sf's or to P's. For instance, a sound like "barking" refers to a single modality. On the other hand, the feature "horns" of the concept "cow" involves different modalities: horns have a color, a form, a hard texture, and so on. Consequently, the data considered by Clark suggest that both the number of sf's as well as the number of P's which are involved in a concept increases. It is plausible to assume that in first instance, different sf's are integrated into a P and that, at a slightly later stage, an increasing number of P's is integrated into an M. Further, one may speculate that sometimes (or maybe often) the first P associated with an object is quite akin to an adult "skeleton" or to an adult main part of the concept (see previous chapter). For instance, in case of "dog", the first P may consist of a form-feature that specifies its non-detailed global form, the color of a particular dog, and the sound-feature "barking". However, the evidence in the context of the feature addition hypothesis is not sufficiently detailed to decide this issue.

4 In defence of the primacy of function: Cassirer, Piaget and Nelson

In the previous paragraph, we saw that, according to the feature addition hypothesis, concept formation is governed mainly by the combination of features. Nelson and colleagues (e.g. Nelson, 1974, 1977; Kessen and Nelson, 1978; Nelson and Gruendel, 1981) put forward a different approach. She formulates two criticisms with regard to feature approaches in general. The first criticism has been met in the previous paragraph. If concepts are represented by perceptually derived features, the problem raises how abstract concepts and functional aspects of concepts are represented. The second criticism is a related one. The semantic feature hypothesis does not differentiate between criteria by which an object can be recognized and the meaning of an object. Both are assumed to be determined by the same features. However, the meaning of an object may be determined also by the way we use it or act upon it. Usually, this information is not included in the perceptual input alone: in general, it takes instruction or sensori-motoric trial and error to become familiar with the functional properties of objects.

The second criticism is implicitly present in the work of Piaget (1954) and of Cassirer (1923). Cassirer (1923) developed a relational theory of concepts according to which the essence of a concept is function rather than substance. A concept is composed and determined in the first place by "logical acts", rather than in terms of the common perceptual features of its exemplars. The latter have to be added to a concept in order to make it perceptually recognizable, but they do not constitute its meaning. A similar idea can by found in the work of Piaget. The practical mastering of object-permanency is acquired during the "sensori-motor stage" (this is the first Piagetian developmental stage; it lasts until the age of two). During this period, objects become embedded in sensori-motor schema's and the object-notion is in first instance determined by the place of the objects in these schema's. Only at the end of the sensori-motor developmental phase (note 2), object recognition is independent from the occurrence of the object in a sensori-motor schema. By then, objects can be recognized by feature detection. Nelson (1974) tries to be more explicit about this process. Concept formation in infants, she argues, consists of four component-processes.

a. An infant must be able to demarcate a form from its background, so that he can draw attention to candidates for objects. It is plausible to assume that this condition is fulfilled for the year-old child (e.g. Piaget, 1954; Bower, 1974).

b. Next, the infant has to detect the functional aspects of the object by instruction or by trial and error. For instance, consider the concept "ball". The child experiences relationships into which the ball enters (e.g. mother picks it up; she throws it; the ball bounces on the floor; I take it; the ball rolls, and so on). The various relations into which it enters must be synthesized over time. The synthesis may include that a ball rolls, bounces, and so on. The result of this functional synthesis forms the "functional core" of the child's concept.

c. Subsequently, an infant may recognize a new instance of the concept if it notes that the functional relationships into which the new instance enters are the same as the ones into which the first exemplar entered. In parallel with the development of a functional concept-criterion, perceptual attributes are noted and enter the demarcation-criteria of concepts. For instance, an infant may recognize a ball also when it is not aproached by an activated sensori-motor schema. In order to be able to explain this faculty, functionalists acknowledge that an infant's concept-properties are not restricted to purely functional ones. Perceptual features may accumulate and synthesize during the learning process. However, Nelson (1974) argues that they are secondary (p.284). In contradistinction with the functional core, perceptual features need not always to be present in an instance of the concept. For example, balls may have all kinds of colors. For some objects, one may construct feature-hierarchies: some features are very often, others less often realized.

d. Finally, a name is attached to the concept. This may happen by instruction or the child himself may invent one.

5 Function versus perceptual features

If we compare the previous paragraph with paragraph 2, we observe that Piaget and Nelson overemphasize the importance of function in the genesis of concepts in the sensori-motor child. In Piagets theory, the sensori-motor phases lasts until the 24-th month. However, perceptual pattern-recognition has been observed for children as young as 9 (e.g. Roberts, 1988) and 10 months (e.g. Strauss, 1974). This shift of a couple of months is not the most important conflict between the evidence considered in paragraph 2 and the functionalist stance. The fact that some patterns which are successfully learned by infants have no functional correlate is of higher significance. For instance, in case of the dot-patterns of Bomba and Siqueland (1983) or in case of the nonsense-objects used in Younger (1985), it is quite improbable that the infants would have extracted functional aspects from the patterns to which they habituated. Hence, perceptual features not necessarily need an additional functional core before they can lead to the formation of a concept.

It is plausible to assume that the importance of form relative to function in child-concepts varies over a wide range of possibilities. The representation of "tree" may be dominated by aspects of form. The same could hold initially for "flowers", but from a given moment, a child may be aware that flowers can serve as a present. Then, the form aspects (and possibly the aspects of texture and smell) of the concept are integrated with a functional aspect. In other examples, functional aspects may be included from the beginning, for example in case of instances of "food".

We noticed that the feature addition scenario of conceptual genesis neglects the role of function. We can add another illustration of this point. We saw in 3.1 that overextensions of word-meanings may be interpreted as evidence in favor of particular feature-approaches. However, one can find in literature also observations of "underextensions" of word-meanings by young children. A child may understand a word only within the context of one procedure, whereas an adult may use the word in a more general way. Then, the word has a more narrow meaning for the child than for an adult. Such underextensions show that function plays a significant role in a child's concepts.

For instance, one of the children observed in Huttenlocher (1974) underextends the word "Mommy": it is only used in the context of wanting to be picked up from the highchair or playpen. Similarly, Nelson (1977) observes a one and a half year old child who can identify her nose, hair, eyes and other parts of her face upon demand. The child does not understand the word face. However, when asked to wash her face, she goes through the motions of rubbing her hand against her face. Nelson suggests that the word "face" is embedded in a single procedure and can not be responded to independently (see also Mandler, 1983). Other examples can be found, for example, in Piaget (1951) and Greenfield and Smith (1976). In conclusion, none of both extreme stances is tenable: functionalist accounts of concepts have to take into account perceptually derived features and feature accounts have to be complemented with functionalist elements.

6 Aspects of function which can be described as generalized *sf*'s

6.1 Functional features

Clark (1973) acknowledges that features may be of a functional kind - although he does not consider the problems related to this contention. For instance, Clark suggests that one of the child-features of "brother" could be "someone who lives with you". Such a characteristic has a functional connotation. Furthermore, we read (Clark, 1973, p.108):

"To summarize, the first semantic features used by the child appear to be based on his perceptions of the world. To this kind of semantic feature are added those features of meaning that are contributed by social or functional factors within the cultural context. These social factors have been described in terms of different roles that may be named or assigned to participants in some situation. While some roles are assigned on temporary basis (e.g. verbs like "promise" or "ask"), others may be more permanent in character."

Hence, feature approaches allow that "features contributed by functional factors" participate in the meaning of a concept. However, this bears three kinds of problems:

a. First, functional features do not fit in (for instance) Clark's circumscription of "feature". In order to explain his feature-notion, he referred to work in the field of perception by Gibson (1969). It is puzzling then how "functional" features may enter the scene.
b. Second, by allowing social, functional and perceptual features without any good circumscription, the problem raises that the notion "feature" may become trivial: in the end, almost everything can be considered as a feature.
c. Finally, function generally involves relations between elements. However, as we have noticed, the description of relations with help of features is rather problematic.

Still, one may wonder if the term "feature", if it is specified in accordance with our terms *sf*, *P* and *M*, can be extended in a meaningful way so that aspects of function can be grasped by it. We argue that the answer to this question is positive.

6.2 Function, *sf*'s and *P*'s

A subject may be aware of the function of an object that directly satisfies a
particular need or desire, such as hunger or warmth. Hence, in order to extend our
frame so as to include aspects of function, we would like to include representational
elements which correspond to needs or emotions. The most simple proposal is to
represent needs and emotions as "features" which belong to a modality different
from the ones considered thus far. If one extends the *sf*-concept in such a way,
emotions can be integrated with other *sf*'s in *P*'s. Consider a concept that is
represented by an *M* that integrates several *P*'s. If the *P* that corresponds to the
skeleton contains an sf that refers to an emotion, then the emotion is associated with
the concept as a whole. If, on the other hand, an *P* that refers to a part of the
concept contains an *sf* that corresponds to an emotion, the emotion is associated with
that particular part.

If a subject judges that an object has a function, then the object usually participates
in a transformation or it produces a transformation. Transformations are
accompanied by movements. Hence, movement plays an important role in the
representation of function. We discussed earlier how movement can be described in
our frame (chapter III). It appeared useful to differentiate between two types of
movements. We saw that simple movements can be described by *sf*'s, and we
differentiated between two kinds of *sf*'s: *sf*'s which refer to external movements and
sf's which correspond to kinesthetic movements by the subject. A *P* may contain
movement-*sf*'s of both kinds. In order to describe profound transformations, one has
to make recourse to explicit temporal associations between different scenes.

Our present discussion suggests how to integrate aspects of function in our frame:

a. Aspects of the function of an object can be expressed by *sf*'s which are integrated
in *P*'s. More specifically, two kinds of *sf*'s are especially important for the
representation of function:
i. *sf*'s which refer to emotions
ii. *sf*'s which refer to simple movements
b. As pointed out in the previous chapter, also *P*'s that refer to image schema's may
contribute to the representation of function. Paragraph 8 comments on this point.
c. A subject may have memorized a scene in which a particular object occurs. Such
a scene may contain information concerning the function of the object. This point
and its consequences are considered in the next paragraph.

7 Internal and external properties of objects

7.1 Direct and indirect associations

Consider two memorized objects or scenes and suppose that the first one triggers the second one during an association process. Then, we can differentiate between two possibilities:

a. The concepts may trigger one another directly. In other terms, when the state of the system evolves from the first concept to the second, it does not pass the close neighborhood of other memorized concepts.
b. The concepts may be associated with each other indirectly. Then, before the network state reaches the second pattern, it passes the close neighborhood of another one. The intermediate memorized pattern may function as an associative bridge between the two patterns which are associated.

As an example of the second case, the intermediate pattern may represent a scene and the associated patterns may represent objects that occur in it. In special, the scene may mediate between objects which are functionally related to each other. For instance, suppose that a subject memorizes a scene in which a bird sits on a nest. Then, the concept "nest" may trigger this scene and next the scene may trigger the concept "bird".

We are reminded of the fact that a representation of a scene or of an object contains a P that corresponds to its skeleton (or to a main part) as well as P's that describe its parts. The latter P's may correspond to the skeleton or the main part of these parts (a detailed representation may include P's which refer to parts of these parts, and so on). In case of a scene, these parts usually correspond to the objects which participate in it. Hence, the skeleton or the main part of an object that participates in a scene is a P that is common to the representation of the scene and the representation of the object. Consequently, since the strength of the link between two items is determined, among others, by the number of shared P's, an object may be associated with a scene in which it occurs and vice versa.

7.2 Gradations of strength in indirect associative links

We notice that there are two straightforward possibilities to introduce gradations in the strength of associative link between indirectly associated objects:

a. First, two indirectly associated objects may both participate in different scenes. This increases the probability of an association between both: if, in an association process, one particular scene in which both objects participate is not triggered, there is still a chance that one of the other scenes is activated.

b. An object and a scene in which the object participates may share more than one P. For instance, the concept "cigarette" and the scene "someone smokes a cigarette" may both contain a skeleton-P for "cigarette" and for "smoke". This strengthens the indirect associative link between "cigarette" and other objects which appear in the scene "someone smokes a cigarette". For example, if someone only smokes during break, "cup of coffee" may be such another object. Since the transition between "cigarette" and "smoking a cigarette" is made more quickly, also the composite transition from "cigarette" to "smoking a cigarette" and from "smoking a cigarette" to "cup with coffee" is made more quickly.

Finally, we notice that there is also a third possibility to strengthen the associative link between an object and a scene in which it participates (see learning rule L8 of chapter VI). According to the this possibility, the skeleton of a scene may invade into the representation of a participating object. Then, the scene and the object share at least two P's: one that corresponds to the skeleton of the scene and one that corresponds tot the skeleton of the object.

7.3 Intrinsic and extrinsic properties of objects

The previous paragraph suggests to differentiate between two kinds of properties of objects (see also Barr and Kaplan, 1987, p.402).

a. The "internal properties" of an object are apparent from the representation of the object itself. For instance, the fact that a bird has wings can be inferred directly from the representation of "bird", since it contains the skeleton-P of "wing".
b. Suppose that a subject memorizes that an object participates in a particular scene. Then, the representation of this scene contains information about the object: it specifies with which other objects it is combined. We call such a specification an "external property". For instance, the fact that a bird sits on a nest is an external

property of "bird" (and of "nest") since it is represented by a scene in which "bird" participates (and in which, along with "bird" and "nest", also e.g. "eggs" and "tree" may participate).

The differentiation of between properties of objects can be used to differentiate between intrinsic and extrinsic categories (Barr and Kaplan, 1987; note 4). A category with no or with only a few extrinsic properties is called an "intrinsic category". A category which has mainly extrinsic properties is an "extrinsic" category. A category may be in between these extremes; then it is neither intrinsic nor extrinsic. However, the evidence discussed in Barr and Kaplan (1987) suggests, that, for several categories, a clear tendency is present. For example, "furniture" and "clothes" are dominantly extrinsic, whereas "bird" and "fruit" are dominantly intrinsic. Barr and Kaplan (1987) showed that intrinsic categories have lower inter-subject variance than extrinsic categories (see also Batig and Montague, 1969; Mc Closkey and Glucksberg, 1978). If subjects are asked to list all instances of a category that occur to them, then the instances appear to be more constant across subjects in case of intrinsic categories than in case of extrinsic categories. Further, the membership distributions of extrinsic objects show more variance than membership distributions of intrinsic categories (Barr and Kaplan, 1987; Rosch, 1975; Hampton and Gardiner, 1983).

8 Functions common to different concepts as guides for abstractions

A particular function may be common to different concepts. In special, the following two cases are often met:

a. Different subordinate concepts which belong to the same basic level category may share a function (note 5). For example, a Louis XIV-chair and a kitchen chair both have the function "to sit on".

b. Different basic level concepts which belong to the same superordinate category may share a function. For example, in case of the superordinate category "vehicle", basic level instances like ship, train, plane and car all have the function "to move and to carry something".

As concerns the second case, we notice the two following facts:

i. The functional aspects of "vehicle" are less specific than the ones of its instances. A bicycle carries one person; a bus may carry many persons; a ship may have a large cargo; a barrow has small load, and so on. The functional aspect of "vehicle", on the other hand, just specifies that "something" is carried.

ii. The concept "vehicle" is achieved ontogenetically at a later instant than its basic level instances (see chapter IX).

Points i. and ii. suggest that the general and less specific function associated with "vehicle" is extracted from the function of its more concrete instances. Consider the question how this extraction may happen. Here, we are reminded of chapter III. Suppose that a subject has to extract a schema that is present in a scene or in an object. Then, the scene or the object is analyzed in terms of image schema's. As concerns the search for configurations of schema's which are common to different instances, we can differentiate between two cases:

a. First, a subject may load the mental images of the instances on the surface matrix and he may examine if an image schema or a combination of image schema's can be detected in all of them.

b. Second, he may examine also the scenes in which the instances participate. He may recognize that each instance participates in a scene with a particular basic structure. Again, this structure is expressed by the way of image schema's.

In both case a and case b, the image schema's which are detected may be represented as P's and they may be added to the representations of the instances. Hence, the latter may acquire common P's. For the sake of illustration, consider a subject who searches for an image schema that is common to different vehicles.

a. As a first possiblity, the subject may concentrate on the mental images of the instances of "vehicle". He may try out several combinations of image schema's, for instance combinations which include schema's that refer to the presence of a steering wheel or to wheels. However, if he considers a sufficient amount of instances, he will discover that not all vehicles have a steering wheel and even that not all vehicles have wheels. After some analysis, he may recognize that the only thing that representations of instances of vehicles have in common is the fact that they move. Then, he may add a P that corresponds to the image schema "can move" to the representations of the individual vehicles.

b. Second, the subject may concentrate on the scenes in which vehicles participate. Suppose that, for each instance of "vehicle", he has memorized a scene in which the instance carries something. Again, the subject may detect this point by inspection of these scenes with help of image schema's. Then, the P (or the P's) that correspond to the image schema('s) that refer to the fact that something is carried may be added to the M's that represent the individual vehicles.

In accordance with Lakoff (1987), the combinations of image-schemas for "can move" and "carries something" may be visualized, for instance, by the following simple drawing:

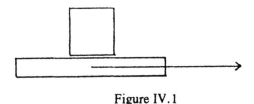

Figure IV.1

Since *P*'s which correspond to such image schema's may participate in the representations of all instances of a concept, they can function as a common abstract core of the concepts. We notice that the capacity to arrive at superordinate cores in this way is intimately related to the capacity to carry out the required analysis with mental images. We will see in the next chapters (especially chapter X) that also other mechanisms contribute to the emergence of a hierarchical knowledge organization. The latter mechanisms are inherent to the dynamics of the module for non-specific associations that we will decribe with more detail.

NOTES

Note 1. In the same study, Ross reports that for the category "man" (more specifically "male doll"), children showed dishabituation-effects. In view of 2.1, this is plausible, since "male doll" is closer to the basic level than a category like "furniture".

Note 2. More specifically, during the fifth and the sixth phase of the sensori-motor stage (see Piaget, 1954).

Note 3. For the important class of concepts which are situated at the basic level of abstraction, aspects of function are in general tightly related with aspects of form (Tversky and Hemmenway, 1984; see chapter IX).

Note 4. Notice that the meaning of "intrinsic" in the dichotomoy intrinsic/extensional dichotomy (chapter I) is somewhat different form the meaning of "intrinsic" in the present dichontomy between intrinsic and extrinsic.

Note 5. See chapter IX for an explanation of these taxonomic terms.

V. THE INTERNAL STRUCTURE OF CATEGORIES

1 Introduction

In contradistinction with an older view that concepts are defined by necessary and sufficient conditions, it is generally recognized nowadays that concepts are defined in a more loose way (paragraph 2). Among the more recent models, the prototype model and the exemplar model can be opposed to each other. According to the prototype model, the components of a concept interact in an additive way. The exemplar model, on the other hand, postulates multiplicative interactions. There is evidence in favor of the point that a prototype model is better than other non-multiplicative models (paragraph 3 and 4). Further, studies of real world concepts reveal that concepts are often organized around one or more prototypes (paragraph 5). However, some properties which are ascribed to prototypes can be predicted also by exemplar models. Moreover, in particular experimental conditions, subjects classify according to the exemplar model rather than according to the prototype model (paragraph 6).

More specifically, it appears that, if subjects are stimulated to represent a concept as a set of independent properties, then they tend to classify in accordance with the exemplar model. If, however, the descriptors of a concept are correlated with each other (e.g. by the experimental conditions or by advance knowledge), then they show additive interactions. Practically, this means that the exemplar model is adequate for non-familiar concepts, and that, when concepts become more familiar, the prototype model offers a better description. Hence, an adequate model for inner-conceptual structure has to allow for both multiplicative as well as additive interactions between the components of a concept (paragraph 7).

Finally, we argue that the dimensions of the models of paragraphs 4 and 6 sometimes correspond to sf's and sometimes to P's. Hence, the P's which participate in an M may interact multiplicatively as well as additively (paragraph 8 and 9).

2 The classical view

2.1 The classical conception of concepts

According to the "classical view" on concepts, a concept is defined as a collection of features which are individually necessary and collectively sufficient (Katz and Postal, 1964; see e.g. Smith and Medin (1981) for a review). For example, the category "zebra" may be defined by the set of features "eats grass", "four-legged", "stripes", "mane", and so on. If something has all these features, it is a zebra. If it lacks at least one of them, it is not. The "classical view" has been supplemented with a theory of learning (Schank, Collins and Hunter, 1986). For the sake of illustration, we consider the approach of Winston (1970) (related proposals can be found, for instance, in Bourne, 1970; Levine, 1975, and Trabasso and Bower, 1968). Consider a subject who learns a category. Then, the first exemplar that he observes determines his initial category definition: an item belongs to the category if and only if it has the features of the first exemplar. Next, as he encounters more exemplars, he changes the category definition as follows:

a. Suppose that the subject is instructed that something is an instance of the category, and suppose that the instance does not possess all the features which are characteristic of the category. Then, the defining features which are not present in the instance must be eliminated from the concept definition.
b. If an object does not belong to the category and if it has all the features that characterize the concept, some additional features must be added to the concept definition. The additional features must be present in all instances of the category but not in the considered object.
c. If an instance is an exemplar of a category and if it has all its defining features or if it is not an instance and if it does not have all its defining features, the concept definition should not be modified.

2.2 Criticisms on the classical view

The classical view on concepts has been the subject of many criticisms. We can differentiate between the following four general points:

a. A first kind of criticism is related to the fact that the classical conception represents concepts by the way of features. This bears two kinds of problems:

i. It is not trivial to reconcile feature-approaches with the importance of relational information. In order to explain the importance of relations as concerns the definition of concepts, a more general frame is required than the one that is offered by the classical view (see chapter III).

ii. The features which define a concept may not be present in an input that corresponds to it. As a simple example, a part of an object may be concealed but the object may still be recognizable. As a more complex example, consider the concept "birthday present". Whether an object is a present or not depends on the existence of a person who has the intention to give it to someone else. Such intentions can not be perceived directly; they have to be inferred.

b. The point that concepts are defined by necessary and sufficient conditions has been the subject of substantial criticism by many authors (e.g. Rosch, 1973; Rosch and Mervis, 1975; Smith, Shoben and Rips, 1974; Medin and Schaffer, 1978; Mc Closkey and Glucksberg, 1978). The core of this criticism goes back to Wittgenstein (1953), who argued that, for instance, the concept "game" has not a set of characteristic features. Some features occur in several instances of "game"; other features are present in only a few instances. However, a set of necessary and collectively sufficient features appears not to exist. Nowadays, it is generally agreed that the instances of a concept may have a wide range of typicalities (this point is discussed in detail in chapter VII). Hence, concept-membership is not an all-or-nothing issue.

c. It appears that there is a fundamental level in conceptual taxonomy. It is the level at which the a child's first concepts are situated. Also in later ontogenetic phases, it can be differentiated from other levels by several experimental properties. This "basic level" is not the most concrete nor the most abstract level, but an intermediate one (chapter IX). The classical view on concepts does not explain the existence of a fundamental level in classification.

d. Finally, the learning-proposal of the classical view is highly simplistic. For instance, it does not take into account the influence of general background knowledge (e.g. Murphy and Medin, 1985) and of pragmatic aspects (e.g. Schank and Abelson, 1977).

3 Models which do not rely on criteria of necessary and sufficient conditions

If a concept is not defined by necessary and sufficient conditions, then the question raises how a subject can decide if a given exemplar belongs to it or not. During the past two decades, different answers have been proposed. For the sake of illustration, we give an example of stimuli which are typically used in experiments in this context. Consider the following faces:

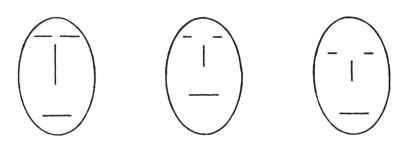

Figure V.1

They contain four variables: the forehead is low or high, the eyes are narrow or not, the nose is long or short, and finally the mouth is high or low. Often, the values of a variable are described by numerical values. For example, one may characterize the forehead-height by a scalar that measures the forehead-height. Alternatively, one can work with binary variables: one can attach the value 0 to the property "low forehead" and the value 1 to "high forehead". Variables which are characterized by numerical values are called "dimensions". Consider two categories A and B which are defined by the following enumerations:

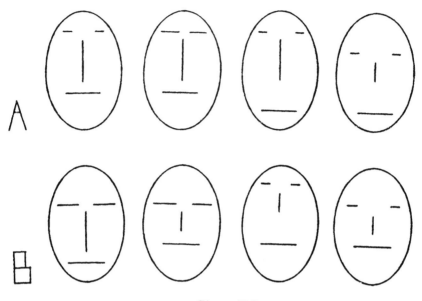

Figure V.2

Suppose that subjects are instructed to memorize these categories, and suppose that, subsequently, new items are shown to the subjects. When they are asked to classify these new items, two possibilities apply: either they do not show any regularity in their classifications, or they classify according to some rule. Intuitively, one may expect that, at least for some new items, the second possibility holds: if a subject sees an input which is close to the exemplars of one category but not to the ones of the other one, one may expect that he will tend to classify it as a member of the former category. Then, the question raises according to which rule such classifications are carried out. The models considered in paragraph 4 and paragraph 6 try to give an answer to this problem.

4 Four non-multiplicative models of classification

In his study of non-classical approaches to categories, Reed (1972) classifies the alternatives for the classical conception in four groups. Although we will see that his classification is not complete, it is interesting to pay some attention to this classification.

4.1 Cue-validity models

The cue-validity-model has been introduced by Beach (1964). We explain it by the way of an example. Suppose that a subject has learned the two categories of picture V.2. Now suppose that he receives an input stimulus that corresponds to one of the exemplars which define the respective categories. More specifically, suppose that the stimulus has a high mouth. Then, given the high mouth, the probability that the exemplar belongs to the first category rather than to the second one is 2/5; the probability that it belongs to the second category is 3/5. Consider a new exemplar that does not participate in the definition of one of both categories, and suppose that this new exemplar has a high mouth. Then, cue-validity models predict that the probability that this input will be classified as a member of category A on the basis of the "high mouth"-cue is 2/5; the probability that it is a member of category B is 3/5 (these probabilities are so-called "cue-validities"). In other terms, the cue-validities which hold for the defining exemplars are assumed to hold also for new inputs.

In a similar way, one can define cue-validities for the other dimensions. For each new item, and for each memorized concept, one can calculate the average of the cue-validities corresponding to the different dimensions. The resulting number is called the cue-validity of the input relative to the memorized concept. Suppose that, in the example, one compares the cue-validities of an input for each of both categories. Then, the "cue-validity model" predicts that the item is classified as a member of the category for which it has highest cue-validity.

4.2 The proximity-algorithm

In order to formulate the following two models, we have to introduce the Minkowsky-distance between patterns. Consider two patterns M^1 and M^2 and suppose that the value of the i-th pattern for the q-th dimension is given by $x(i,q)$. Suppose that the patterns are composed of dimensions. Then, the Minkowsky r-distance between both patterns is given by:

$$d^r(M^1, M^2) = \sqrt[r]{\sum_{q=1}^{n} |x(1,q) - x(2,q)|^r}$$

(eq. V.1)

In accordance with this formula, one can calculate the r-distances between a given input and the memorized exemplars of a category. The proximity-algorithm can be formulated as follows. If an input is presented, one determines which stored exemplar is most close to it. Then, the input is classified in the category to which this exemplar belongs. In alternative versions, one first determines for each category the s-set of s exemplars which are most close to the input. Next, for each s-set, one selects the exemplar which is most removed from the input. Finally, one selects the category for which the latter exemplar is most close to the input.

4.3 The average-distance rule

According to the average-distance model, subjects calculate, for each category, the average distance of the input to the exemplars of the category. Next, they classify the input in the category which is (according to the average distance measure) closest to the input.

4.4 The prototype rule

A "prototype" of a category can be defined in different ways. In case of variables with continuous values, one can define it as the pattern of which the i-th component is equal to the mean value of the of the i-th components of the exemplars of the category. In case of variables with discrete components, prototypes are usually defined in such a way that their i-th component is equal to one of the values of the i-th components of the exemplars. In order to obtain this point, one can take for each dimension the discrete value which is closest to the continuous value obtained by the procedure for continuous values.

According to the prototype-rule for classification, one calculates the distances between an input and the prototypes of all categories. Then, the input is classified in the category that contains the prototype that is most close to the input. Some prototype-models are slightly more complicated in that they allow that some dimensions are of higher importance than others. This means that, if patterns differ along an important dimension, then their distance increases more than if they would have been different according to a less important dimension. This can be expressed formally if one introduces weight-factors $w(i)$ in the expression for the Minkowsky-distance between two patterns (note 1):

$$d^r(M^1, M^2) = \sqrt{\sum_{q=1}^{n} w(q) |x(1,q) - y(2,q)|^r}$$

(eq. V.2)

4.5 Experiments which decide between these models

Reed (1972) examined which of the previous models fits best with the experimental data. It appeared that the weighted-feature variant of prototype rule was the best model: inputs are compared with prototypes but in such a way that the features which discriminate best between categories have highest weight (Reed 1972, p.401). Reed's findings agree with two other classes of results:

a. Consider a subject who has learned some categories by the way of their defining exemplars. Suppose that, for none of these categories, prototypical patterns have been presented during the learning process. Then, in spite of this fact, the subject will classify the prototypes as fast and as accurately as the old training patterns. Further, the defining exemplars and the prototypes are classified better than other new exemplars (e.g. Posner and Keele, 1968; Peterson, Meagher, Chait and Gillie, 1973; Homa and Chambliss, 1975; Homa and Voghsburg, 1976).
b. A second body of results concerns the difference in retention between prototypical and non-prototypical patterns. When delays of the order of several days are inserted between the learning tests and the transfer tests, one observes significantly higher forgetting for the old training stimuli than for the prototypes (e.g. Posner and Keele, 1970; Homa and Voghsburg, 1976; and Goldman and Homa, 1977).

5 Rosch' theory of prototypes

5.1 Prototypes of real world categories and typicalities

Rosch has pointed out that the instances of concepts often cluster around central exemplars (e.g. Rosch, 1978; Rosch and Mervis, 1975). The latter are the "prototypes" of the concept. The closer an exemplar resembles a prototype, the more typical it is for the corresponding category. The prototypes themselves are the most typical category-instances (Rosch 1978, p.36). In order to obtain an estimate for the typicality of a particular instance of a category, the experimenter may ask his subjects to rate it (for instance, by a number between one and nine). It is well documented that subjects agree fairly well with each other about the typicalities of instances (Rips, Shoben and Smith 1973; Rosch and Mervis, 1975; Rosch, Simpson and Miller, 1976; see also chapter VII). Rosch (1978) noticed that typicality is a variable which is tightly correlated with many other psychological variables. Hence, the question if an item is a prototype or not can be decided in different ways. We summarize the evidence in favor of this point:

a. Typicality is correlated with reaction time. The speed with which subjects make category membership decisions is shorter for a prototype than for a non-typical item.
b. The rate at which new items are learned correlates positively with the typicality of the items. In Rosch (1978), this point was evidenced for artificial categories. Anglin (1976) showed that, also in case of real world concepts, young children learn category-memberships of good examples before memberships of poor examples.
c. When subjects are asked to list instances of categories, the most typical ones are mentioned first.
d. Suppose that a noisy stimulus is given to a subject and that he receives the category name of the corresponding instance as a cue. Then, for typical the instances of the category, the cue produces a higher increase in recognition speed.
e. Prototypical category members represent the means of attributes that have a metric, such as size (Rosch, Simpson and Miller (1976); this point is also illustrated in Reed (1972), see paragraph 4).
f. There is a relation between typicality and the way in which words are used in expressions with "hedges". Hedges are qualifying terms such as "almost" and "virtually" (Lakoff 1973). Rosch (1978) shows that, when subjects are given sentence frames such as "X is virtually Y", they reliably place the more typical member of a pair of items into the referent slot.
g. The typicalities of members of superordinate categories are positively correlated with the degree to which they can substitute the superordinate categories in sentences.
h. Finally, also in the context of American Sign Language, evidence can be found for the priority of prototypes (Newport and Belugi, 1978).

6 The exemplar model and its properties

6.1 The exemplar model

The intuition behind the exemplar model is that classification judgements involve no prototypes or abstractions; rather, they are based on comparisons of an input with stored exemplars. This is reminiscent of models like the average-distance model and the proximity-algorithm: also there, an input is related to the stored exemplars instead of to prototypes. An exemplar model, however, differs in an essential respect from these models: in an exemplar model, the dimensions interact multiplicatively instead of additively. As a consequence, different dimensions interact more "dramatically" than in case of additive rules: if an input has not a proper value along one dimension, this may be sufficient to decide that the input is not classified as a member of a particular category (note 2).

There are several reference papers in which the exemplar model is explained (e.g. Medin, 1975; Medin and Schaffer, 1978; Smith and Medin, 1981; Medin, Dewey and Murphy, 1984; related non-additive models can be found in Anderson, Kline and Beasly, 1979; Hayes-Roth and Hayes-Roth, 1977; Martin and Caramazza, 1980; Neuman, 1974; Reitman and Bower, 1973). Especially often cited is Medin and Schaffer (1978). Their model is based on the following assumptions:

i. The probability to classify an item as a member of a category A is proportional to the sum of the similarities of the item with the memorized exemplars of A. It is inversely proportional to the sum of the similarities of the item with all memorized exemplars of all categories.
ii. In case that the i-th dimension of an item has a value equal to the i-th dimension of a memorized exemplar, the similarity of the item with the exemplar along this dimension is one; in case of different values, the similarity is equal to $s(i)$ with $0 < s(i) < 1$. The parameters $s(i)$ are called "similarity parameters". They may vary across the dimensions.
iii. The global similarity between an item and exemplar is equal to the product of the similarities along the different dimensions. This point expresses the "interactive coding" aspect of the exemplar model.
iv. The similarity parameter corresponding to a dimension decreases when the dimension is attended.
v. The decay of memory along a dimension i is represented by an increase of the similarity parameter corresponding to the dimension. This process bears a loss of distinctiveness along this dimension.

6.2 An example

In order to illustrate these ideas, we consider a simple example. We consider two categories which are ranged over four dimensions. In the first two experiments of Medin and Schaffer (1978), one dimension corresponds to color, one to form, one to size and one to position. The dimensions are binary. For each dimension, one possible value is formally represented by a 1 and the other one by a 0. The similarity parameters along the respective dimensions are denoted c, f, s, and p.

The formal values of the variables of the respective exemplars are given in the following table (Medin and Schaffer, 1978, p.218):

TRAINING STIMULI

A-STIMULI

Stimulus number	Dimension values			
	C	F	S	N
1	1	1	1	1
2	1	0	1	0
3	0	1	0	1

B-STIMULI

Stimulus number	Dimension values			
	C	F	S	N
4	0	0	0	0
5	1	0	1	1
6	0	1	0	0

TEST STIMULI

A-PREDICTED

Stimulus number	Dimension values			
	C	F	S	N
7	0	1	1	1
8	1	1	0	1
9	1	1	1	0

B-PREDICTED

Stimulus number	Dimension values			
	C	F	S	N
10	1	0	0	0
11	0	0	1	0
12	0	0	0	1

Table V.1

The subjects are instructed to learn the categories A and B. The experimenter shows one exemplar at a time. The subjects guess if the item is an A- or a B-item. Subsequently, the experimenter corrects if necessary. This process is repeated until the subjects classify all items errorless. According to points i-v of paragraph 6.1, the chance that a subject classifies exemplar 1 in category A is given by:

$$P(1,A) = \frac{1+p+cfs}{1+p+cfs+cfsp+cf+sp} \qquad \text{(eq. V.3)}$$

The quantity $P(1,A)$ is called the similarity of item 1 with category A. Similar expressions are derived straightforwardly for other exemplars as well as for items of category B.

6.3 The exemplar model and the evidence in favor of prototypes

One may wonder if an exemplar model is reconcilable with the existing evidence in favor of prototypes. Medin and Schaffer (1978) argue that this is the case as far as concerns two properties of prototypes.

First, we are reminded of the fact that prototypical patterns are central in their own category and that they have low similarity to instances of other categories (e.g. Rosch and Mervis, 1975). Now suppose that, in the context of the exemplar model, one defines prototypes in the same way as in case of the prototype model of e.g. Reed (1972) : for each dimension, a prototype has the value which is most typical for the exemplars of the category. Then, a quick inspection of formula (eq. V.3) shows that, according to the exemplar model, prototype patterns have in general high similarity with the exemplars of their category. Further, a consideration of the corresponding mathematical expressions shows also that their similarity to exemplars of other categories is in general relatively low.

Second, we consider the fact that prototypical patterns are forgotten less quickly than non-prototypical patterns (4.4). Also this point can be explained by the exemplar model. We notice that, if the similarity parameters are low, relatively few between-category classifications will be made (see e.g. expression eq. V.3). On the other hand, if these parameters increase, more between category confusions will occur. Now an increase affects prototypical and non-prototypical patterns in a different way, since the latter are unlikely to be highly similar to other exemplars of their category (note 3). Hence, if the process of forgetting is represented as an increase of the similarity-parameters, then forgetting affects non-prototypical exemplars more than prototypical ones.

6.4 Experimental evidence in favor of the exemplar model

We point out how one can design an experiment in order to discriminate between exemplar-models and prototype-models. We notice that, in accordance with 4.4, the prototype of the first category of table 1 is item 1 (1111): for the first category, 1 is the value that occurs most frequently in each dimension. Similarly, the prototype associated with category B is item 4 (0000). A prototype model predicts that the performance on the new item 7 will be the same as the performance on item 10: both differ from their prototype along the same dimension. If all dimensions have the same similarity parameters, the same performance is predicted for all other test-items of table 1. If the similarity parameters are not the same for all dimensions, one still has that item 8 and item 11 are classified with equal ease; a similar point holds for item 9 and item 12.

The exemplar model makes different predictions. Stimuli 10, 11 and 12 are highly similar to one A stimulus and to one B stimulus. Stimuli 7, 8 and 9, on the other hand, are highly similar to two A stimuli and are not highly similar to any B stimulus. Consequently, the exemplar model predicts that stimulus 7 will be classified more easily as an A than stimulus 10 is classified as a B. Similarly, 8 will be classified more easily as an A than 11 as a B, and 9 will be classified more easily as an A than 12 as a B. The exemplar model predicts that, with distance from an input to the prototype held constant, performance will vary with the number of stored exemplars similar to the input. Prototype models, one the other hand, are insensitive to such density effects.

Medin and Schaffer (1978) carried out some experiments in order to decide between the prototype model and their exemplar approach. Their first experiment dealth with geometric forms. The dimensional variables were form, size, color and position. A form was either an equilateral triangle or a circle, either red or green, had a diameter or height of either 1.25 or 2.5 cm and was centered either on the left or on the right of the card on which it was presented. The variables were combined in accordance with table V.2. The experimental results favored the exemplar model at the expense of the prototype model.

In order to examine the generality of this result, the authors considered two variations of the experimental conditions. First, one may notice that the categories A and B are not linearly separable: it is not possible to construct a linear discriminant function of the dimensional variables so that the elements of A have positive values for the function and the elements of B have a negative value. One could argue that prototype models are, in a sense, linear, since they depend on additive rules. Hence, they might be better suited for linearly separable categories than for other categories. To examine this hypothesis, Medin and Schaffer (1978, p.222) considered the following two categories:

TRAINING STIMULI

A-STIMULI   B-STIMULI

Stimulus number	Dimension values				Stimulus number	Dimension values			
	C	F	S	N		C	F	S	N
1	0	1	1	0	7	0	0	0	0
2	1	1	1	0	8	1	0	1	1
3	0	1	1	1	9	0	1	0	0
4	1	0	1	0	10	0	0	1	1
5	1	1	0	1	11	0	1	0	0
6	1	0	1	1					

Table V.2

This time, a linear discriminant function can separate the two categories. To see this, notice that, if the form dimensions are given zero weight, at least two of the other three variables have non-zero value in case of items of category A, whereas in case of the exemplars of B, only one of the remaining variables is different from zero. However, the experiment again favored the exemplar model at the expense of the prototype model. The second variation of the experiment gave other interpretations to the dimensional variables: the variables were interpreted as face-characteristics. More specifically, the four dimensions were interpreted as nose-length, mouth-height, eye separation and eye-height. Also in this case, the experimental results favored the exemplar model.

6.5 The simplified nature of the used prototype-concept

In the present paragraph, we comment on the way in which the terms "prototype" and "abstraction" are used by Medin and colleagues in their subsequent studies. We point out that this use differs in some important respects from the common-sense use as well as from the way it is used in studies of real-world prototypes. Actually, Medin et al. use their terms here in a quite broad way. As an illustration, consider again experiment 1 of Medin and Schaffer (1978) (see table 1). In this experiment, a red equilateral triangle of 1.25 cm height on the left of the card is the prototype of a category with three elements. The elements are, along with the prototype, a red equilateral triangle of 2.5 cm height on the left of the card and a green circle of 1.25

cm diameter on the left of the card. Clearly, in order to speak of a "prototype" in this context, the term has to be used in a quite broad way. It can be argued in three ways that the "prototypes" of the experiments under consideration are not prototypes according to the common-sense meaning of the term.

a. Intuitively, one would expect of a prototype that it is more or less identifiable if one considers the other exemplars of the category to which it belongs. In case of the quoted example, this is not the case (see table V.1): the second element (1010) and the third element (0101) of A are as close to (0000) (the prototype of the rival category) as to (1111) (the prototype of A). Since A contains (in addition to the prototype itself) but these elements, its prototype can not be inferred from them if the prototype itself is left out.

b. Due to the nature of the exemplars which are presented, subjects can not abstract common aspects from the exemplars. In real world-situations, on the other hand, the point that two objects are classified in the same category is often correlated with the fact that they share a function, that they appear in the same context, or that they share some features. Such elements are entirely absent in the examples used in the experiments at issue. In fact, one has the impression that the only aspect common to the members of the same category is that they receive the same label "A" or "B" (this point is discussed further in the next paragraph). Real world categories, on the other hand, are not just a matter linguistic convention.

c. In its common use, "prototype" or "abstraction" often refers to a core to which something has to be added if one wants to arrive at an instance. In other terms, instances involve more dimensions than abstractions or prototypes. In the models under consideration, however, this fact is neglected.

These arguments qualify the relevance of this kind of experiments for the study of real-world prototypes. As demonstrated in quite some studies, the latter have a central place within rich and complex structures (e.g. Rosch, 1978; Lakoff, 1987; Barsalou, 1985). Hence, although the considered results are quite important to anyone who wants to make a theory about concepts, one has to keep in mind that the concepts which are used in these experiments are rather simplified and artificial.

6.6 Labels as category definitions

If we are correct with our contention that, as far as concerns the present experimental conditions, instances belong to their category by virtue of their external labels, one would expect that a subject's ability to classify the instances decreases if the link between the instances and the label is weakened. In the present paragraph, we mention evidence that confirms this presumption. In Medin, Dewey and Murphy (1983), subjects learned to classify photographs of faces in two famiiies. The discrimination of the families occured on the basis of the variables "hair color", "shirt color", "smile type" and "hair length". Four kinds of learning-instructions were used.

a. In the last-name only condition, the learning/process was simiiar to the one used in Medin and Schaffer (1978): subjects were given pictures of faces (one at a time), they guessed the family to which they belonged, and immediately after the guess, they were given the correct answer. The training lasted until the subjects could classify the training/exemplars correctly.
b. In the first name/last name condition, subjects were asked to learn the full name of the training exemplars. The first names of the training items were all different.
c. In the first-name-only condition, subjects first learned the first names of each of the nine training exemplars without being informed about family membership. Later, they learned the last name of each item by a paired-associate procedure in which the first names, but not the photographs, were presented.
d. Finally, in the last-name-infinite condition, the same scenario was used as in a., except for the fact that the training exemplars were never the same: two instances of the same item always differed in some or other detail (but were similar in the four dimensions which were present in learning condition a.). In other terms, "idiosyncratic" information was added to the items.

Suppose that the most important glue between members of such a categories are their common labels. Then, one would expect that the performance for the last-name only condition would exceed the one for the first-name/last-name condition, since the labels were tied more directly to the items in former situation:

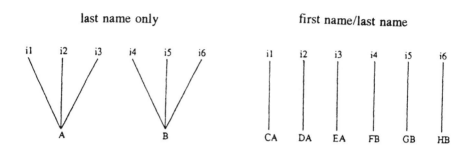

Figure V.3

The labels in the first name/last name condition do not directly fulfill a classification task: they differentiate within a class. In order to arrive at a classification, the labels have to be decomposed into parts and one part (the first name part) has to be skipped. It is not trivial that this happens automatically. To put this more clear, consider the four family names "Van Clarsfeld", "Van Guck", "Murphy" and "Murdock", and suppose that subjects learn in an experimental context (with the last-name-only method) to classify a few members of the corresponding families. Then, they probably will not automatically skip the fragments "Clarsfeld" and "Guck" in order to form the category of the "Van" 's, nor will they skip "phy" from Murphy and "dock" from Murdock in order to form the category "Mur". If a subject does not realize that some of its memories are "Mur's" and if the "Mur's" do not share some specific features, then the fact that a new item is called "Murwall" by the experimenter will not influence the way in which the subject classifies it. The situation in the first name/last name condition is somewhat less drastic than in this example, because it is more obvious which part of the label has to be skipped: it suffices to skip the first name. Still, the experiments for the subjects in the first name/last name group show that they have a transfer performance which is hardly discriminable from chance. In contrast, the transfer performance for the last-name-only group was excellent. Hence, our presumption about the nature of these categories is confirmed.

If an experimental situation enhances an inner-label segmentation with last name isolation, one may expect that transfer performance increases relative to the first name/last name condition. For instance, when the last names are learned at another instance than the first names, such an increase may be expected. This expectation is confirmed by the fact that the transfer performance in case of condition c. is better than in case of condition d.

The last-name-only group showed virtually the same transfer performance as the last-name infinite group. This does not fit nicely in the exemplar approach. The items used in the last-name-only condition may be interpreted as prototypes for the instances which are used in the last-name infinite group. Then, one has that learning in a prototypes-only condition leads to the same transfer performance as learning with prototypes plus different instances, so that predictions concerning performance may be based on prototypes only. Here, however, a more genuine kind of prototypes is at issue: the nine prototypical items provide each of them a core of attributes that is present in their instances. This observation sustains the presumption that the prototype-concept used in the context of the exemplar model is not a good one and that it does not allow for general conclusions concerning the involvedness of prototypes in categorizations.

In conclusion, the evidence considered in Medin, Dewey and Murphy (1983) implies that, in conditions in which labels hold together sets of exemplars, the classification of new items is made by reference to these exemplars. This statement contains two non-trivial aspects:

a. First, it asserts that transfer performance is present: if appropriate conditions are created, people classify new items into classes which are determined by the fact that their exemplars share a label. These classifications are not random. The closer the input is to a stored exemplar, the stronger it is attracted by it.
b. Second, this attraction seems to be of a dimensionally multiplicative form: the similarities across the different dimensions have to be multiplied in order to know how strong an item is attracted by an exemplar.

Other things, however, are not at issue in this kind of experiments, in contradistinction with some claims of their authors (note 4).

7 The necessity to integrate additive and multiplicative interactions

7.1 Conditions in which prototypes appear in tests of the exemplar model

Under particular conditions, classifications guided by prototypes were observed in experimental tests of the exemplar model. Intuitively, one may guess that these conditions apply if prototypes are imprinted with sufficient depth so that they can attract input items. Further, one may expect that this situation occurs if the subjects learn the prototypical value of each dimension before they are instructed about the defining exemplars of the categories. These presumptions were confirmed in Medin, Altom and Murphy (1984). The stimuli used by these authors were similar to the ones of e.g. experiment 1 in Medin and Schaffer (1978) (see 6.2). The subjects received geometric patterns which varied along four dimensions: color, size, form an number. Also this time, more than one learning-group was studied. We consider the two groups which are of relevance for our present discussion:

a. The subjects of a first group were instructed in the same way as in the experiments in Medin and Schaffer (1978): a pattern was presented and after a subject had made a guess concerning its classification, the correct answer was given; this was repeated until all learning exemplars could be classified correctly.
b. The subjects of the prototypes-first group were instructed to learn the typical values of each category prior to any training on exemplars. For instance, the subjects were taught that "on average", category A-members were red, large, triangular and present once a each card, whereas category B-members tended to be blue, small, circular and presented twice a card.

The data obtained for the first group replicated the results of Medin and Schaffer (1978): classifications appeared to be based on similarity to the stored exemplars rather than on similarity to the prototypes. The subjects were able to judge which exemplars were prototypical, but nevertheless, they did not base their classifications on the prototypes. For the second group, however, different results were obtained. First, during the learning phase, the errors were determined more by similarity to the prototypes than by similarity to other training stimuli. Second, in the test phase, the classification of old as well as of new exemplars was governed by similarity to the prototypes.

7.2 Evidence for classifications guided by prototypes in related experiments

Later research by Medin et al. showed that, if subjects are encouraged to use their background knowledge in the course of experimental classifications, they show a tendency to base their classifications on familiar prototypes. Further, classifications are learned more slowly if the attention of the subjects is not drawn to the fact that they may benefit from their advance knowledge about familiar prototypes (Wattenmaker, Dewey, Murphy, Medin, 1986; Medin, Wattenmaker, Hampson, 1987). This point is similar to the one of the previous paragraph in that it shows that prototypes may guide classifications if subjects pay attention to them or if they are familiar with them.

For instance, in Wattenmaker, Dewey, Murphy and Medin (1986), items were considered which were ranged over the dimensions: "made of rubber" versus "made of metal", "medium weight" versus "heavy weight", "flat surface" versus "irregular surface", and "easy to grasp" versus "difficult to grasp". The subjects were divided in two groups. The subjects of the first group were informed that the properties which define the typical values of the first category could all be attributed to a hammer, and that this information could be helpful for subsequent classifications. The subjects of the second group were not aware of this fact. The experiment showed that the classification performance of the subjects of the first group was significantly better: they classified all items correctly after a significantly shorter training time.

In another example (Wattenmaker, Dewey, Murphy and Medin, 1986) four pairs of character traits were used as the possible values of four dimensions. Again, two categories were ranged over these dimensions. The prototype of one of the categories integrated characteristic traits of introvert behavior whereas the prototype of the other class was composed by traits associated with extraversion. Also here, it appeared that prototype-based classifications were stimulated by the fact that the dimensions of the prototype could be readily integrated by reference to familiar knowledge. Similarly, in Medin, Wattenmaker and Hampson (1987), two categories were defined in such a way that the prototype of one of them integrated dimensional values which could be associated with flying behavior (a small body, webbed feet, feathers, small ears and a beak). Again, this background-knowledge appeared to favor prototype-based sorting. The authors concluded (p.272) (note 5):

"These data suggest that one route to family resemblance sorting is provided by information that brings out inter-property relationships. When these inter-property relations allow integration across component dimensions, then family resemblance becomes natural. "

7.3 Experimental learning conditions and realistic learning conditions

The conditions of the experiments considered in 7.2 were significantly different from the ones of the older experiments carried out in the context of the exemplar model (see 6). In the latter experiments, subjects were stimulated to be "analytical": each of the stimulus-dimensions was subject to systematic variation. This variation was not clearly correlated with variations in other dimensions. Hence, it is not astonishing that subjects did not extract automatically a prototype. In real-world situations, on the other hand, a subject makes recourse to his already acquired knowledge to interpret an object or a situation. He changes familiar representations only if it appears that they are not suited for a new situation. Hence, in real world situations, reference to background knowledge is automatic. Therefore, we suggest that the experimental conditions of 7.2 are closer to real-world conditions than the conditions of 6.

Further, in real-world situations, the systematic and unordered variation characteristic of the experiments of 6 does not necessarily occur. For instance, infants or children may learn a concept from a single example (Anglin, 1977; Nelson, 1974). This point may explain why authors like Rosch (see 5), who concentrate real-world concepts, agree on the existence and the importance of prototypes (see also chapter VII). As might be suspected from 7.2, in later work, Medin and colleagues acknowledged this possibility (Medin, Wattenmaker and Hampson, 1987, p.275):

"Based on the work of Rosch, Mervis, and others and the near ubiquitous typicality effects obtained with other procedures, it is difficult to escape the intuition that family-resemblance sorting ought to be natural. ... One remaining possibility is that family resemblance categories are usually learned in circumstances that make a family resemblance structure more natural. Family resemblance structure may become important when the learner is not being analytic. "

7.4 The mixture model

We saw that, in certain conditions, the exemplar model offers an adequate description, whereas, in other situations, a prototype model fits better with the experiments. In order to arrive at a model that contains both possibilities, Medin, Altom and Murphy (1984) proposed a "mixture"-model. It is obtained by a weighted combination of the prototype rule for classification and the exemplar rule. For each experiment, one has to fit the relative weights of both models in such a way that the predictions of the mixture model are in agreement with the experiment. Obviously, this is not an attractive method: it does not allow for predictions since the weights of the respective models are adapted post factum in order to fit experimentally obtained data. Further, it does not include a systematic explanation for the problem when and why the relative weights of the component models change. We will propose in next chapter an alternative, connectionist model that does not have these drawbacks.

8 The nature of the dimensions used in these models

In the experiments which we considered in this chapter, input-stimuli, exemplars and prototypes were always ranged over a set of dimensions. In the present paragraph, we consider the question how these dimensions relate to the elements of representation that we introduced in the previous chapters. It appears that these dimensions correspond at some instances to sf's, and to P's at other instances.

First, in some of the experiments, the dimensions refer to sf's. These experiments show that sf's may interact in a multiplicative as well as in an additive way:

i. We remember that some experiments evidence multiplicative interactions between sf's. For example, in the two first experiments of Medin and Schaffer (1978), the dimensions were form, size, color and position. Medin, Altom and Murphy (1983) used the dimensions form, color, size and number. It appeared that, under the conditions of these experiments, sf's combine in a multiplicative way.
ii. In other examples, however, sf's interacted additively. For instance, Medin, Altom and Murphy (1983) considered inputs which were ranged over the dimensions form, color, size and number. It appeared that they were classified with reference to prototypes if the latter received a sufficient amount of attention during the learning phase.

When prototypes receive a sufficient amount of attention, the interactions between the *sf*'s appear to change from multiplicative to additive. We can describe this change as follows. As long as an exemplar model holds, the *sf*'s of different modalities are not sufficiently strongly coupled to allow for inter-modality attractors. Hence, the probability to realize an inter-modality pattern is equal to the product of the probabilities to realize the component patterns in the respective modalities. When prototypes are formed, the inter-modality connections which sustain inter-modality patterns grow stronger and the *P* which integrates the *sf*'s of the different modalities becomes an attractor. Since a *P* is spread out over different modalities, the non-fit of an input with a *P* in one modality can be compensated by good fit in other modalities.

In other experiments, the dimensions correspond to *P*'s. The results of these experiments reveal that *P*'s may interact multiplicatively as well as additively.

i. For example, in the third experiment of Medin and Schaffer (1978), the stimuli which were used were faces and the dimensions were nose-length, mouth-heigth, eye-separation, and eye-heigth. One may wonder which modalities were involved in a single component in this example. Apparently, form is one of the most obvious candidates. Mouth-height could be stored as the form of the area between the chin and the mouth, eye-separation as the form of the area's between both eyes, and so on. Further, each form is localized somewhere on the face-skeleton, so that a location has to be coupled to the representation of the respective forms. Hence, we suggest that each dimension integrates some form information and some information concerning its location. According to our frame, such dimensions correspond to *P*'s (note 6).

ii. In other experimental conditions, *P*'s appeared to interact in an additive way. For example, in Wattenmaker, Dewey, Murphy and Medin (1986), a set of objects was described by the dimensions "made of metal" versus "made of rubber", "medium weight" versus "heavy weight", "flat surface" versus "irregular surface", and "easy to grasp" versus "difficult to grasp". Apparently, these dimensions did not refer to *sf*'s but they involved the integration of information from different modalities such as color, texture, and modalities which contain kinesthetic information. In the study at issue, it was shown that, under particular experimental conditions, *P*'s interact in an additive way (see 7.2).

9 The exemplar rule and the prototype rule in terms of order parameters

A closer examination of the stimuli of the experiments in which P's were involved suggests that one has to associate two P's with a dimension instead of one (a similar point can be made for the experiments which involve sf's). In the studies by Medin and colleagues, two specifications which refer to the same kind of property are often represented as antithetic values of a single dimension. For instance, "made of rubber" and "made of metal" are mapped on a single dimension. Similarly, large eye-separation and small eye- separation are represented as opposite values of a single dimension. Now it is not probable that a subject has a single, two valued dimension which refers, for instance, to rubber as well as to metal. Although a subject may be quite aware that rubber is different form metal, it is not probable that he represents rubber as the negation of metal. Hence, it appears that different P's are involved in a single dimension.

If one attaches one P to each value of a binary dimension, then the number of P's is twice the number of dimensions. However, we point out that this makes no difference as concerns the fundamental characteristics of the exemplar model or of the prototype model. As far as these models are concerned with P's, they can be reformulated in terms of order-parameters associated with P's. Consider a situation in which stimuli, exemplars and prototypes are described by four dimensions. More specifically, suppose that an input can be represented formally by four dimensional values (a_1, a_2, a_3, a_4) , and suppose that the dimensions refer to P's.

First, we consider a prototype model. We restrict ourselves to dimensions of equal weight (the argument can be generalized in an evident way to the case of dimensions with different weights). Suppose that a prototype of a particular class is characterized by the set of components (p_1, p_2, p_3, p_4) . Then, the resemblance of the input with to the prototype is given by:

$$p = \frac{1}{N}(x_1 + x_2 + x_3 + x_4) \tag{eq. V.4}$$

with

$x_i = 1 \ \ if \ \ a_i = p_i$

$x_i = 0$ *if* $a_i \neq p_i$

1/N is a normalization constant

If the model is deterministic, then the input is mapped on the prototype with highest p-value (e.g. Reed, 1972). If the model is probabilistic, then the chance that an input is mapped on a prototype is equal to its p-value (e.g. Medin and Schaffer, 1978). Suppose now that the first value of the i-th dimension corresponds to $P(i,1)$ and the second value of the i-th dimension to $P(i,2)$. Then, we can define order parameters $m(i,j)$ ($j=1$ or $j=2$; $i=1,...,k$, where k is equal to the number of dimensions) for an input relative to the prototype by the specification that:

$m(i,1)=1$ *if* $x_i=1$; $m(i,1)=0$ *if* $x_i=0$
$m(i,2)=1$ *if* $x_i=0$; $m(i,2)=0$ *if* $x_i=1$

Suppose, for instance, that prototype is characterized by the *P*'s $(P(1,1),P(2,1),P(3,2),P(4,2))$. Then, the rule (eq.V.4) can be rewritten as:

$$p = (1/N) \ (m(1,1) + m(2,1) + m(3,2) + m(4,2)) \qquad \text{(eq.V.5)}$$

Hence, the prototype model can be reformulated in terms of order parameters without major change. A similar point holds for the exemplar model. For the sake of simplicity, we constrain ourselves to a category with a single exemplar (the argument can be generalized in a straightforward way). Suppose the exemplar is characterized by the dimensional values (b_1,b_2,b_3,b_4) . According to the original formulation of the exemplar model, the probability that an input (a_1,a_2,a_3,a_4) is mapped on the exemplar is given by:

$$p = \frac{1}{N} x_1 . x_2 . x_3 . x_4 \qquad \text{(eq.V.6)}$$

with

$x_i = 1$ *if* $b_i = a_i$

$x_i = s(i)$ if $b_i \neq a_i$

1/N is a normalization constant

Suppose, for instance, that the exemplar is composed of the P's $(P(1,1), P(2,2), P(3,2), P(4,2))$. Then, the previous rule can be rewritten as:

$$p = (1/N) \ (m(1,1). \ m(2,1). \ m(3,2). \ m(4,2)) \tag{eq.V.7}$$

This time, the order parameters are defined by the prescription:

$m(i,1)=1$ if $x_i=1$; $m(i,1)=s(i)$ if $x_i=0$
$m(i,2)=1$ if $x_i=0$; $m(i,2)=s(i)$ if $x_i=1$

Again, we see that the central characteristic of the exemplar rule remains if is reformulated in terms of P's: the order parameters interact in a multiplicative way.

NOTES

Note 1. The prototype model proposed Reed (1972) is sometimes called an "independent-cue" model, since in formula (eq.2), each dimension contributes independently to the quantity $d(M^1, M^2)$: the expression for the similarity of an input to a prototype does not contain multiplicative relations between different dimensions. There is no a priori reason for such a restriction. Reed acknowledged this point (Reed 1972, p.403):

"... (the models I considered) were all based on the same assumption: that patterns could be adequately represented in terms of a vector of independent feature values. That this assumption is an oversimplification is indicated by those subjects who used the distance between the eyes and the nose as a basis for classification. This distance is determined by the relationship between two features; the height of the forehead and the length of the nose. More generally, there are many patterns for which the consequences of ignoring structural information will be much more serious and present techniques for testing additivity should aid in identifying such patterns."

Note 2. Suppose that one dimension expresses the "context" of the exemplars. Then, the right context must be activated in order retrieve a particular exemplar. For this reason, the exemplar-model is sometimes called the "context-model". However, the concept "context" is used here in such a general sense that it may be misleading. For instance, Medin and Schaffer (1978, p.211) gave an example in which "blue circle" was an exemplar, and in which "blue" was conceived as the context in which "circle" appears. Instead of using the concept "context" in such a broad way, we will continue to speak about the "exemplar" model.

Note 3. The latter "since" can be understood by the following considerations. First, we notice that, if the total number of items in the knowledge base is large, then, for different input items, the denominator of expression (eq. V.3) (as well as the denominators of the expressions corresponding to other exemplars) tend to be approximately equal to each other. Hence, often, the value of the numerator will be decisive. Second, for high similarity parameters, the chance that a memorized exemplar is classified in the wrong category may be quite high. In general, the chance of a wrong classification increases if the similarity parameters increase. Finally, consider the numerator which appears in the expression which governs the chance that a prototype is classified in its own category. In general, this numerator contains less similarity parameters than the corresponding numerators of non-prototypical instances. Hence, the chance that a prototype is classified in its own category is in general less affected by an increase of the similarity parameters than the corresponding chances for non- prototypical items.

Note 4. Consider, for instance, the following two quotes in which they evaluate their results (Medin, Dewey, Murphy, 1983, p.623):

"Results on degree of abstraction form a coherent picture. The stimuli can be viewed as composed of category-level and idiosyncratic information, and the different conditions encouraged subjects to use different mixtures of these two types of information. Requiring first names to be learned stressed idiosyncratic information, and the conditions in which first names were learned led to poor transfer. ..."

and second (Medin, Dewey and Murphy 1983, p.623; in this quote the authors try to explain why subjects trained in the first-name only condition show better transfer-performance than subjects of the first-name/last-name group):

"Perhaps the first-name/ last-name group learned the last names on the basis of the same idiosyncratic information that allowed first-name learning. The difference between the groups might be that the first-name-only subjects tried to form an impression of the category during last-name paired-associate learning. They might have done this by trying to retrieve the image associated with a given first name and then attempting to form generalizations that could be applied at the level of the category."

The view expressed in these quotes is that the representations of the training-exemplars must be decomposable somehow in a part at a categorical level and an idiosyncratic part. Further, it is assumed that these parts can be favored differentially by different naming conditions. Hence, the authors assume that there is, within the context of their experiments, more to concept formation than label-attachment and comparison to exemplars furnished with this label.

Note 5. In the present context, the term "family resemblance sorting" refers to the fact that classifications are based on prototypes.

Note 6. We notice that, due to the artificial nature of the experimental stimuli, quite less modalities contribute to the P's than in case of real world stimuli. Further, we notice that, even if the respective dimensions would correspond to single sf's, in this example they would have to be encoded as degenerate P's, since each of them involves separate attention (this is required by the "analytical" nature of the experimental conditions: see 7.3).

VI. A CONNECTIONIST MODEL AND A PROPOSAL FOR A LEARNING RULE.

1 Introduction

The previous chapter suggests the form of the field by which a concept is "consolidated": it contains a term that is a multiplicative function of the order parameters of its P's and a term that is an additive combination of these order parameters. The consolidation of an item can be represented as an external field that is induced by a meta-layer in the layer that contains the representations of the concepts and of their components (paragraphs 2,3). The consolidation is normalized in order to obtain comparable effects for M's of different orders (paragraph 4). Product terms and sum terms have different properties. Sum terms may produce effects of interference between different items. As a consequence, P's which occur in different M's may have a strong tendency to invade in the network state. Product terms in general do not cause interferences. They produce a steep but local basin of attraction around an M (paragraph 5). These points are illustrated by three examples (paragraph 6).

The general learning rule of our model includes different sub-rules (paragraph 7). We can differentiate between two kinds of sub-rules. First, there are rules that can be formulated entirely in terms of the model that is proposed. The second class of rules invokes our general frame (chapters II-IV). It includes principles that refer to pre-processing and principles that refer to the analysis of mental images (paragraph 7). When an item becomes familiar, the product term of its consolidation increases until it saturates; then, the sum term comes into play and its relative importance gradually increases (this is the "saturated-F model", paragraph 8). An item that is never retrieved becomes gradually forgotten; this is expressed by a gradual decrease of the strength of its sum- and of its product-consolidation. To a limited extent, our learning rule can be formulated in terms of the meta-layer only. To this extent, it is reminiscent of computationalist models of concepts. However, the basis-layer is responsible for the remarkable interactions between the attractors of our model (paragraph 9).

2 A connectionist model

2.1 Connectionist schema models

In most psychological models that use distributed representations, the components of a concept are associated with a single unit and the concept as a whole is represented by the set composed by these units (e.g. Rumelhart & Mc Clelland, 1986). In a typical example, Rumelhart, Smolensky and Hinton (1986) represent concepts corresponding to rooms. The concepts are called "schemata" and hence their model is called the "schema-model". The components of the schemata correspond to descriptors of the rooms, such as "has drapes", "contains a TV", and so on. The units of the model are binary, and the activations of the units update in accordance with the Hopfield updating rule (Hopfield, 1982). Further, the connections between two units are set in accordance with a Bayesian rule. It is claimed that this model has the following four properties. First, each schema is a stable attractor (this means that a schema is content-addressable). Second, along with schemata corresponding to rooms, it can store subschemata. Subschemata are formed by units that cohere: they are usually together active or together non-active. Third, schemata may be rigid and show strong bonds among their elements or they may show a more flexible structure. Fourth, schemata may have variable elements. If an input pattern corresponds to a particular schema, but if the input contains components that do not belong to the schema and that remain clamped during the updating process, the schema may nevertheless be retrieved.

The schema model describes some of the psychological processes that we consider. For instance, since the model uses distributed representations, it shows automatic spread of activation. Further, the notion of context may be grasped if a context is defined as a cluster of concepts which overlap with each other or if it is defined in terms of sub-schemata that tend to cohere during associative transitions. However, this kind of model is not capable to grasp other important features, such as the evolution of the type of interaction between components. Nor has a rule been formulated that entails that the associations between concepts evolve from complexive to taxonomic. Another drawback of this approach is that the stability of the attractors can be studied analytically to a rather limited extent. If one uses a Bayesian learning rule to store schemata and subschemata in a finite network, one is largely dependent on simulations to see if the desired attractors are stable. Further, there is no mechanism that allows for a controlled transition from an instance (e.g. a schema) to a more abstract concept (e.g. a subschema) and vice versa. Typically, recurrent connectionist models that are constructed with the aim to store conceptual hierarchies are significantly more complicated (e.g. Bacci, Mato & Parga, 1990; Gutfreund, 1988; Parga & Virasoro, 1986) or use another kind of distributed representation (Van Loocke, 1990, 1991a, 1991b, 1993).

2.2 An alternative connectionist approach

The model that we formulate avoids the drawbacks of the more traditional connectionist schema model, and it allows to describe the psychological properties that we consider in this monograph. We describe this model in a non-technical way; for technical details, we refer to Appendix I (see also Van Loocke, 1990, 1991a, 1991b, 1993). An important feature is that the components of concepts are themselves represented in a distributed way. As we anticipated in chapter I, they are represented by large patterns defined over binary units with activation values +1 and -1. The concepts are defined over the same units. The representation of a concept M can be obtained from the representations of its components by local vote-operations. In each unit i, the activations of the components vote. The representations of multi-component concepts which are obtained in this way have appropriate topological and metric properties (chapter I; see also Appendix I).

To start with, we notice that a single layer, fully recurrent and distributed connectionist model that stores orthogonal patterns has received quite some attention in literature (e.g. Hopfield, 1982; Amit, Gutfreund & Sompolinsky, 1985; Amit, Gutfreund & Sompolinsky, 1987; Amit, 1987). Suppose that the activation value of a memorized pattern P^μ in unit i is denoted by P_i^μ . Then, the connection strength w_{ij} between two units i and j is determined by:

$$w_{ij} = \frac{1}{N}\sum_{\mu=1}^{n} P_i^\mu P_j^\mu \qquad\qquad \text{(eq. VI.1)}$$

N is the number of units in the network; n is the number of memorized patterns. The updating rule of such a model is given by:

$$p[S_i(t+1)=+1] = [1+\exp(-\frac{1}{T}f_i(t))]^{-1} \qquad\qquad \text{(eq. VI.2a)}$$

$$p[S_i(t+1)=-1] = [1+\exp(\frac{1}{T}f_i(t))]^{-1} \qquad\qquad \text{(eq. VI.2b)}$$

with

$$f_i = \sum_{j=1}^{N} w_{ij} S_j$$

(eq. VI.3)

S_i denotes the activation value of unit i. The parameter T is the computational temperature. f_i is the field experienced by unit i. The more positive f_i , the higher the chance that i will become active. Conversely, a negative f_i stimulates unit i to become non-active. The expression for f_i can be rewritten as:

$$f_i = \frac{1}{N}\sum_{j=1}^{N} (\sum_{\mu=1}^{n} P_i^{\mu}P_j^{\mu})S_j = \sum_{\mu=1}^{n} P_i^{\mu}m^{\mu} = \sum_{\mu=1}^{n} f_i^{\mu}$$

(eq. VI.4)

with

$$m^{\mu} = \frac{1}{N}\sum_{i=1}^{N} S_i P_i^{\mu} \qquad f_i^{\mu} = P_i^{\mu}m^{\mu}$$

(eq. VI.5)

m^{μ} is the "order-parameter" associated with the μ-th pattern; its value is equal to the correlation between the actual network state and the μ-th stored pattern. The previous expression means that a memorized pattern P^{μ} is stimulated in each unit to the extent m^{μ} . If this interpretation is kept in mind, it is straightforward to reformulate this single layer network as a two-layer network with inter-layer connections only. Indeed, suppose that a first layer contains the original distributed representations, and that a second layer has one unit for each memorized pattern. Further, suppose that the connection strength between unit i of the first layer and unit μ of the second layer is equal to P_i^{μ} . Then, if the units of the second layer are linear units that contain a scaling factor $1/N$, the activation of unit μ of the

second layer will be given by: $m^{\mu} = \dfrac{1}{N}\sum_{j=1}^{N} S_j P_j^{\mu}$. If, subsequently, these values

are communicated backwards to the first layer through the same connections, unit i of the first layer will experience precisely the field f_i (see eq. VI.4).

The first layer is called the "basis-layer", since it contains the distributed representations of components and concepts as we described them. Since the units of the second layer have activation values that correspond to order parameters, it is called a meta-layer. The two-layer reformulation has the advantage that it can be generalized straightforwardly for multi-component concepts. The point is to extend the meta-layer so that it includes one unit for each component and one unit for each multi-component concept. The meta-layer units that correspond to components receive their input from the basis layer units. Like in the case without multi-component concepts, the connections are put in such a way that the activations of these meta-layer units are equal to the order parameters of the corresponding components. A meta-layer unit that corresponds to a concept calculates the field that supports this concept; it receives its input from the meta-layer units that correspond to components. These fields, in turn, serve as input for the basis layer units (figure VI.1).

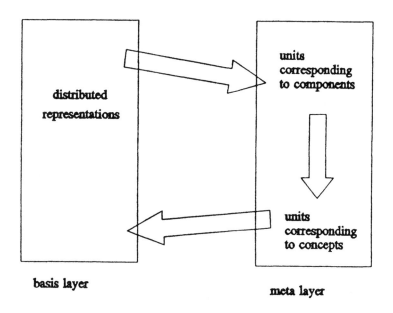

distributed
representations

units
corresponding
to components

units
corresponding
to concepts

basis layer

meta layer

Figure VI.1

The field f_i^μ that corresponds to a multi-component concept M^μ contains two parts: a multiplicative one (corresponding to the exemplar model) and an additive one (corresponding to the prototype model), connected by a coupling parameter b^μ (the index i refers to the fact that the field is experienced in unit i of the basis layer). The additive part sums the extents to which the components of M^μ are active; the multiplicative part multiplies these quantities. In case of a single component concept, these fields are trivially identical, and expression (4) reappears. The exact expression of f_i^μ for multi-component concepts is given in paragraph 3. Actually, we will talk often in terms of the "consolidation" of a concept. The consolidation c of a concept M^μ is the absolute magnitude of its field. In each unit, it is related to the field by the expression $f_i^\mu = c^\mu M_i^\mu$.

Like in case of the schema-model, the updating procedure of this two-layer system is "randomly asynchronous". At each time click, a unit of the basis layer is randomly chosen. It updates its activation value, and subsequently all units of the meta-layer adapt their activations.

3 The formal expression of the consolidation rule (non-normalized version)

The chance that an input is classified as a particular item can be called the extent to which the item "attracts" the input. In our connectionist model, the attractive force (i.e. the extension and the depth of the basin of attraction) of an item is governed by the field or the consolidation that it experiences. As we have noticed, the previous chapter suggests to include a multiplicative as well as an additive term in the consolidation of a concept. In the course of the present and of the next chapters, this hypothesis wil prove to be quite successful.

Suppose that an M integrates k P's (k is an odd number: see chapter I). Suppose the order parameter of the network state S for the μ-th P is m^μ . Further, suppose that the indices of the P's are chosen in such a way that the first k P's participate in M (the indices are natural numbers including zero). Then, the consolidation c of the multi-component state M is governed by:

$$
\begin{aligned}
c(M) = \ F \ \{ \ (1-b). \quad & (1/2) \ (1+sign(m^0+e)) \ (m^0+e). \\
& .(1/2) \ (1+sign(m^1+e)) \ (m^1+e). \\
& . \ \ldots \\
& .(1/2) \ (1+sign(m^\mu+e)) \ (m^\mu+e). \\
& . \ \ldots \\
& .(1/2) \ (1+sign(m^{k-1}+e)) \ (m^{k-1}+e) \ + \\
+b \quad & .(m^0 + m^1 + \ldots + m^{k-1}) \}
\end{aligned}
\qquad \text{(eq.VI.6)}
$$

e is a small positive constant
b is a real number between 0 and 1
F is a real number
sign is the signum function

Expression (eq.VI.6) deserves some comments.

a. The product-term is slightly more complex than just the product of the order-parameters. The reason is that order parameters may be negative. Hence, one slightly negative order parameter could reverse the effects of a pure product. The signum operation prohibits this. As a consequence, if an order parameter of a P would be negative, the product term would vanish. The small constant e, however, allows the order parameters to be slightly negative (as long as their absolute value is smaller than e) without causing the product term to vanish. Graphically, we have:

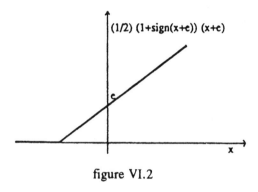

figure VI.2

In other terms, the function $(1/2)$ $(1+sign(m^\mu+e))$ $(m^\mu+e)$ is equal to zero for values of m^μ which are smaller than -e; it is equal to $m^\mu+e$ for values of m^μ which are larger than +e. In practice, it is preferable to choose e strictly positive rather than zero. There are four reasons for such a choice:

i. The P's of finite networks are in general not perfectly orthogonal (see Appendix III). Hence, in practice, one works with "noisy" P's. As a consequence, the order parameters may contain small errors (of the order of the correlations between the P's). In special, an order parameter may be negatively biased by this source of noise. Hence, since small negative values can be caused by noise effects, it would be undesirable that the product term would vanish as soon as a single order parameter becomes slightly negative. The parameter e prohibits this.

ii. In our connectionist model, the neurons of the basis layer update in random order. Also this point produces small fluctuations in the order parameters. Again, the consolidations of the M's must be qualitatively independent of these fluctuations. Also here, a strictly positive e prohibits that the product term would vanish due to a random fluctuation (note 1).

iii. For zero e, the basins of attraction of items which are learned by a product consolidation are quite small: as soon as one order parameter of a component of such a pattern becomes zero, the pattern looses all of its attractivity. In other terms, an item will be recognized in an input only if all its P's are positively biased by it. Hence, in order to obtain a network a with good recognition performance, e has to be chosen strictly positive.

iv. Finally, such a choice is in accordance with evidence that we considered in the previous chapter. If, along a particular dimension, an input does not fit with a memorized exemplar, then the probability that the input is mapped on the exemplar does not vanish entirely. Rather, along this dimension, the similarity between the input and the exemplar is determined by a non-zero similarity parameter. A non-zero value of e may be interpreted as a non-zero similarity parameter.

b. The parameter F determines the "depth" with which a pattern has been imprinted. The larger the F-value of a multi-component state M, the stronger M attracts the network state when it is in its neighborhood. An increase in the F-value of an item usually bears an increase of its basin of attraction.

c. The parameter b is a measure for the weight of the sum term relative to the product term. We will see that this parameter is of high significance for our model. In general, a product term produces a local and sharp basin of attraction; the sum term, on the other hand, produces a less steep but larger basin of attraction.

d. Consider a network that has learned several M's in accordance with (eq. VI.6). Suppose that the b-values of some of them are strictly positive. Further, suppose that the actual network state has positive correlations with these multi-component states. Then, each of these M's may attract the network state. We anticipate that this can give raise to effects of interference between different attractions (see 5.2).

4 The normalization of the consolidation rule

Expression (eq.VI.6) does not treat concepts of different orders (i.e. M's with different numbers of components) on equal footing. This holds for the product component as well as for the sum component. Hence, we normalize (eq.VI.6). From the present paragraph on, we often abbreviate "item number k" as "ik".

4.1 The sum part of the consolidation

Consider, for instance, a memorized item i0 of order 3 and a memorized item i1 of order 5. Suppose that the indices of the P's are chosen in such a way that the three first P's participate in i0 and the five next ones in i1. Suppose that the state of the system coincides with item i0. Then, i0 experiences a sum-consolidation equal to

$$\text{sum part of } c(i0) = F.b.(m^0 + m^1 + m^3)$$

m^μ denotes the order parameter of the μ-th P. Since, by supposition, the network state coincides with i0, one has that m^0, m^1 and m^2 are equal to the value $m^*(3)$ (i.e. the correlation between a third order vote mixture and its components; see Apendix I). Hence, we have:

sum part of $c(i0) = F.b.3.m^*(3)$
with (see Appendix I):
$m^*(3) = 0.5$
Hence:
sum part of $c(i0) = F.b. \; 1.5$

On the other hand, when the network state coincides with i1, one obtains by a similar argument:

$$\begin{aligned}
\text{sum part of } c(i1) &= F.b.(m^3 + m^4 + m^5 + m^6 + m^7) \\
&= F.b.5.m^*(5) \\
&= F.b.5. \; 0.375 \qquad \text{(see Appendix I)} \\
&= F.b. \; 1.875
\end{aligned}$$

Hence, if the network state is in the neighborhood of i0, it will be attracted with less strength than if it is in the neighborhood of i1. Consequently, the sum part of formula (eq.VI.6) appears to favor multi-component states of higher order. Since there is no a priori reason for such a point, we will renormalize the sum part in such a way that concepts of all levels stand on equal footing. There are two reasons why, according to (eq. VI.6), concepts of different levels receive different sum-consolidations.

a. First, the values $m^*(k)$ for different levels k differ. Hence, we propose to normalize each order parameter which occurs in (eq. VI.6). Suppose that the μ-th P participates in an item i0 of mixture level k. Then, we define the normalized order parameter of the μ-th P relative to i0 as the order parameter divided by $m^*(k)$. For ease of notation, we use the abbreviation n(μ,k) to refer to the normalized order parameter of the μ-th P relative to a concept of mixture level k:

$$n(\mu,k) \;=\; \frac{m^\mu}{m^*(k)}$$

The normalized order parameters of a P that participates in an M is always equal to one when the network state coincides with the M, irrespective of its level. Hence, we replace in the sum part of (eq. VI.6) each order parameter by the corresponding normalized expression.

b. The higher the order of an M, the higher the number of P's which participate in it. Hence, the higher the number of terms which contribute to the sum-part of its consolidation. This effect can be canceled if one takes the mean value of the (normalized) order parameters instead of their sum. Hence, we divide the sum part of the consolidation of an item by its order.

4.2 The product part of the consolidation

Also in case of the product part of the consolidation, we will make recourse to normalized order parameters. Then, the product part is unaffected by the point that the saturation values of the order parameters $m^*(k)$ are different for different levels k. Consider, for instance, a memorized item i0 of order three. Suppose that the indices of the P's are chosen in such a way that the first three P's participate in i0. The product part of its consolidation (for normalized order parameters) reads:

product part of $c(i0)$ = *F. (1-b) .((1/2)(1+sign((n(0,3)+e))*
$\qquad\qquad\qquad$ *.(n(0,3)+e)*
$\qquad\qquad\qquad$ *.((1/2)(1+sign((n(1,3)+e))*
$\qquad\qquad\qquad$ *.(n(1,3)+e)*
$\qquad\qquad\qquad$ *.((1/2)(1+sign((n(2,3)+e))*
$\qquad\qquad\qquad$ *.(n(2,3)+e)*

Suppose now that the network state coincides with i0. Then, one has $n(0,3)=n(1,3)=n(2,3)=1$ so that:

product part of $c(i0)$ = F. *(1-b) .(1+e).(1+e).(1+e)*

Next, consider a memorized item i1 of order five. By a similar calculation, one obtains that, if the network state coincides with i1, the product part of the consolidation experienced by i1 equals:

product part of $c(i1)$ = *F. (1-b). (1+e).(1+e).(1+e).(1+e).(1+e)*

Hence, since is e strictly positive, the product consolidation is larger if the network state coincides with higher level concepts than if it coincides with lower level ones. In order to correct for this effect, the normalized order parameter in each second part of a factor that corresponds to a *P* is multiplied with (1-e). Then, the product part of the consolidation of item i0 reads:

product part of $c(i0)$ = *F. (1-b) .((1/2)(1+sign(n(0,3)+e))*
$\qquad\qquad\qquad$ *.((n(0,3).(1-e)) +e)*
$\qquad\qquad\qquad$ *.((1/2)(1+sign(n(1,3)+e))*
$\qquad\qquad\qquad$ *.((n(1,3).(1-e)) +e)*
$\qquad\qquad\qquad$ *.((1/2)(1+sign(n(2,3)+e))*
$\qquad\qquad\qquad$ *.((n(2,3).(1-e)) +e)*

It is readily verified that, if the network state coincides with i0:

product part of $c(i0)$= F. *(1-b)*

The same equation holds for items which combine other numbers of components.

4.3 The normalized expression

If we bring together the points of 3.1 and 3.2., we obtain the following expression for the consolidation of a memorized multi-component state M:

$$C(m) = \ F \ \{ \ \ (1\text{-}b) \ . \ (1/2) \ (1 + sign(n(0,k) + e)) \ ((n(0,k).\,(1\text{-}e)) \ + e)$$
$$. \ (1/2) \ (1 + sign(n(1,k) + e)) \ ((n(1,k).\,(1\text{-}e)) \ + e)$$
$$. \ ...$$
$$. \ (1/2) \ (1 + sign(n(i,k) + e)) \ ((n(i,k).\,(1\text{-}e)) \ + e)$$
$$. \ ...$$
$$. \ (1/2) \ (1 + sign(n(k\text{-}1,k) + e)) \ ((n(k\text{-}1).\,(1\text{-}e)) \ + e)$$

$$+ \ b \ \ .(n(0,k) + n(1,k) + ... + n(i,k) + ...n(k\text{-}1,k)) \ \} \qquad \text{(eq. VI.7)}$$

This is the expression for the consolidation on which our model is based. It will be used in all our simulations.

5 The qualitative difference between sum- and product-consolidations

5.1 Basic properties of product terms

Consider an network in which the consolidations of the items are governed entirely by product terms (i.e. all b-values are equal to zero). Suppose that an input is presented to the system. Then, as a first approximation, the strength of the attraction exerted by a memorized item can be estimated if one counts the number of P's of the item which have a nearly zero order parameter. The larger this number, the lower the relative attractivity of the item. In practice, a value of e of the order of 0.1 is appropriate (note 1). As a consequence, the product consolidation of an M decreases with an order of magnitude for each of its P's that has an approximately zero order parameter. It follows that product terms in general do not give raise to effects of interference.

Consider two different items i0 and i1 which differ by at least one P. If the network state is very close to i0 (i.e. if all order parameters of the P's that participate in i0 are close to their maximal value), i1 attracts the network state at least one order of magnitude less forcefully than i0. This point holds a fortiori for patterns which share less P's with i0. In general, product consolidations lead to the following scenario.

As long as the state of the system is somewhere in between different memorized *M*'s, the latter compete with each other. However, as soon as one of them has gained an advantage over the others, it attracts with significantly more strength. Once the network state is close to it, only this *M* keeps exerting significant attraction on the network state.

5.2 Basic properties of sum terms

Suppose that, for a particular knowledge base, all memorized items have b-value one. In other terms, suppose that all consolidations consist of a sum-contribution only. Then, the following properties hold:

a. If, for every memorized *M*, the non-zero order parameters of its *P*'s have approximately the same value, then the consolidation experienced by an *M* is proportional to the relative number of non-zero order parameters of its components. Hence, this number determines the strength with which the *M* attracts the network state. b. A memorized *M* has a non-zero value for its consolidation as soon as one of its *P*'s has an order parameter that differs from zero.

Suppose that the network state coincides with a consolidated multi-component state i0. Consider another consolidated item i1 and suppose that the number of activated *P*'s of i1 is not an order of magnitude smaller than its mixture level. Then, the consolidation experienced by i1 is of the same order of magnitude as the consolidation experienced by i0. As a consequence, several memorized *M*'s may simultaneously attract the network state. Hence, phenomena of interference between different attractions occur. We illustrate this point in the examples of the next paragraph. If the value of the consolidation of different *M*'s is significantly positive and if these *M*'s share some *P*'s, then the latter *P*'s show an especially strong tendency to become or to remain activated. This tendency may decide in which direction the network state moves.

6 Some examples

6.1 Conventions concerning notation

Before we give some examples, we make two additional conventions concerning the notation that we use.

a. In order to specifiy the composition of an item, the k-th memorized item of a knowledge base is denoted by the characters "ik" followed by a colon and by the indices of the P's which participate in it. Both k and the indices of the P's are natural numbers including zero. For example,

i0: 0,1,2,3,4

denotes item i0. It contains five components, the indices of which are respectively 0, 1, 2, 3 and 4.

b. An input presented to the system will be denoted "in". The P's which participate in it are specified in the same way as the P's which participate in a memorized item. For instance:

in: 0,8,12

denotes an input pattern that includes the components 0, 8 and 12.

6.2 Example 1

Suppose that a knowledge base includes the following items:

i0: 0,1,2,3,4
i1: 0,1,2,3,4,   5,6
i2: 0,1,2,3,4,   7,8
i3: 0,1,2,3,4,   9,10

i4: 11,12,13,14,15
i5: 11,12,13,14,15,   16,17

Item i0 can be interpreted as a prototype for the items i1, i2 and i3: it forms a core common to the latter items. Item i4 is a prototype for i5. Suppose that the following item is presented to the system:

in: 2,3,11,12,13

The input shares two P's with i0, i1, i2 and i3. It shares three P's with i4 and i5. We study the dynamics of the system for two conditions. First, we consider the case of a pure product consolidation (i.e. the case of zero b-values). Second, the case of a consolidation which includes an additive contribution (i.e. the case of non-zero b-values) is considered.

6.2.1 The case of zero b-values

First, we consider the case in which all stored items have a negligible b-value. Then, the strength with which a stored item attracts an input is determined by the number of zero (or nearly zero) order parameters of its P's: for each zero order parameter, the value of the consolidation of the item decreases with an order of magnitude. In case of the present example, the input produces the following numbers of zero order parameters for the respective items:

i0: 3 zero order parameters (associated respectively with the P's 0, 1 and 4)
i1: 5 zero order parameters (associated respectively with the P's 0, 1, 4, 5 and 6)
i2: 5 zero order parameters (associated respectively with the P's 0, 1, 4, 7 and 8)
i3: 5 zero order parameters (associated respectively with the P's 0, 1, 4, 9 and 10)
i4: 2 zero order parameters (associated respectively with the P's 14 and 15)
i5: 4 zero order parameters (associated respectively with the P's 14, 15, 16, 17)

Consequently, item i4 has the smallest number of zero values among its order parameters. Hence, it will show the strongest tendency to attract the input. Our simulations confirm this fact. This is illustrated in figure s1 (see Appendix III for some technical specifications concerning the simulations). The horizontal axis of figure s1 shows the number of neural updatings. The vertical axis shows the correlation of the network state with i0 and i4.

6.2.2 The case of non-negligible b-values

The situation changes when the b-values of the stored items get larger. Then, also
the sum-terms come into play. To start with, we confine ourselves to the situation
of sum terms only (in other terms, we suppose that all b-values are equal to 1). We
notice that, in case of the present example, the order parameters of the P's which
participate in the input are all the same (and, up to fluctuations, equal to $m^*(5)$).
Hence, in order to estimate the value of the sum-consolidations of the respective
items, we count the number of P's that they share with the input (see 5.2). We
have:

i0: 2   shared order parameters (associated with the P's 2 and 3)
i1: 2   shared order parameters (associated with the P's 2 and 3)
i2: 2   shared order parameters (associated with the P's 2 and 3)
i3: 2   shared order parameters (associated with the P's 2 and 3)
i4: 3   shared order parameters (associated with the P's 11, 12 and 13)
i5: 3   shared order parameters (associated with the P's 11, 12 and 13)

Hence, items i4 and i5 attract the input with more strength than the other items.
However, the input will not lead to a retrieval of one of them. This is due to the fact
that the attractions exerted by the respective stored items interfere. If an item attracts
the network state, then the P's which participate in it tend to invade in the network
state (or tend to remain in it if they are already activated). More general, the more
items by which an P is stimulated, the stronger its tendency to invade in the state
of the system. For each P, we consider the number of items in which it participates.

P:	number of items in which it participates	name of these items
0	4	i0, i1, i2, i3, i4
1	4	i0, i1, i2, i3, i4
2	4	i0, i1, i2, i3, i4
3	4	i0, i1, i2, i3, i4
4	4	i0, i1, i2, i3, i4
5	1	i1
6	1	i1
7	1	i2
8	1	i2
9	1	i3
10	1	i3
11	2	i4, i5
12	2	i4, i5
13	2	i4, i5
14	2	i4, i5
15	2	i4, i5
16	1	i5
17	1	i5

We perceive that the *P*'s 0, 1, 2, 3 and 4 participate in four memorized items. Since these items exert their attracting forces simultaneously, these *P*'s experience four times a tendency to invade into the network state. Consequently, their tendency to invade in the network state is especially high. This point has to be qualified by the fact that the consolidations of the items at issue have a lower value than the ones of the items in which the *P*'s 11, 12, 13, 14 and 15 occur (since the latter items contain one more non-zero order parameter). However, a more detailed comparison shows that:

i. the latter *P*'s are favored by half as much items as the *P*'s 0, 1, 2, 3 and 4
ii. the values of the consolidations of the items which favor them are only 1.5 times the value of the consolidation of the items which contain 0, 1, 2, 3 and 4.

Hence, the *P*'s 0, 1, 2, 3 and 4 will win the competition and they will invade in the network state. As their order parameters increase, the values of the consolidations of i0, i1, i2 and i3 increase. Gradually, they will exceed the values of the consolidation of i4 and i5. After some time of evolution, the network state becomes more correlated with i0, i1, i2 and i3 than with i4 and i5. Due to the normalization of the consolidations, i0 gradually will attract stronger than i1, i2 and i3: all components of i0 have relatively strong activation whereas two components of i1, i2 and i3 are not activated. Since the sum term of the consolidation takes the mean values of the (normalized) order parameters, it will be larger for i0 than for i1, i2 and i3 (note 2). Hence, the network state evolves to i0.

This scenario is confirmed by our simulations, as is illustrated in figure s2. We observe in figure s2 that the network state hesitates to converge entirely to i0. This is because its instances i1, i2 and i3 keep a comparatively high consolidation. Hence, although the network state shows a clear preference, the high value of the consolidation of other memories pulls its correlation with i0 below one. If the b-values of the items are positive but still significantly smaller than one, then the product term of the consolidation may produce a sufficiently steep basin of attraction around i0 so that the network state converges exactly to i0. Figure s3 illustrates this point for the case in which all b-values are equal to 0.3.

6.2.3 The transition from low b-values to high b-values

It follows from 6.2.1. and 6.2.2. that consolidations with low b- values and consolidations with higher b-values may lead to different classifications (in the present example, the system chooses for i0 as soon as the b-values of all items exceed 0.03). If a set of items has high b-values, then their common P's show a strong tendency become to activated. Since common components may express a prototype or an abstract core, one has that, for high b-values, prototypes or abstract cores may strongly influence the choice of the memorized item to which an input will converge. The present example also illustrates another property of the system. If all items have the same F- and b-values, and if the b-values are significantly positive, then prototypes or cores which have many instances have stronger tendency to invade in the network state than prototypes or cores with less instances. This effect is entirely absent for zero b-values.

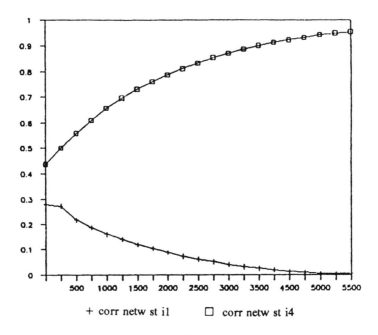

+ corr netw st i1   □ corr netw st i4

Figure s1

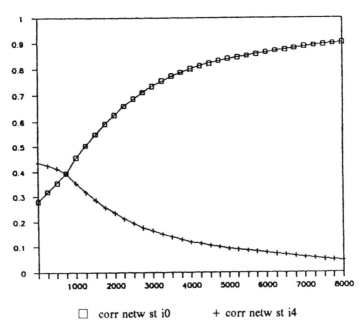

□ corr netw st i0   + corr netw st i4

Figure s2

Schematically, we have:

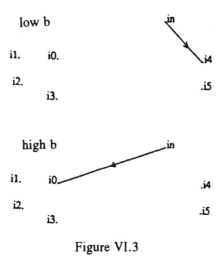

Figure VI.3

Finally, we notice that present example suggests to choose the b-value of the memorized items strictly smaller than one. In effect, according to our learning rule, the b-value of non-familiar items is equal to zero, and the b-value of familiar items increases only gradually (see 7).

6.3 Example 2

We consider an example in which the memorized items have different b-values. More specifically, the items of the present example are:

i0: 0,1,2,3,4
i1: 0,1,2,   5,6
i2:   1,2,3,   7,8
i3: 0,   3,4,   9,10
i4: 0,1,   4,   11,12

The input presented to the system is:

in= 0,1,2,5,6,13,14

This input contains all components of i1. It can be interpreted as i1 that is disturbed by noise: since the components 13 and 14 do not contribute to the representations of the memorized items, they are noise relative to the considered knowledge base. Suppose that the input is realized in the basis network. Then, the following table shows for each memorized item the number of P's with zero order parameters:

item	number of zero order parameters	number of components shared with "in"
i0	2	3
i1	0	5
i2	3	2
i3	4	1
i4	3	2

It is readily inferred from the column which contains the number of zero order parameters that, in case of pure product consolidation, the input will be mapped on i1. Now suppose that item i0 has a high b-value and that the ones of the other items also are significantly positive. For instance, consider the following b-values:

i0: b=0.7
i1: b=0.3
i2: b=0.3
i3: b=0.3
i4: b=0.3

Then, the situation is more subtle. To understand what happens, we count the number of items in which the respective P's participate:

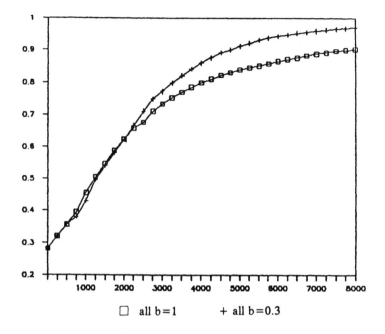

□ all b=1   + all b=0.3

Figure s3

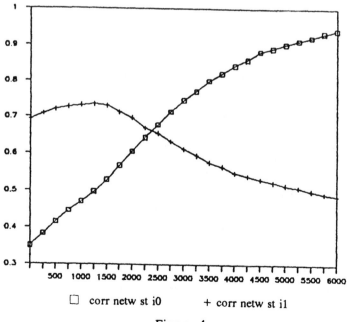

□ corr netw st i0   + corr netw st i1

Figure s4

name of the component	number of items in which it occurs	names of the items
0	4	i0,i1,i2,i3
1	4	i0,i1,i2,i4
2	3	i0,i2,i3
4	3	i0,i3,i4
5	1	i1
6	1	i1
7	1	i2
8	1	i2
9	1	i3
10	1	i3
11	1	i4
12	1	i4

If all items have high b-value, the components 0,1,2,3 and 4 invade in the network state and, eventually, item i0 is retrieved. This point has already been discussed in the previous example. However, a similar effect takes place also for the present b-values. We give a qualitative explanation for this point.

If the b-value of i0 is high, then i0 has significant attractivity as soon as some of its P's are realized. Now when the network state coincides with the input "in", three of the five P's of i0 are activated. Hence, the value of the sum component of the consolidation of i0 is relatively large. Consequently, the P's 0,1,2,3 and 4 show a strong tendency to enter in the network state. Since both the sum and product consolidation of i1 are significantly higher than the one of i0, this fact alone does not suffice to explain the convergence towards i0. However, we notice that the input has also different P's in common with i2, i3 and i4. Now if also these items have non-zero b-value, the P's which occur in more than one of these items are encouraged more than once to enter the network state. Hence, if this condition is fulfilled, the P's of i0 are favored not only by the consolidation of i0 itself but also by the fact that they occur in other items as well. The latter point can be decisive: if the sum-consolidations of i1, i2 and i3 favor their common P's with sufficient strength, then the input will be mapped on i0 instead of on i1. Simulations confirm indeed that, for the present b-values, the input converges to i0. This is illustrated in figure s4.

On the other hand, for the following b-values

i0: b=0.7
i1: b=0.1
i2: b=0.1
i3: b=0.1
i4: b=0.1

the input converges to i1 (figure s5). In other terms, if the b-values of items i1, i2 and i3 increase from 0.1 to 0.3, the classification behavior of the system changes: at b-values of at least 0.3 (and at a b-value of i0 of 0.7), the P's which occur in more than one of these items are drawn in the network state and the input converges to i0. At b-values for i1, i2, i3 and i4 of about 0.2, the network "doubts" how to classify the input: dependent on small random effects (see appendix III), the input may be classified as i0 one time and as i1 another time. If these b-values are below 0.1, then the components of i0 are not sufficiently stimulated and the input converges to i1.

The high b-value of i0 is essential in this process: for the values

i0: b=0.6
i1: b=0.3
i2: b=0.3
i3: b=0.3
i4: b=0.3

the input converges to i1 instead of to i0 (picture s6). Hence, in the present example, the components of i0 need a substantial encouragement by i0 itself in order to enter the network state. We will see in chapter X that the present example has an interesting interpretation: if a particular item has high b-value, then it may prohibit that other, related items are addressed even if an input has large overlap with them. This may necessitate a change in representation (see also the general learning rule in 7).

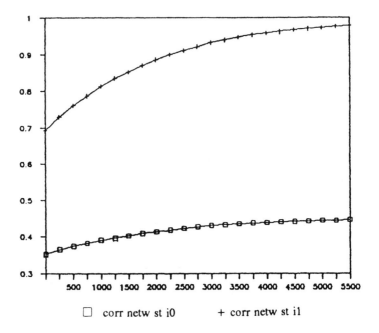

Figure s5

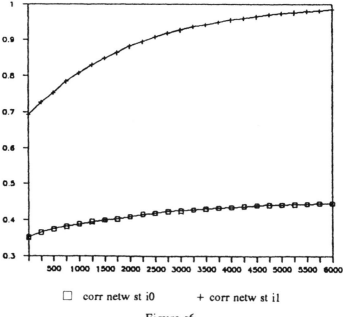

Figure s6

6.4 Example 3

We consider the following set of items and the following input:

```
i0:   1,2,3    5,6
i1: 0,1,  3,    7,8
i2:   1,2,  4, 9,10
i3: 0,  2,3,   11,12
i4: 0,     3,4, 13,14
```

in: 0,1,3,7,8,15,16

Like in example 2, the input can be considered as i1 plus noise (the noise is expressed by components 15 and 16). To start with, we consider a pure product consolidation. Then, since all components of i1 are activated for the input and since, for all other items, at least two order parameters are zero, one has that the input will be mapped on item i1. This is illustrated in figure s7. Again, the situation changes if the b-values increase. We notice that all P's of the set A:

A: 0,1,2,3,4

occur three times in a memorized item. Hence, if the sum parts of the consolidations of the items are sufficiently large, these P's show a strong tendency to enter in the network state. In the present example, A does not correspond to a memorized pattern. Still, for high b-values, the input will not converge to i0 but to a non-stored state M in which the order parameters of the P's of A have highest value. In the state M, the order parameters of component 7 and component 8 are also significantly positive, but they are smaller than the ones of the components of A since they are favored by fewer items. On the other hand, component 7 and component 8 are not repelled entirely out of the network state since A does not attract by itself.

Consequently, the network state converges to an asymmetric state M. Our simulations show indeed that, if the b-values of all items are equal to 0.8, the network state converges to a state with the following (approximate) correlations with the respective items:

corr. of eventual state with i0 = 0.453
corr. of eventual state with i1 = 0.826
corr. of eventual state with i2 = 0.435
corr. of eventual state with i3 = 0.433
corr. of eventual state with i4 = 0.440

All other order parameters are zero up to fluctuations.

Figure s8 illustrates the evolution of the correlation of the network state with i0 and i1; figure s9 shows the evolution of the order parameters of component 2 and component 4. We perceive that these *P*'s are drawn into the network state. We anticipate that, if the network maps an input on an asymmetric mixture state, then this is a sign to change representation (see the full learning rule in 7).

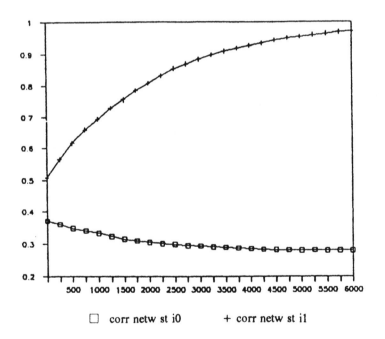

☐ corr netw st i0   + corr netw st i1

Figure s7

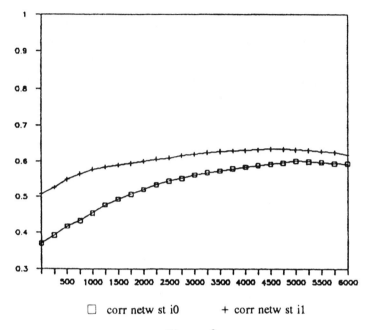

$\square$ corr netw st i0   + corr netw st i1

Figure s8

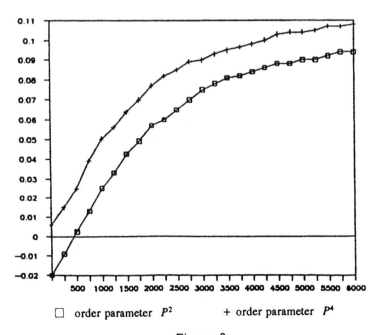

$\square$ order parameter P^2 + order parameter P^4

Figure s9

7 The full learning rule

We are ready to formulate the full learning rule of our model now. Expression (eq. VI.7) plays a central role in it. However, it has to be supplemented by some principles which govern the evolution of the representations of concepts. We differentiate between two kinds of rules. First, we consider rules which can be formulated in terms of the module that we describe only. Second, we consider the rules for which we have to make recourse to our more general frame (chapters II-IV).

7.1 Multi-component concepts and their evolution

First, we formulate four principles which govern the evolution of representations and which can be formulated in terms of our connectionist system.

L1. Suppose that an input is given to the network and suppose that the network does not recognize one of its memorized patterns in it. Then, the input corresponds to an item that has not been learned yet. Consider the components which participate in the input and which have order parameters which exceed a treshold value I(tr) (note 3). If this bears an odd number of components, then the M that consists of these components is considered. If the criterion is satisfied by an even number of components, then an additional component is included in accordance with rule L9 (note 4). The resulting odd M is consolidated in agreement with formula (eq. VI.7). Unless the item is especially important for the subject (e.g. if it is accompanied with high emotions), the initial values of both F and b are low (see 8.1).

L2. Each time that an M is retrieved, its F-value or its b-value increases. Also if an item becomes important for some or other reason (for instance, if it is accompanied with high emotions), its F-value or its b-value increases.

This rule can be specified; each specification leads to a different instance of the more general model. In 8, we point out the specification that we will adopt.

L3. For each concept, we define a correlation-sphere with radius R by the set of network states which have a correlation higher than R with the concept. Then, the extension of the basin of attraction of a concept can be estimated by the radius of the largest correlation sphere within which every network state converges to the concept. This definition allows us to formulate learning rule L3:

We require that the basin of attraction of every concept of the network exceeds a minimal value R(tr). If, for a given concept, the network concludes at a given moment that this threshold value is not exceeded, then the concept has to change its representation. This may happen in three ways:

i. First, suppose that an input that corresponds to the concept is presented to the network. Suppose that *P*'s which do not participate in the representation of the concept show fastly increasing order parameters. Then, these *P*'s have to be included in the new representation of the concept. If this results in an even mixture, rule L9 has to be applied in order to obtain an odd one. If point i. does not apply or if it applies but if the resulting new representation does not have the required topological properties, then point ii. or point iii. must be applied.
ii. Second, the pre-processing system may scan the corresponding object or scene in order to deliver more *P*'s to the network (see L6).
iii. Third, in accordance with rules L7 and L8, analysis with help of image schema's may offer supplementary *P*'s.

Also points ii and iii. must not violate the principle that an *M* has to be odd (see rule L9). Rule L3 may entail that a new item that is consolidated in agreement with L1 has to change its representation immedeately. For instance, if, in the neighborhood of the representation of the new item, particular components, which do not participate in the representation of the new item, show a strong tendency to invade in the network state, then the item may have a quite small basin of attraction or it may be not addressable at all. Then, its representation has to change: it has to include the *P*'s at issue in order to obtain a network topology that is reconcilable with the present learning rule. Intuitively, this entails that a new item may be drawn in an elaborated category or context (see X,7.3). Further, it may entail that, at a given moment, a familiar item has to change its representation due to gradual changes in the familiarity of other items (see X,7.1).

L4. The network may extract and consolidate an abstract core or a prototype from instances which are already stored. To this end, one of the subordinate instances is activated. Then, in order to stimulate the network state to move, the F-value of the instance is put equal to zero. Next, the b-values of all relevant items are temporary significantly increased (note 5). Finally, the order parameters of the relevant *P*'s are considered. If a *P* has a stable, significantly positive order parameter or if it has a significantly growing order parameter, then it is included in the *M* that expresses the more abstract concept (also here, oddity constraints have to be taken into account: see L9). Other *P*'s do not participate in the representation of the abstract concept.

The abstract concept is consolidated in agreement with rule L1. After the abstract concept is identified and has received its consolidation, the b-values of the items are set to their normal values again.

If the order parameters of the *P*'s which are candidates for the abstract category appear to cluster in significantly disjunct bands, then the situation is more complex. Then, one can introduce more than one abstract category at different levels of inclusion. The most abstract concept includes all *P*'s of the highest band. At a lower level of abstraction, an attractor can be formed with all *P*'s of the highest and of the one but highest band, and so on. All these categories are consolidated in agreement with L1 (see X.II.8 for an illustration of this rule).

L5. The F- and the b-values of patterns which are never retrieved gradually decay. The b-values decay quite slowly (see 8.3).

7.2 Rules which invoke our general frame

In the present paragraph, the rules of 7.1 are supplemented by rules which refer to the general frame that we developed in II-IV. They can be divided in three classes.

7.2.1 Rules which refer to the mechanisms of pre-processing

L6. Suppose that, by application of the learning rules, two familiar concepts become less discriminable than required by L3, or suppose that a subject has to introduce a supplementary differentiation in his concepts (because a teacher tells him so or because the environment stimulates him to make this differentiation). Further, suppose that the application of L3.i. does not lead to the discriminability required by L3.

Then, in order to enhance discriminability, the subject may scan one of the corresponding objects or scenes in order to extract *P*'s that correspond to more detailed aspects. These *P*'s may participate in the new representation of the objects or scenes in question. We are reminded of the fact that the pre-processing system first focusses on the global aspects of objects or scenes (i.e. their "skeleton" or main part; see the discussion in chapter II). First, the *P*'s corresponding to these aspects are transmitted to the system. Next, more detailed levels are taken into account. The pre-processing system may deliver *P*'s until a level of detail is reached at which the objects or scenes are discriminable in the sense of L3. The application of L6 must not violate the principle that *M*'s which represent concepts are odd (see L9).

7.2.2 Rules related to the analysis of mental states

L7. Suppose that the representation of an object or of a scene is transmitted to the surface matrix and suppose that it is analyzed with help of image schema's. Then, the P's which correspond to the schema's which are detected may be added to the representation of the object or of the scene (this rule is postulated in agreement with chapter II). Such additions may enhance the discriminability of concepts (see L3.iii.).

Rule L7 must not violate the principle that M's have to be odd mixtures. Hence, either pairs of P's have to be added after analysis of the scene or object, or rule L9 has to be applied.

L8. If a subject analyzes a scene and if he concludes that a particular object fits in it, then the may add the skeleton of the scene to the representation of the object (see chapter III). Also this rule may lead to a better discriminability between concepts (see L3.iii.).

Again, the addition of P's must not violate the oddity of M's. In order to respect this principle, rule L9 may have to be applied.

7.2.3 The oddity of the vote mixtures that represent concepts

L9. Suppose that a new item has to be learned or that a memorized item has to change representation. Then, the rules L1-L8 are applied. Suppose that, in a particular situation, an application of these rules does not lead directly to an M with an odd number of P's. Then, the input may be scanned for one more P in order to obtain a network state of an odd mixture level. Alternatively, if this process does not deliver a supplementary P, or if, for some reason (e.g. because the concept is too abstract), it can not be carried out, recourse can be made to L7 and L8 in order to search for supplementary P's.

8 Comments

8.1 The increase of the F-values and of the b-values

It is plausbile to propose that the F-value of a memorized concept increases each time that the concept is retrieved. Intuitively, this means that a concept becomes imprinted with more depth. In case of patterns which are accompanied by high emotions, the F-value may increase drastically. Then, the network learns "fast". We notice that the capacity of our network for fast learning contrasts, for instance, with the learning rule of a multi-layer perceptron. The latter requires that inputs are shown time and over again before a pattern is imprinted. The larger the parameter R(tr), the higher one has to choose the initial value of F in order to give a new concept a stable representation. Further, the required height of F is dependent on the concrete structure of the knowledge base. For instance, if a new concept is far removed from previously learned concepts, a low initial F-value may suffice. If, on the other hand, the new item is in the neigborhood of deeply imprinted memories, it needs a higher intial F-value in order to obtain a basin of attaction with some extension (see also X.II.8).

Rule L2 also states that the b-value of a memorized item gradually increases as a pattern is met more often. This point is derived form the fact that a prototype model becomes more adequate than an exemplar model as a concept becomes more familiar (see previous chapter). We will see in the course of the following chapters that this simple hypothesis helps us to explain quite some psychological phenomena. Intuitively, the gradual increase of the b-values gives more weight to P's which are shared by different M's (this is illustrated in the examples of the paragraph 6). Hence, it increases the importance of "cores" or prototypes shared by different concepts. As we will show in chapter X, in conjunction with the other learning rules, L2 stimulates the reorganization of semantic memory.

8.2 The saturated-F model

Learning rule L2 is quite unspecific. For instance, it does not specify if the F-value of an M increases more quickly than its b-value; also, it does not specify if the increase of these parameters is linear or not. In the present paragraph, we specify L2. A model that accepts these specifications is called a "saturated-F model".

i. The first time that an M is imprinted, only its F-value receives a a striclty positive value (note 6).

ii. As the M is retrieved more often (or if it becomes important for another reason), its F-value increases until it reaches a saturation value F(sat). During this process, its b-value remains zero.

iii. If the M becomes still more familiar (or if it becomes more important for another reason), its b-value becomes strictly positive and it gradually increases.

Intuitively, a saturated-F model proposes that the P's of an M first interact according to an exemplar-rule. Only when the M is sufficiently familiar, its P's show an interaction term that corresponds to the prototype-model. In the following chapters, we will use the saturated-F model in order to explain the psychological properties that we will consider. We will see that it is consistent with several psychological phenomena.

8.3 The decay of the parameters b and F

In rule L5, it is specified that the F- and the b-value of an M decrease if the M is never activated. One may wonder how exactly these parameters decay as time proceeds. The existing empirical evidence on the problem of forgetting is not sufficiently detailed in order to allow for the derivation of an exact formula. We notice that there is some evidence for the stance that prototypes decay less fast than non-prototypical elements (Strange, Keene, Kessel and Jenkins, 1970; Homa, Cross, Cornell, Goldman and Schwartz 1973; Homa and Voghsburg, 1976; Goldman and Homa, 1977). However, this allows to infer only the following general constraint on the way in which the b-values of items decrease. Consider a set of consolidated items which are centered around a prototype. Suppose that all these items (including the prototype) have the same F- and b-values, and suppose that none of these items is retrieved during a period of considerable extension. Further, suppose that the F-values and the b-values of all items decay uniformly. Then, the evidence referred to entails that, during this period, the b-values can not have decreased entirely to zero. If this would have been the case, the prototypes would be remembered to the same extent as the other instances (since common components have no significant additional attractivity in case of b=0); this, however, disagrees with the evidence. Hence, we suggest that the b-values of the items do not decay quickly to zero.

9 The function of the basis-layer.

Our learning rule presumes that concepts can be defined in terms of P's. In fact, L1-L9 specify when P's have to be included in the representations of concepts and how this has to happen. Now the point that P's are represented as large binary vectors is not directly apparent from our learning rule: this fact becomes evident only if one implements formula (eq.VI.7) and if one examines the meaning of its terms. However, one may wonder if also this formula can be interpreted in such a way that only variables of the meta-layer are involved. Then, one would obtain a computationalist model rather than a connectionist one. For instance, one may suggest to specify the state of the system as a vector which has the order parameters of the P's as its components, and one may try to implement formula (eq.VI.7) directly in terms of these parameters. If this scenario would work, the hypothesis of a basis layer with binary vectors would be superfluous: it would introduce terms which are redundant for the dynamics of the model. It is important to see why this argument is wrong.

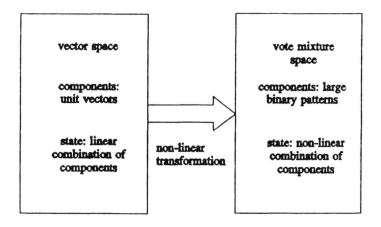

Figure VI.4

Our representation is non-linearly related with vector space representations. As a consequence, dynamics which are easily described by our system are hard to describe by vector models, and vice versa. Hence, the introduction of the basis-layer is not just an introduction of redundant degrees of freedom. On the contrary: because formula (eq. VI.7) refers to large binary patterns and to their vote mixtures, it generates the dynamical properties that allow to describe several psychological phenomena (see also Van Loocke 1991a, 1993).

NOTES

Note 1. The simulations to which we refer are made with a basis layer of 2048 neurons. The P's (i.e. the groundpatterns) of the network are orthogonal up to 2.5 per cent. Then, the fluctuations produced by i. and ii. can be rendered harmless by an e-value of the same order. In our simulations, we put e equal to 0.1 (this value of a includes a safety margin; see also Appendix III).

Note 2. This point has to be qualified by the fact that the P's of i0 increase to a less degree by the transition to normalized order parameters than the P's of i1, i2 and i3 (since $m^*(5)$ is larger than $m^*(7)$). However, this fact produces only a quite small change in the values of the respective consolidations. It does not outweigh the two zero order parameters of i1, i2 and i3.

Note 3. The treshold value I(tr) must be larger than $m^*(k(\text{max}))$, where k(max) is the largest mixture level that occurs in a given knowledge base. Then, if an input is itself a vote mixture, all its components will participate in the M that is consolidated.

Note 4. Alternatively, one could include the groundstate with the highest order-parameter that is smaller than I(tr); if I(tr) is not too small and if the order parameter at issue is close to I(tr), then this is a quite reasonable criterion. However, in practice, the order parameters which are smaller than I(tr) may all be significantly smaller than I(tr). Then, the system has to make recourse to rule L9.

Note 5. Alternatively, one may temporary raise the b-values of all memorized concepts. If the instance from which the abstraction starts does not have large overlaps with instances of other categories, then this procedure will lead to the same abstract category, since instances of other categories will not tend to draw their P's in the network state.

Note 6. One may wonder which F-value one has to give to an M that is imprinted for the first time and that is accompanied with normal emotional circumstances. Our simulations suggest that the value F(initial) = 0.5 F(sat) is an appropriate value (see X.II.8).

VII. PROTOTYPES AND MORE GENERAL TYPICALITY-EFFECTS

1 Introduction

The typicalities of items can be determined experimentally by the speed of membership decisions. Likewise, in case of our connectionist model, we determine typicalities by the speed of membership decisions in simulations (paragraph 2). The typicalities which are estimated by our model have three obvious properties. First, items that share more P's with a prototype are more typical members of the corresponding category. Second, items with more supplementary P's relative to the prototype are less typical. Third, the instances of a category which resemble the instances of another category are less typical (paragraph 3,4).

The "central tendency" of an item increases if it is central in its own category and it decreases if it is related to instances of other categories. In case of "simple" categories, central tendency arrangements coincide with typicality arrangements (paragraph 5). In more complex situations, this point has to be qualified. It appears that the typicalities of taxonomic categories are not determined by the same factors as the typicalities of goal-derived categories. Typicalities of taxonomic categories are determined largely by central tendency. On the other hand, typicalities of goal-derived categories are determined mainly by frequency and by ideality. The frequency factor can be partially explained by reference to the links between non-verbal semantic patterns and their labels. The factor "ideality" is due to the structure of particular sets of representations (paragraph 6). Finally, we point out that our model suggests other factors which determine typicality distributions. If an item belongs to an extraordinary elaborated sub-category, then it may be less typical for its category. A very subordinate item may be less typical than a less subordinate one, even if the former has higher ideality (paragraph 7).

2 Typicality in our model

2.1 Estimates for the typicalities of instances of categories

In chapter V, we saw that concepts are in general not determined by a set of necessary and sufficient conditions. Often, they are centered around one or more prototypes. Further, subjects often agree that a particular instance is more typical for a category than another instance. The degree to which an item is typical for a category is called the "typicality" of the item relative to the category. There are two methods to determine the typicality of items:

a. According to the first one, subjects are asked to rate the typicality of an instance of a category by a number, for instance a number between 1 and 9.
b. The second method determines the time a subject needs to classify an item as a member of a category. The method presumes that the typicality of an item is negatively correlated with this decision time: the more typical an item is of a category, the more quickly it is recognized as one of its members.

These methods lead to results which are strongly correlated (see e.g. Barsalou and Sewell, 1985; Barsalou, 1985). The second method can be used to obtain typicality estimates from the connectionist model that we proposed in the previous chapter: one can measure the time a network needs to classify a particular item as a member of a category. The point that the consolidation rule bears effects of typicality is a remarkable fact, since we derived this rule from studies in which subjects only decided whether an item belonged to a category or not; the difficulty with which this decision was made was not recorded. In the following chapters, we will encounter this situation different times: our learning rule explains phenomena which are not directly related to the ones from which its form was derived. In the two following paragraphs, we confine ourselves to adult categories which are centered around a prototype. We assume that these categories are represented in an intrinsic way. For instances of such categories, the b-values are strictly positive and the F-values have reached the value F(sat) (see previous chapter). In the two last paragraphs of this chapter, we also consider other kinds of categories.

2.2 Two alternative ways to specify typicalities predicted by our model

We notice that, if a subject is asked if an item i1 is a typical instance of a concept i0, then i0 always is a superordinate or a basic level category. Suppose that the subject verifies if i1 is an i0. From a formal point of view, this process may proceed according to one of the following two scenario's.

a. According to the first possibility, initially only item i1 is realized. Then, the network state corresponding to the activation of i1 is made unstable (this effect can be produced by a temporary drastic decrease of the F-value associated with i1). Next, the time the network state needs to move to i0 is measured.

b. According to the second possibility, initially i1 is realized but also i0 may be favored. After all, if the question is asked "is i1 an i0 ?", i0 is explicitly mentioned. Item i0 may be favored in one of the two following ways:
i. First, the F-value of i0 may have a higher value during a relatively short period: since its label has been triggered very recently, its attractiveness may be higher for a short while.
ii. Alternatively, one could propose that, along with i1, also i0 would be realized partially within the initial state of the system.
These two sub-possibilities i. and ii. are similar form a practical point of view, since a significant increase of the F-value of i0 leads quite quickly to a partial activation of i0. Next, the network state is stimulated to withdraw from i1 (by a temporary drastic decrease of the F-value of i1). Again, the typicality of i1 can be estimated if one measures the time required by the model to move from the initial state to i0.

2.3 Differences in the speed of membership decisions

Scenario b. in general increases both the chance that i1 leads to a trigger of i0 as well as the speed of this process. For instance, consider the following eight items:

i0: 0,1,2,3,4
i1:   1,2,3,4, 5,6,7
i2: 0,1,2,3,   8,9,10
i3: 0,1, 3,4, 11,12,13
i4: 0,1,2, 4, 14,15,16

i5: 17,18,19
i6: 17,18,19, 5,6
i7: 17,18,19,   6,7, 20,21

Suppose that their b-value is positive so that prototype-effects occur (more specifically, we take all b-values equal to 0.3). The items i1, i2, i3 and i4 are members of the category defined by the prototype i0. Items i6 and i7 are instances of i5. For convenience, we assume that i0 is retrieved once the network state has a correlation higher than 0.9 with it (see chapter I). Suppose the system has to estimate the typicality of i1. If the F-values of all items equal F(sat), then i1 leads to a trigger of i0 after about 3804 updatings (this is a mean value for 8 runs of the network; the dispersion s after eight runs is given by s=155 updatings). This is illustrated in figure s10. If the F-values of the items i2-i7 are to equal F(sat) and if the F-value of i0 equals 2F(sat), i0 is retrieved after about 3364 updatings (the dispersion s after eight runs is equal to s=146). Also this point is illustrated in figure s10.

2.4 The partial equivalence of both methods as far as concerns typicality arrangements

From a qualitative point of view, possibility a. and b. lead to the same arrangement of typicality estimates in the following sense. Consider two items i1 and i2 which belong to a category i0. Then, if an item i1 is more typical than an item i2 according to scenario a., this holds also according to scenario b (note 1). Further, if an item i1 is more typical than an item i2 according to scenario b., and if, according to scenario a., the item is classified as a member of i0, then i1 is more typical according to the first method also. The only qualitative difference between both methods is that the second one may classify items which are at the boarder of a category i0 as members of i0 whereas the first method may judge that they do not belong to i0. For instance, in the example of 2.3, the input

in: 0,1,17,18,21

converges to i0 if the F-value of i0 equals 2 F(sat) but not if its F-value is equal to F(sat). In the latter condition, the input converges to i5. Figure s11 shows the evolution of the correlations of the network state with i0 and i5 for F(i0)=2F(sat). Figure s12 shows the same correlations for F(i0)=F(sat). In the examples of the following paragraph, the instances can be classified as members of their respective categories with help of the first method, and we will use this method in order to obtain estimates of typicalities.

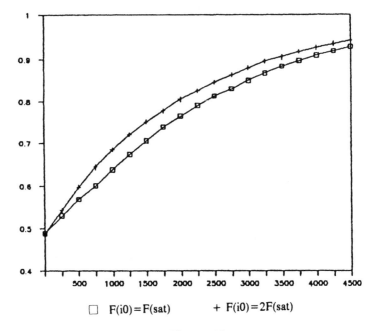

Figure s10

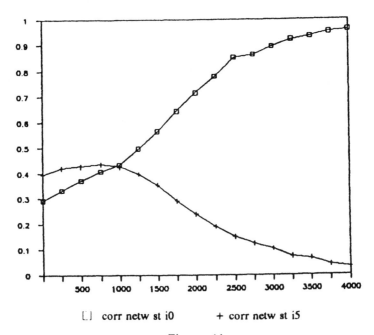

Figure s11

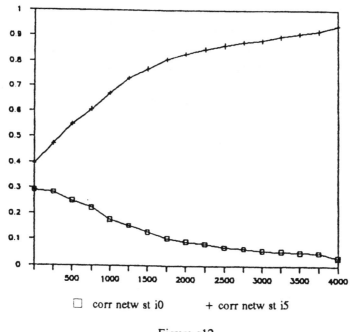

Figure s12

3 Obvious properties of the relative typicalities estimated by our model

3.1 Items which share more *P*'s with the prototype are more typical

In the present paragraph, we restrict ourselves to concepts with one prototype (the discussion can be generalized straightforwardly). Consider a concept A with one prototype i0 and with four instances i1, i2, i3 and i4. Further, suppose that the b-values of the prototype and of the instances are at least slightly positive. Then, if i1 shares more *P*'s with i0 than i2, i1 has higher typicality than i2. For instance, consider the following items:

```
i0: 0,1,2,3,4
i1: 0,1,2,3,4, 5,6,7,8
i2: 0,1,   4, 9,10,11,12
i3: 0, 2,3,   13,14,15,16
i4:   1,2,3,  17,18,19,20
```

If the b-values of all items are equal to 0.1, and if the initial network state coincides with i1 (with the supplementary constraint that the F-value of i1 should be temporary equal to zero in order to make i1 unstable), it takes about 2958 iterations for the network state to retrieve i0 (this is a mean value for eight runs; the dispersion s is given by s = 174). This is illustrated in figure s13). If the b-values of all items are equal to 0.1, and if the initial network state coincides with i2 (with the supplementary constraint that the F-value of i2 is temporary equal to zero in order to make i2 unstable), it takes about 3806 iterations for the network state to retrieve i0 (see figure s13) (the dispersion s for eight runs is given by s = 152). Hence, according to our model, item i1 is more typical for A than i2. This point is intuitively quite plausible: the more *P*'s an instance shares with a category, the less *P*'s have to be inferred during the evolution of the state of the system towards the prototype. Finally, we notice that the b-values of the items must not be entirely equal to zero. If this would be the case, then the items i2, i3 and i4 could converge to item i1 rather than to item i0 (this follows form the fact that the number of *P*'s that i1 shares with these items is equal to the number of *P*'s that i0 shares with them; hence, in case of pure product interactions, the probability that i1 attracts these items is similar to the probability that i0 attracts them (note 2)).

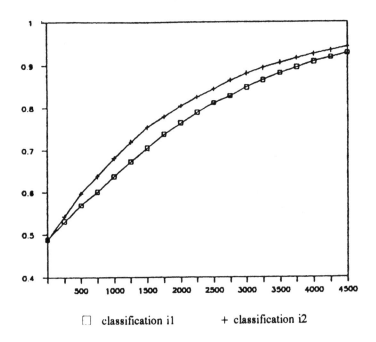

Figure s13

3.2 Items which contain more supplementary *P*'s relative to the prototype are less typical

Suppose that two items i1 and i2 share the same number of *P*'s with a prototype i0. Further, suppose i2 contains more supplementary *P*'s than i1. Then, i2 is less typical than i1. For example, consider the following items which belong to an intrinsically represented category A:

i0: 0,1,2,3,4
i1: 0,1,2, 4, 5
i2: 0,1,   3,4, 6,7,8
i3:   1,2,3,4, 9,10,11,12,13

Then, i1 is more typical than i2, and i2 is more typical than i3. More specifically, in case of a basis layer with 2048 units, item i1 leads to the retrieval of i0 after about 2719 neural updatings (the dispersion s for eight runs is given by s=110) (figure s14); item i2 retrieves i0 after about 3288 (s=161) updatings (figure s14) and i3 takes approximately 3706 (s=121) updatings (figure s14) (all b-values have been put equal to 0.1 in these simulations). Intuitively, this point is quite plausible. Item i3 (respectively i2) contains more supplementary components relative to the prototype than i2 (respectively i1). Hence, in case i3 (respectively i2) is presented to the network, more components have to dissipate out of the network state than in case of a presentation of i2 (respectively i1).

3.3 The items of a category which resemble the ones of another category are less typical

Suppose that two items i1 and i2 contain the prototype i0 of a category A to the same extent. Further, suppose they have the same number of supplementary components relative to i0. Then, if i1 resembles another concept and if i2 does not, i1 is less typical than i2. For instance, consider the items of 2.3 again:

i0: 0,1,2,3,4
i1:   1,2,3,4, 5,6,7
i2: 0,1,2,3,   8,9,10
i3: 0,1,   3,4, 11,12,13
i4: 0,1,2, 4, 14,15,16

i5: 17,18,19
i6: 17,18,19, 5,6
i7: 17,18,19, 6,7, 20,21

The items i1, i2, i3 and belong to the category A which is centered around the prototype i0. Items i6 and i7 belong to the category B which is centered around the prototype i5. In contradistinction with item i2, item i1 shares two P's with B-exemplars i6 and i7. As a consequence, i2 is more typical than i1. If i1 is presented as an input to the system (and if the F-value of i1 is temporary put equal to zero in order to allow for an association process) then the network requires approximately 3798 iterations to retrieve i0 (the dispersion for eight runs is equal to 151) (figure s15). If i2 is presented as an input to the system (and if the F-value of i2 is temporary put equal to zero in order to allow for an association process), then the network needs about 3384 updatings to retrieve i0 (the dispersion for eight runs is equal to 148) (figure s15).

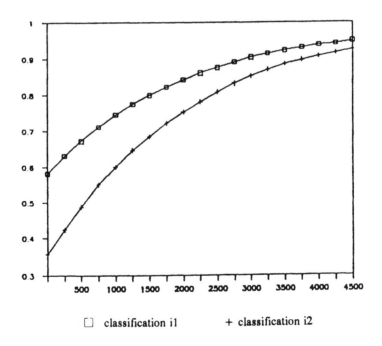

☐ classification i1   + classification i2

Figure s14

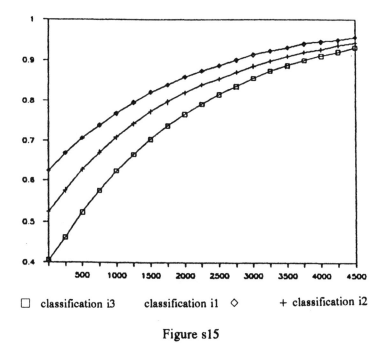

| | classification i3 | classification i1 ◇ | + classification i2 |

Figure s15

Again, this point is intuitively plausible. If an item of a category A resembles items of another category B, and if the network judges the typicality of that item, then two categories compete for the network state. This leads to a less straightforward convergence to A. We observe that the curves of s15 are very similar to the ones of s10. This is quite natural. In s10, the condition $F(i0) = F(sat)$ differs from the condition $F(i0) = 2F(sat)$ because, in the latter case, the items i6 and i7 attract too weakly to slow down the process of convergence to i0. In s15, the convergence of i2 to i0 is also not hindered by i6 and i7 since i2 does not share any P with the latter items. Like in s10 (and for $F(i0) = F(sat)$), i1 is classified less quickly because it is attracted by i6 and i7.

4 A simple mathematical explanation of these facts

Suppose that i1 and i2 are members of a class organized around a prototype i0. Suppose that the overlap between i1 and i0 is larger than the overlap between i2 and i0. It is possible to re-order the indices of the units of the basis-layer in such a way that the first P units all have the same value for i0 and i1 and so that the N-P last units have different values for i1 and i0:

0	P	N

We have:

$$Q(i0,i1) = 1/N \ (P - (N-P))$$

$$P = (N/2) \ (1 + Q(i1,i0)) \tag{eq. VII.1}$$

($Q(i0,i1)$ denotes the overlap between i0 and i1)

Suppose that the network state coincides with i1 and that i0 is very attractive. Then, each time a neuron is selected for an update, it will take the activation value of i0 in this unit. This process produces a gradual increase of the number of units in which the actual network state and i0 have the same activation value. Now suppose i2 has lower overlap with i0. Then, it follows from (eq. VII.1) that the number of units in which it has the same activation value as i0 is lower. If the network state coincides with i2, a larger number of updatings will be required before the network state has a correlation of 0.9 with i0. Hence, it takes more time to classify i2 as a member of the class organized around i0 than to decide that i1 is a member of this class. The mean difference in updatings is the mean number of updatings that is required for the evolution from i2 to a state that has an overlap equal to $Q(i1,i0)$ with i0.

This argument allows to give a simple mathematical explanation for the examples of 3.1 and 3.2. We are reminded of the following two relations between share (and non-share) of *P*'s and overlap (see chapter I; see Appendix I):

a. Suppose that i1 and i2 are of the same order. Suppose that i1 shares more components with a third pattern i0 than i2. Then, the overlap between i1 and i0 is larger than the overlap between i2 and i1.
b. Suppose that both i1 and i2 share k *P*'s with i0. Then, if i2 is of a higher mixture level than i1, i1 has higher overlap with i0 than i2.

In conjunction with the previous argument, these theorems give a simple explanation of the situations considered in 3.1 and 3.2. In case of 3.3, i0 is not the only concept that exerts attraction, so that the argument of 4.1 does not apply. The typicalities observed in 3.3, however, can be explained by the argument that has been given at the end of 3.3.

5 Prototypes and central tendency

5.1 The concept of central tendency

In two influential papers, Rosch et al. (Rosch and Mervis 1975; and Rosch, Simpson and Miller, 1976) argue that typicalities express the extent to which items are central in their category and the extent to which they are not related to items of other categories. The extent to which an item is central in its category is measured by its "central tendency". The central tendency of an item of a category A is determined by the number of properties that it shares with the other items of A. It is plausible to assume that a prototype has high central tendency. The intuition behind this assumption is that a prototype has the "typical" properties of a category: i.e. those properties which are shared by many of its instances. A non-prototypical item, on the other hand, has properties which are exceptional for the category.

It is tempting to associate the properties which are meant in this definition with the P's as we defined them in chapters I-IV. In fact, this proposal can be interpreted as a more exact reformulation of the original definition. Then, according to our frame, the central tendency of an item $i1$ that belongs to a category A can be calculated as the sum of the numbers of P's that $i1$ shares with the other instances of A. This definition, however, does not work in all cases. For instance, suppose that a category A consists of the following three items:

i0: 0,1,2,3,4
i1: 0,1,2,3,4, 5,6
i2: 0,1,2,3,4, 7,8

Then, the central tendencies of respectively $i0$, $i1$ and $i2$ are all equal to 10. Hence, if the present definition is used, the central tendency-concept is not able to demarcate the prototype $i0$ from the non-prototypical items $i1$ and $i2$. In other situations, on the other hand, the definition works. Consider, for instance, the following items:

i0: 0,1,2,3,4,
i1:   1,2,   4, 5,6
i2: 0,1,   ,3,4,   7
i3: 0,   2,3,   8,9
i4:   1,2,3,4,   10

We have:

central tendency of i0: 14
central tendency of i1: 9
central tendency of i2: 11
central tendency of i3: 8
central tendency of i4: 12

In this example, the prototype has highest central tendency. However, as the first example shows, when the prototype has invaded its instances, the definition of central tendency becomes inappropriate. At closer look, it appears that the problem is that the central tendency of an item does not decrease if it contains P's which do not occur in other instances. This point can be taken into account if one counts overlaps rather than numbers of shared components (see chapter I and Appendix I: the overlap between two items M and M' decreases as M' contains more components that do not participate in M). Then, for the first example, we have (see Appendix I for the precise calculation of the overlaps):

central tendency of i0 = Q(i0,i1) + Q(i0,i2)
$\qquad\qquad$ = 0.687 + 0.687 = 1.374
central tendency of i1 = Q(i1,i0) + Q(i1,i2)
$\qquad\qquad$ = 0.687 + 0.531 = 1.218
central tendency of i2 = Q(i2,i0) + Q(i2,i1)
$\qquad\qquad$ = 0.687 + 0.531 = 1.218

We observe that the redefined central tendency leads to more acceptable results. Hence, we prefer this definition over the original one of Rosch and Mervis (1975).

5.2 The typicality of an instance and its relation to other categories

The study of Rosch and Mervis (1975) contains experimental data that indicate that the typicality of an item is positively correlated with its central tendency and negatively with the degree to which it is related with items of other categories. In order to estimate the degree to which an item i1 is related with items which belong to different categories, the authors suggest to count the number of properties that i1 shares with the items of the other categories. Again, it is natural to associate the properties which are meant in this definition with P's. However, for the sake of continuity with 5.1, we will sum also here the overlaps between items, rather than counting the common numbers of P's.

It is not known in which precise way the typicality of an item (as it is defined in 5.1) is affected by the fact that it shares a property with an item of a rival category. An exact expression lacks in Rosch and Mervis (1975). At some instances in literature (e.g. Medin, Wattenmaker and Hampson, 1987), it is suggested that the typicality of an item decreases linearly if it shares properties with items of rival categories. According to this interpretation, the typicality of an item i1 is obtained if one subtracts one unit from the central tendency of i1 for each property that it shares with items of other categories. We assume, as a first approximation, that typicalities can be calculated in this way.

This leads us to the following expression for the typicality of an item i:

typicality of i = sum of overlaps with items of the same category
                           minus
                  sum of overlaps with items of other categories

                = central tendency
                           minus
                  sum of overlaps with items of other categories

In order to differentiate this quantity from the typicalities which are generated by effective runs of our network, we call these calculated ones the "theoretical Rosch-typicalities". We will show in the following sub-paragraph that, as far as concerns the examples considered in 3, the theoretically obtained typicality arrangements agree fairly well with the ones predicted by our model.

5.3 The relation between the theoretical typicality arrangements and arrangements obtained by simulations in case of the examples of 3

5.3.1 The example of 3.1

In the example of 3.1, no alternative categories are considered so that the theoretical typicalities of the items coincide with their central tendencies. We have (see Appendix I for the exact calculations of the overlaps):

ct of i0 = Q(i0,i1) + Q(i0,i2) + Q(i0,i3) + Q(i0,i4)
       = 0.570 + 0.359 + 0.359 + 0.359
       = 1.647

ct of i1 = Q(i1,i0) + Q(i1,i2) + Q(i1,i3) + Q(i1,i4)

     = 0.570 + 0.259 + 0.259 + 0.259

     = 1.347

ct of i2 = Q(i2,i0) + Q(i2,i1) + Q(i2,i3) + Q(i2,i4)

     = 0.359 + 0.259 + 0.098 + 0.098

     = 0.814

ct of i3 = Q(i3,i0) + Q(i3,i1) + Q(i3,i2) + Q(i3,i4)

     = 0.359 + 0.259 + 0.098 + 0.195

     = 0.911

ct of i4 = Q(i4,i0) + Q(i4,i1) + Q(i4,i2) + Q(i4,i3)

     = 0.359 + 0.259 + 0.098 + 0.195

     = 0.911

"ct" abbreviates "central tendency"

We conclude that the theoretical Rosch-typicalities lead to the same typicality arrangements of the items as the typicalities which are generated by simulations of our model.

5.3.2 The example of 3.2

Also in the second example, no rival categories are considered so that also here the theoretical typicality of the instances is equal to their central tendency:

ct of i0 = Q(i0,i1) + Q(i0,i2) + Q(i0,i3)

     = 0.625 + 0.5 + 0.430

     = 1.555

ct of i1 = Q(i1,i0) + Q(i1,i2) + Q(i1,i3)

     = 0.625 + 0.359 + 0.312

     = 1.296

ct of i2 = Q(i2,i0) + Q(i2,i1) + Q(i2,i3)

     = 0.5 + 0.359 + 0.259

     = 1.118

ct of i3 $= Q(i3,i0) + Q(i3,i1) + Q(i3,i2)$
$= 0.430 + 0.312 + 0.259$
$= 1.001$

Again, we conclude that the typicality arrangement produced by the theoretical Rosch-typicalities coincides with the one that is obtained from simulations.

5.3.3 The example of 3.3

This time, two categories are considered. Hence, the theoretical Rosch-typicality of an item is obtained if one subtracts its overlaps with the items of the other category from its central tendency. One obtains the following values for the items which belong to A:

tR i0$= Q(i0,i1) + Q(i0,i2) + Q(i0,i3) + Q(i0,i4) - Q(i0,i5) - Q(i0,i6) - Q(i0,i7)$
$= 0.5 + 0.5 + 0.5 + 0.5 - 0 - 0 - 0$
$= 2$

tR i1$= Q(i1,i0) + Q(i1,i2) + Q(i1,i3) + Q(i1,i4) - Q(i1,i5) - Q(i1,i6) - Q(i1,i7)$
$= 0.5 + 0.297 + 0.297 + 0.297 - 0 - 0.234 - 0.195$
$= 0.962$

tR i2$= O(i2,i0) + Q(i2,i1) + Q(i2,i3) + Q(i2,i4) - Q(i2,i5) - Q(i2,i6) - Q(i2,i7)$
$= 0.5 + 0.297 + 0.297 + 0.297 - 0 - 0 - 0$
$= 1.391$

tR i3$= Q(i3,i0) + Q(i3,i1) + Q(i3,i2) + Q(i3,i4) - Q(i3,i5) - Q(i3,i6) - Q(i3,i7)$
$= 0.5 + 0.297 + 0.297 + 0.297 - 0 - 0 - 0$
$= 1.391$

tR i4$= Q(i4,i0) + Q(i4,i1) + Q(i4,i2) + Q(i4,i3) - O(i4,i5) - Q(i4,i6) - Q(i4,i7)$
$= 0.5 + 0.297 + 0.297 + 0.297 - 0 - 0 - 0$
$= 1.391$

"tR" abbreviates "theoretical Rosch typicality"

In conclusion, also here the typicality arrangements predicted by the simulations of our model and the arrangements of the theoretical Rosch typicalities agree with each other.

6 Other factors which contribute to the typicality of an item

6.1 Introduction

Rosch and colleagues consider in their research two factors which contribute to the typicality-structure of categories: the central tendency factor and the criterion that the typical instances of a category do not share much properties with other categories. More recent research has revealed that also other factors may be of relevance for the issue of typicality. In special, Barsalou (Barsalou, 1983; Barsalou and Sewell, 1985; Barsalou, 1985) made a series of studies that has become quite influential. It appears that, along with the factors considered by Rosch, two other factors are of relevance for typicality distributions:

a. The first one is how often an instance is retrieved. One may ask subjects to rate the relative frequency with which an item is met in their daily life. If one averages these ratings over the subjects, one obtains the "frequency of instantiation" of the item.
b. Second, an instance may be more typical for a category if it shares more of its "ideal dimensions". An ideal dimension refers to a characteristic function of the category (e.g. "to go jogging" is an ideal dimension for a physical education teacher; "to fly" is an ideal dimension for a bird, and so on). Barsalou (1985) asks his subjects to rate the ideality of an item by a number between one and nine.

The degree to which the respective factors contribute to the typicality of an item depends on the nature of the category to which it belongs. It appears useful to differentiate between two kinds of categories: taxonomic ones and goal derived ones (Barsalou, 1985). The first kind is the "ordinary" one, consisting of categories such as clothing, birds, furniture, and so on. Second, one may study "goal-derived" categories. They are composed by items suited to fulfil some or other goal. "Foods not to eat on a diet", "birthday presents", and "clothes to wear in the snow" are examples of such categories. First, we consider taxonomic categories. The data of Barsalou (1985) concerning the relative contributions of different factors to typicality point out three things.

a. Central tendency correlates significantly with typicality. However, for some categories, also ideality and frequency show significant correlations with typicality. Consequently, although the work of Rosch and Mervis (1975) and Rosch, Simpson et al. (1976) shows that central tendency is an important determinant of graded structure, this factor does not determine unequivocally the graded structure of every taxonomic category.

b. For some categories, a significant amount of the variance in typicality is due to frequency of instantiation. This holds, for instance, for the categories "birds", "weapons", "vehicles" and "fruits".

c. Third, for some categories, there is a significant second-order partial correlation between ideality and typicality. In special, for "weapons", "clothing" and "vehicles", this correlation is remarkably large. Thus, the structure of some categories appears to depend on the goals that the corresponding objects serve.

Next, we consider goal-derived categories. Such categories appear to have different properties.

a. The mean value of the second-order partial correlation between typicality and central tendency is about 0.05. This is a non- significant correlation. Hence, central tendency accounts for no unique variance in the graded structure of goal-derived categories. Consequently, the structure of goal-derived categories is different from the one of taxonomic categories.

b. In general, goal-derived categories are structured by both ideals and frequency. Some of them, however, are structured primarily by frequency, such as "camping equipment" and "picnic activities". Others, such as "snow clothes" and "weekend entertainment", are structured in main by ideals.

7 Alternative determinants of graded structure in our model: frequency and ideality

We saw in 5 that our model agrees quite well with the stance that central tendency is an important determinant of the typicality distributions of categories which are centered around prototypes. It is plausible to assume that this kind of categories form a significant part of ordinary, taxonomic adult-categories (see chapter X). The study of Barsalou (1985) confirms that central tendency plays a substantial role in case of such categories. However, even there, other factors may be significant. One may wonder if our model allows for such other factors. These factors must not be correlated with central tendency, since they may contribute significantly with typicality after central tendency has been partialed out. We argue that, according to

our model, there are different factors which are not correlated with central tendency and which may contribute to the typicality of an item. In the present paragraph, we show that ideality and frequency are such factors. In 8, we consider still other ones.

7.1 Categories and their labels

The categories at issue in the present chapter are all provided of a verbal label. This label had to be learned by the subjects. We differentiate between six conditions in which this learning process may take place:

a. If a subject is confronted with a category for the first time, he has to learn by heart the label that corresponds to it.

b. If a subject is familiar with a category, he may have constructed a prototype (or possibly more than one) around which its instances are centered. Suppose now that he learns a new instance of the category and suppose that the instance shares the properties of the prototype (or of one of the prototypes) to a significant extent. Then, he does not have to learn by heart to which category the new instance belongs: the category name of the instance can be retrieved if the subject makes an abstraction from the instance to the prototype (see chapter I).

c. Suppose that a subject has constructed a prototype of a category. If he learns a new instance that lacks most of the properties of the prototype, he has to learn explicitly that the instance belongs to the category: this point does not follow from the nature of the representation of the prototype and of the new instance.

d. If the category is not centered around prototypes, it may be centered around ideal dimensions. If a new instance shares these ideal dimensions, the fact that it belongs to the category can be derived from its representation; it does not have to be coupled independently to the verbal label of the category.

e. If a category is centered around ideal dimensions and if a new instance does not share these dimensions, then it has to be coupled directly to the verbal label of the category.

f. Finally, if a category is neither centered around prototypes nor around ideal dimensions, and if a new instance is added to the category, it has to be linked directly to the verbal label of the category.

Schematically, we have:

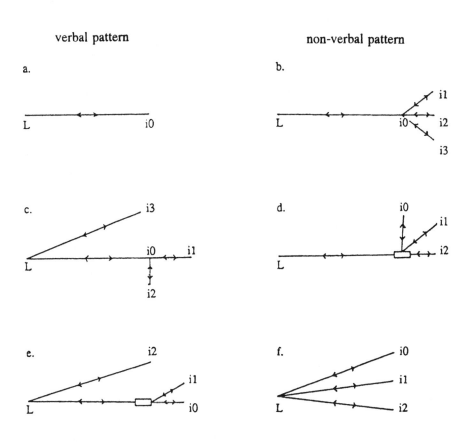

Figure VII.1

We observe that in cases b and d, a subject does not have to learn explicitly the category-label of a new instance, since he may derive this information from his non-verbal representations. In the other cases, however, he has to link the non-verbal representation of the new instance explicitly with the category label.

7.2 Frequency

At least as far as concerns cases a, c, e and f, it is plausible that the process by which an instance is coupled to the label of its category is not an all-or-nothing process. Rather, as concerns these cases, we assume that a new instance becomes more tightly linked to its category label if the subject is reminded more often of the fact that the instance belongs to the category. We propose that a more tight link between an instance and its category label means that the corresponding patterns are connected in a less noisy way. More specifically, suppose that, in case of relatively noiseless connections, a realization of a non-verbal pattern to the extent r stimulates its verbal label with a field of (mean) magnitude h (note 3). Then, in case of more noisy connections, we suppose that a realization of the same non-verbal pattern to the extent r leads to a stimulation h' of its verbal label, with h' < h.

Now suppose that a particular label is triggered if its units experience stimulating fields that exceed a threshold value T. Then, if the inter-area connections are noisy, an non-verbal pattern has to be realized to a higher extent before the stimulating fields which are experienced at its label exceed T. Conversely, in case of inter-area connections with low noise, the state of a non-verbal module does not need to coincide exactly with a non-verbal pattern before its label can be retrieved. Consequently, in the latter case, a label can be triggered before all the noise in the non-verbal network has been filtered out. Hence, if a subject has to trigger the verbal label of a category in the course of a classification task, membership decisions are made more quickly in case of noiseless inter-modular connections than in case of noisy ones. Since the speed of membership decisions is strongly correlated with typicality (see 2), we conclude that, as far as concerns the cases a, c, e and f, the typicality of an instance may be positively correlated with its frequency of instantiation.

Finally, we notice that, as semantic memory reorganizes and as categories become familiar, case b and d will tend to dominate cases a, c, e and f (chapter X). The latter cases may be expected to occur in non-familiar categories and in categories that contain instances which do not share much P's with the other instances of the category. Since the latter conditions occur more often in case of goal-derived categories than in case of taxonomic categories, the factor frequency is more important for the former kind of categories. This has been observed indeed by Barsalou (1985).

7.3 Ideality

Consider a concept with the following prototype i0 and that contains the following items:

```
i0: 0,1,2,3,4
i1: 0,1,2,3,4, 5,6,7,8
i2: 0,1,2,3,4  9,10,11,     13
i3: 0,1,2,3,4,    10,11,12,  14
i4: 0,1,2,3,4, 9,10,   12,   15
i5: 0,1,2       9,10,11,12,  16,17
```

We have:

$$ct\ i0 = 0.570 + 0.570 + 0.570 + 0.570 + 0.312$$
$$= 2.592$$

$$ct\ i1 = 0.570 + 0.390 + 0.390 + 0.390 + 0.226$$
$$= 1.966$$

$$ct\ i2 = 0.570 + 0.390 + 0.590 + 0.590 + 0.482$$
$$= 2.622$$

$$ct\ i3 = 0.570 + 0.390 + 0.590 + 0.590 + 0.482$$
$$= 2.622$$

$$ct\ i4 = 0.570 + 0.390 + 0.590 + 0.590 + 0.482$$
$$= 2.622$$

$$ct\ i5 = 0.312 + 0.226 + 0.482 + 0.482 + 0.482$$
$$= 1.984$$

The central tendency of the three last items is larger than the central tendency of i1. In special, the central tendency of i5 is slightly larger than the central tendency of i1. However, our simulations show that i1 is more typical than i5 (figure s16; the b-values of all items are put equal to 0.1). Item i1 is classified as a member of the category organized around the prototype i0 after approximately 2930 updatings (with a dispersion of 119). Item i5 is classified as a member of the category organized around the prototype i0 after approximately 5922 updatings (the value of s for eight runs is 294).

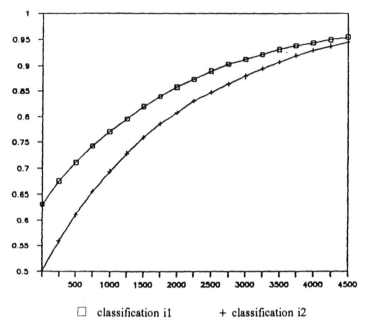

Figure s16

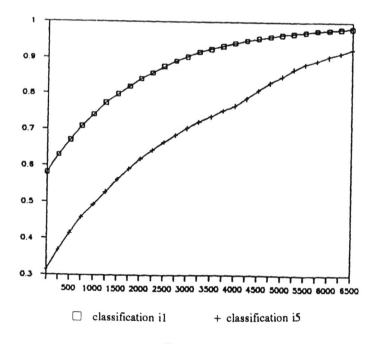

Figure s17

This point agrees with one of the facts observed in Barsalou (1985). In fact, in the present example, particular dimensions (the dimensions of i0) are "ideal" for a category. If an instance lacks some ideal dimensions, then it appears to be less typical than an instance in which all typical P's participate (this is not a replication of paragraph 3.1: in the example considered in 3.1, typicalities could be predicted by central tendency; here, this is not the case). We notice that different instances of a category can have different idealities only if the prototypical P's have not invaded entirely in all of them. Hence, we expect that ideality is of higher importance for categories which are not restructured yet than for categories which have a nearly perfect tree-like structure. Since a non-taxonomic structure is typical for non-familiar categories (chapter X), we expect that ideality is of higher importance for familiar than for non-familiar categories. This agrees with the evidence of Barsalou (1985).

In the present paragraph, we saw that the factor ideality may allow for predictions of typicalities when central tendency does not. In the next paragraph, we show that ideality and central tendency may lead to opposite typicality predictions.

8 The dependency of typicality predictors on the configuration of the concepts

8.1 An example in which central tendency is a more reliable typicality-predictor than ideality

We saw in 7.3 that, in some conditions, ideality is a better typicality predictor than central tendency. In the present paragraph, we show that it is possible to give examples in which the opposite fact holds. Consider a category A with the following instances:

i0: 0,1,2,3,4
i1: 0,1,2,3, 5
i2: 0,1,2,3,4, 6,7,8,9,10,11
i3: 0,1,2,3,4, 12,13,14,15,16,17

we have:

ct of i0 = 0.625 + 0.5 + 0.5
$\qquad$ = 1.625

ct of i1 = 0.625 + 0.382 + 0.382
$\qquad$ = 1.389

ct of i2 = 0.5 + 0.382 + 0.310
        = 1.192

ct of i3 = 0.5 + 0.382 + 0.310
        = 1.192

Item i1 contains less ideal dimensions than the items i2 and i3, but it has higher central tendency. The simulations of our model show that i1 is more typical than i2 and i3 (figure s17; the b-values of all items are put equal to 0.1). Item i1 is classified as a member of the category organized around the prototype i0 after approximately 2707 updatings (again, this is the mean value for eight runs of the network; the dispersion s is given by s=260). Item i2 is classified as a member of the category organized around the prototype i0 after approximately 3353 updatings (s for eight runs is given by s=154). Hence, in contradistinction with the example of 7.3, central tendency appears to be a better predictor of typicality than ideality.

8.2 Interpretation of the examples: other factors which determine typicality

When theoretical Rosch-typicalities and ideality do not lead to the same typicality arrangement, neither of them appears to be a reliable predictor of typicality. This raises the issue if, in such cases, other factors may be isolated which are more strongly correlated with typicality. We show in this paragraph that this may be the case indeed.

8.2.1 A variation of the example of 7.3

We consider the example of 7.3 again. We perceive that the sub-category characterized by the set of components (9,10,11,12) has invaded partially in four category instances. When the instances become familiar, their representations will change and the subset of components (0,1,2,3,4) will invade entirely into the items i2, i3, i4 and i5 (chapter X). Further, i5 will include all P's of i0. Then, the respective i-items are transformed into the following j-items (note 4):

j0: 0,1,2,3,4
j1: 0,1,2,3,4, 5,6,7,8
j2: 0,1,2,3,4, 9,10,11,12, 13,18
j3: 0,1,2,3,4, 9,10,11,12, 14,19
j4: 0,1,2,3,4, 9,10,11,12, 15,16
j5: 0,1,2,3,4, 9,10,11,12, 16,17

All these items have the same ideality. The central tendency of the last four items, however, is larger than the one of the first two items:

$$\text{ct } j0 = 0.570 + 0.5 + 0.5 + 0.5 + 0.5$$
$$= 2.750$$

$$\text{ct } j1 = 0.570 + 0.347 + 0.347 + 0.347 + 0.347$$
$$= 1.958$$

$$\text{ct } j2 = 0.5 + 0.347 + 0.630 + 0.630 + 0.630$$
$$= 2.737$$

$$\text{ct } j3 = 0.5 + 0.347 + 0.630 + 0.630 + 0.630$$
$$= 2.737$$

$$\text{ct } j4 = 0.5 + 0.347 + 0.630 + 0.630 + 0.630$$
$$= 2.737$$

$$\text{ct } j5 = 0.5 + 0.347 + 0.630 + 0.630 + 0.630$$
$$= 2.737$$

However, according to the membership latency test, item $j1$ remains more typical than the four last items. Hence, after the reorganization of the respective representations, neither ideality nor theoretical Rosch-typicality predicts the typicality arrangement governed by the model. Consequently, another factor must be at work.

8.2.2 Typicalities in case of categories with elaborated sub-categories

The factor referred to at the end of the previous paragraph can be identified in a straightforward way. Suppose, for instance, that the typicality of item $i2$ is estimated. Then, $i2$ is presented to the network (its F-value is temporary put equal to zero in order to allow for an association process). The network state will experience two tendencies.

i. The first one is governed by the P's of $i0$: on the one hand, they participate in five instances, and, on the other hand, $i0$ itself is also consolidated.
ii. Second, also the P's that typify the sub-category (9,10,11,12) have strong tendency to remain present in the network state.

For b-values larger than 0.05, the first tendency eventually wins and the item is recognized as a member of the category centered around the prototype i0 (for smaller b-values, the input does not converge to i0 but to either i3, i4 or i5; note 5). However, since the second tendency acts as a friction force that slows down the evolution of the network state towards i0, this process takes more time than if the second tendency would have been absent. Hence, item i2 is recognized less quickly as a member of the category than item i1. These considerations suggest that the following factor influences typicality.

Suppose that two items i1 and i2 belong to a category A, and suppose that i1 and i2 contain all components of the prototype. Further, suppose that i2 belongs to a subcategory of A which is highly familiar and elaborated; suppose that i1 does not belong to such a subcategory. Then, in general, i1 is a more typical member of A than i2. One may object that this property is not really consonant with the intuition behind the term "typicality". Then, however, our argument shows that the typicality-concept should be redefined so as to exclude the situations with which the present factor deals. Anyway, our model invites to test empirically (and for human subjects rather than for our connectionist model alone) the psychological hypothesis concerning the correlation between this factor and category membership decision times.

8.3 Real world instances of the example of 7.3

Let us try to find some real world instances of the formal example of 7.3. We have to search a category with the property that some of its instances belong to an elaborate sub-category and that some do not. For some subjects, these conditions may be fulfilled for the following category and the following instances:

category:
animal

instances of an elaborate sub-category (dog):
fox terrier
poodle
boxer

instances of a sub-category with only a single instance:
horse

If someone is familiar with dogs, for instance with fox terriers, poodles and a boxers, and if he knows only one kind of horse (and if he has not yet reorganized his representation of animals in such a way that all ruminants or hoofed animals share P's which are characteristic of these sub-classes), then this is an example of the formal situation under consideration. One may suggest that an instance that belongs to the elaborate subordinate category is of a more subordinate level than an instance that does not. One may argue that "dog" and "horse" belong to the same taxonomic level and that, for instance, "boxer" is more subordinate than "horse". Whether this holds or not depends on the way in which one defines and compares taxonomic levels. Two possibilities apply.

a. First, one may count the number of P's in a concept, and specify that the degree of subordinatedness of a concept is proportional to this number. Then, for instance, "horse" and "boxer" do not differ in subordinatedness: if they are represented formally in accordance with the example of 7.3, they contain the same number of P's.

b. If, on the other hand, one determines the gradation of subordinatedness by the number of subcategories that an item includes, then "horse" is one level less subordinate than "boxer".

The present example concerns instances which belong to clearly different taxonomic levels only according to criterion b. The formal example of 8.1, on the other hand, concerns instances which belong to different taxonomic levels according to criterion a. We consider it again in the next paragraph.

8.4 The example of 8.1

The example of 8.1 is of a different nature. Here, ideality predicts the wrong typicality arrangement whereas central tendency predicts the right one. The reason why items i2 and i3 have lower central tendency is that they contain significantly more P's than i0 and i1. In the present example, this fact has the following consequences:

i. The overlap of i2 and i3 with i0 is smaller than the overlap of i1 with i0.
ii. The overlap between i1 and i2 (as well as the overlap between i1 and i3) is larger than the overlap between i2 and i3.
iii. Item i0 has larger overlap with i1 than with i2 and i3 (even though the latter items include all components of i0).

Hence, the central tendency of i1 exceeds the ones of i2 and i3. The fact that, in this example, the typicality arrangement predicted by central tendency coincides with the experimental typicality arrangement is quite plausible: if the items i2 and i3 have to be mapped on i0, significantly more P's have to be suppressed before i0 is reached than in the case that i1 has to be mapped on i0.

The point that i2 and i3 have significantly more components than i1 or i0 may be interpreted in as an indication that i2 and i3 are of a more subordinate level than i0 and i1 (see possibility a. in 8.3). This leads us to the following interpretation of the current example: a very subordinate instance is a less typical member of its category than a less subordinate one. In (psychological) practice, however, one focusses in general on one taxonomic level if typicalities of different instances are compared. For instance, one considers whether an apple is a more typical fruit than a lemon, but not whether an apple is a more typical fruit than a Granny Smith. Again, one may propose to restrict the typicality discussion to contexts that exclude the one of the present example. However, independent of the fact whether one does so or not, it would be interesting to carry out an experiment in order to examine if psychological membership decision times bear the same arrangements as the ones predicted by our model.

NOTES

Note 1. This point holds as long as the F-value of the prototype in case b. is not raised dramatically (i.e. an order of magnitude larger than F(sat)). If such a drastic increase would occur, then the network would behave as if this prototype is its only memorized pattern. Then, the time an input needs to converge to the prototype would be dependent on its initial correlation with the prototype only. Hence, conflicting tendencies of rival categories that slow down the process of convergence would have no effect. This however, would contradict empirical evidence (see 5) as well as the behavior of the network with normal parameter values.

Note 2. In effect, the probability that i2 converges to i1 is even slightly higher than the probability that it converges to i0. We notice that the mixture level of i1 is higher than the mixture level of i0. Hence, the normalization of the order parameters of the P's of, for instance, i2 relatively to i1 bears a larger increase than their normalization relative to i0 (see IX,3). Hence, if i2 is presented as an input to the network, i1 experiences a product consolidation which is slightly higher than the one experienced by i0.

Note 3. For an exact formulation of what a "stimulating field" means in the context of our network, we refer to Appendix I.

Note 4. Of course, in addition to the P's that typify the category and the sub-category, also other P's may have to be added to the representations of the instances in order to obtain agreement between the representations and the differentiations required by the environment. The new representations of i2, i3 and i4 contain a P that has to ensure the oddity of their mixture level (see previous chapter).

Note 5. If the b-values of all items become quite large, then the tendencies of the (partially) common P's to remain or to invade in the network state may become very strong and they may force the network state to converge to an asymmetric mixture state. In such a mixture, the weight of a P is determined by the number of M's in which it participates. In case of the present example, this phenomenon is met for b-values which exceed 0.4.

VIII. THE INFLUENCE OF CONTEXTS ON TYPICALITIES

1 Introduction

In this chapter, we examine the effects of contexts on typicalities. The "strong hypothesis" on the influence of contexts assumes that, when a category is embedded in a context, not the category itself but the instance that is most typical for the category is active (paragraph 2). However, evidence in favor of the strong hypothesis suffers from methodological problems (paragraph 3.1). Therefore, alternative experimental methods have been proposed. The Stroop method suggests that the effects of contexts on the structure of categories are quite weak (paragraph 3.2). The reading time method and the verification time method, on the other hand, suggest that typicality distributions of categories restructure gradually when a context is activated (paragraph 3.3). Our theoretical considerations suggest that the latter two methods are more feasible than the former one (4.1). This agrees with predictions made by the model that we have constructed: it predicts that the reading time method (4.2) as well as the verification time method (4.3) record changes in typicalities when a concept is biased by a context.

2 The strong hypothesis on the influence of contexts on the structure of categories

We saw in the previous chapter that, in general, not all instances of a category are equally typical. One may wonder if such typicality effects are context-dependent or not. Intuitively, it is quite plausible that contextual bias may have an influence on typicality-estimates. For instance, consider the context evoked by the sentence "The guest saw the bird that roasted on the grill". As concerns the instances of the category "bird", this context gives a positive bias to "chicken" and a negative one to "robin". In the unbiased category "bird", on the other hand "robin" is more typical then "chicken". In two papers that have become famous, Anderson et al. (Anderson and Mc Gaw 1973; Anderson, Pichert, et al. 1976) argued that contexts have a profound effect on the structure of categories. More specifically, the following two points were made:

a. If one chooses an appropriate context, then any exemplar of a category can become the most typical one.

b. In what they term the "strong" version of their hypothesis, Anderson et al. claim that, in case of contextual bias, subjects do not encode a concept by the way of a "core"-meaning, but by the way of a particular example that fits the context.

These assertions were supported by the results of a series of cued-recall experiments. In these experiments, subjects were given sentences like "the fish attacked the swimmer" and "the weapon was protruding from the corpse". Next, the experimenter examined the recall of these sentences for two kinds of cues. The first kind consisted of superordinate categories like "fish" or "weapon". The second kind of cues were items which are suggested by the context. For instance, in the first example, "shark" was the fish one expected the sentence to be about. Similarly, in the second example, one expected the weapon to be a knife. The experiments showed that, for each considered category, the instance which was suggested by the context was a better retrieval cue than the category name itself. For example, the chance that a subject remembered "the fish attacked the swimmer" was larger when the retrieval cue was "shark" than when it was "fish". Anderson et al. concluded that contextually biased categories were memorized by the way of their most typical exemplars for the context rather than by general terms.

3 Refutations of the strong hypothesis

3.1 A problem concerning the interpretation of the experiments

The results of Anderson et al. would have far-reaching consequences if they would allow for the conclusions drawn from them. However, different authors argued this is doubtful (e.g. Gumenik, 1979; Whitney and Kellas, 1981; Roth and Shoben, 1983). For instance, Gumenik (1979) argued that Anderson's experimental results did not refer to the way in which information is stored, but that they were due to processes at the time of retrieval. In accordance with this stance, Gumenik (1979) showed the following fact. Consider a sentence that contains a particular category and suppose that the sentence favors a particular instance of the category. Then, the latter instance is an effective retrieval cue for the sentence. However, an item that does not belong to the category may be equally effective as a retrieval cue. For example, both "murder" and "knife" are more effective cues than "weapon" for the sentence "the weapon was protruding from the corpse". Anderson and Shifrin (1980) replied that "murder" might have triggered "knife" and only subsequently the sentence to be recalled. If such an indirect trigger process happened with sufficient speed, then "knife" and "murder" might be indistinguishable as retrieval cues. This reply did not satisfy everyone. Other authors have tried out other experimental methods in order to examine the context-dependency of the inner structure of concepts. We consider two alternative methods.

3.2 Contextual bias and experiments based on the Stroop-method

In a study by Whitney and Kellas (1984), the results of Anderson et al. were replicated, but then the authors went on to demonstrate that false conclusions had been drawn from them. For their own experiments, they relied on the Stroop-method. Suppose that a couple of words is shown to a subject and that the second word is printed in colored ink. The subject is asked to read the first word and, subsequently, to name the color of the second one. When the second word is semantically related to the first one, it takes more time to name its color (Warren, 1972; Conrad, 1974). Usually, this is interpreted in the following way. If a word is partially activated by the fact that an associatively related word has been retrieved, then the semantic content of this word can not be immediately erased out of the mental state of the subject. It takes some time to make place for the color in which it is printed.

Whitney and Kellas (1984) selected a set of categories, and for each category (e.g. "bird"), they presented two sentences to their subjects. In the first sentence, a typical exemplar received positive bias (e.g. "robin" is positively biased by "The guest saw the bird that landed on the branch"). The same exemplar was negatively biased in the second sentence (e.g. "The guest saw the bird that roasted on the grill"). Further, for each category, an atypical member was chosen that was negatively biased by the first sentence and positively by the second one (for instance, in the previous example, "chicken" is an atypical bird negatively biased by the first sentence but positively by the second one). After such sentences had been shown to a subject, the name of an instance was shown in a particular color. Then, the time needed by the subject to determine this color was measured.

Consider the question what the theory of Anderson et al. would predict in these conditions. If a sentence that gives a positive bias to a typical category instance is used as a prime and if the target word is a typical category exemplar, then the theory of Anderson et al. would predict color-naming interference. Further, there should be color-naming interference for atypical exemplars when the biasing sentence favors atypical instances. The latter prediction contradicts with the stance that the inner structure of categories is stable against context-effects. According to the latter stance, both typical and atypical contextual biases lead to color-naming interference if the target-word is a typical category example. The model of Anderson, on the other hand, would predict such an effect only in case of typical contextual bias.

Hence, Whitney and Kellas claimed that their experiments could discriminate between the "strong" version of the hypothesis of contextual influence and the position that the influence of contexts on category-structure is quite weak. The experiments decided in favor of the latter hypothesis (Whitney and Kellas, 1984). The authors argued that Anderson et al. might have been guided too much by an "exemplar view" on knowledge: if one holds the view that subjects store exemplars instead of prototype information, then it is not plausible that contextual influences produce weak and continuous changes in typicality distributions. Rather, one has to assume that the exemplar on which a subject focusses is replaced by another one as the context changes. This suggests that a change in context may have strong effect. In their antagonist position against Anderson et al., Withney and Kellas took, in turn, a quite extreme position concerning the effects of contexts: their influence on typicalities is minimized. Intuitively, it is tempting to suggest that contexts have somehow an effect on typicality-distributions, but that this effect is a gradual one. Such an intermediate position has been put forward, for instance, in work of Roth and Shoben (1983).

3.3 The reading time method

We saw that the problem with the results of Anderson et al. is that it is not clear if they refer to processes at the moment of encoding or at the moment of retrieval. Since, in the context of present discussion, we are mainly interested in encoding effects, it is of relevance to examine data tapped immediately after the encoding process or even partially simultaneously with it. The color-naming interference paradigm of the previous paragraph is one way to achieve this. In the present paragraph, we consider an alternative method to determine the influence of contexts on typicality ratings. It goes back to research by Garrod and Sanford (1977). The latter authors presented their subjects couples of sentences. The first sentence of such a couple contained the name of a category that participated in the description of a scene. For instance, "The trees were shattered by the storm" was the first sentence of a couple. The second sentence contained an instance of the category. In case of the mentioned example, "The oaks were wrenched from the ground" was a sentence that contained a typical exemplar. A sentence with "palms", on the other hand, contained an instance that was atypical for the scene described by the first sentence. The authors varied the degree to which the instance of the second sentence was typical for the scene described by the first sentence. Their experiments showed that the time required to read the second sentence was negatively correlated with the typicality of its instance.

Roth and Shoben (1983) extended this experiment. For each category, two sentences were considered in which it occurred. The first one biased a particular exemplar positively. For instance, the sentence "Stacy volunteered to milk the animal whenever she visited the farm" produced a positive bias for the exemplar "cow". The second sentence biased this exemplar negatively, for instance: "Fran played with her father to let her ride the animal". Along with the two sentences which contained the category name, a sentence with the name of the exemplar was considered, for example: "She was very fond of the cow". The experiments revealed that a sentence that contained an exemplar was read faster if it was presented after a sentence that described a scene in which the exemplar was positively biased. Conversely, if an exemplar was negatively biased by a scene, it took more time to read a sentence that contained the exemplar. Interestingly, the facilitation effect of the positively biasing scenes and the inhibition effect of the negatively biasing scenes occurred for both typical and atypical category-exemplars.

This experiment indicated that context and category representation interact with each other. However, it did not determine how a category is represented when it is embedded in a context. It is possible to distinguish between three scenario's:

a. The first one corresponds to conception of Anderson et al.. It states that, if a category is shown from the perspective of a particular context, then this category is represented by an exemplar that is typical for the context. Roth and Shoben call this the "instantiation-hypothesis".
b. We pointed out higher that hypothesis a. has its problems. It also hard to reconcile with the intuition that in several contexts, more than one exemplar of a category may have high typicality. The least drastic modification of stance a. is the "refocussing-hypothesis". It assumes that different exemplars are reconcilable with a context, but that their typicality is determined by their resemblance to the exemplar which is most strongly suggested by the context.

c. Finally, the restructuring-hypothesis proposes that the typicality distribution of a category that is embedded in a context may have more than one prototype or central element. The context can restructure the typicality-distribution in a more or less drastic way.

The different consequences of the second and of the third hypothesis allow for an experimental decision between them. According to the second one, if the most typical instance of a category is the same for two contexts, then both contexts generate the same typicality distributions for the category. The third hypothesis does not entail this proposition. Roth and Shoben showed that it is straightforward to mention categories and contexts which are in contradiction with this proposition. Hence, they advocated the restructuring-hypothesis. In another experiment, the authors went on to survey the degree to which a typicality distribution may change under the influence of contextual bias. The experiment relied on the method of speed of membership decisions. As we saw in the previous chapter, the more typical an item is for a category, the less time a category membership judgement takes (e.g. Rosch, 1973; and Rips, Shoben and Smith 1973). The experimenters recorded the time required to verify membership for category-members which were reconcilable with the context. Then, they measured the speed of membership decisions for category-members which were incompatible with the context. The results showed that, in case of positive contextual bias, contextually typical members were verified more quickly than non- contextually typical ones. Moreover, an analysis of the correlations showed that decision times in case of contextual bias were not correlated with the non-contextually biased typicality measures. Consequently, typicality distributions may be affected quite strongly by contextual bias (note 1).

4 Interpretation and discussion

4.1 The dissonance between the results achieved with the Stroop- paradigm and the results obtained with the reading time method

First, we focus on the fact that the results of the Stroop method do not agree with the results obtained by the reading time method: according to the former ones, the effects of contexts on typicality distributions are weak; the latter ones, on the other hand, suggest that these effects may be quite strong. Since these studies use different methods, the question raises if one of the methods is preferable over the other one. We suggest that this is the case. We remember that, in the experiments which are based on the Stroop paradigm, a subject receives two words or sentences. The second word or sentence is printed in colored ink. When a subject has read the first one, the time he needs to determine the color of the second one is recorded. It is relevant to point out that the subject knows his task concerning the second word or sentence before he has read the first one. This is of importance because this knowledge may restrict his attention to the first word or sentence. A subject may not carry out the semantic processing of the second word thoroughly if he knows that is not relevant for the task that he has to carry out. This point may explain why the Stroop paradigm is less well suited to determine typicalities.

This argument gains strength by the following consideration. In our discussions concerning the basic taxonomic level in category organization (see next chapter), we will see that, in the first phase of an interpretation process, an input is classified at the basic level of abstraction; only afterwards, it is classified at a more subordinate level. Now in the experiments of Whitney and Kellas, the first sentence contains a basic level category and a contextual bias with the aim to favor certain subordinate instances of the basic level concept. However, if the processing of the first sentence stops at the basic level, the subordinate bias may not lead to the activation of a more specific item. After all, the subjects are aware of the point that processing the sentence thoroughly would be superfluous: it would not help them to carry out their task. If this remark is correct, then the Stroop-paradigm is not a good method to assess typicalities in case of contextual bias. The reading time method used by Roth and Shoben (1983) also presupposes that a first sentence is processed sufficiently thoroughly. In this case, however, there is no bias towards another task than processing sentences or words. Further, the results obtained with this method are compatible with the ones obtained with the method of speed of membership decisions.

4.2 The influence of contexts on typicalities

4.2.1 Contextual influences on typicalities which are determined by the reading time method

The intuition behind the reading time method is that reading time may be tightly related with "comprehension time" or "interpretation time". In fact, Roth and Shoben (1983) used the terms "reading time" and "comprehension time" as synonyms. If this identification is allowed, then the fact that has to be explained is that contexts influence the time that it takes to interpret the instances of a category. It is straightforward to show that our model shows this property. For the sake of concreteness, we consider a simple example. Consider a category i0 and four instances i1, i2, i3 and i4. Further, consider a scene i5 that biases i1 positively. We propose that this means that the i5 has more P's in common with i1 than with i2, i3 and i4:

i0: 0,1,2
i1: 0,1,2, 3,4,5,6
i2: 0,1,2, 7,8,9,10
i3: 0,1,2, 11,12,13,14
i4: 0,1,2, 15,16,17,18
i5: 2,3,4, 19,20

Consider the following two inputs (note 2):

in: 2,3,4,19,20 / 0,1,2,3,4,5,6

in': 2,3,4,19,20 / 0,1,2,7,8,9,10

The first one corresponds to the activation of both the scene i5 and the instance i1. The second one corresponds to the activation of the scene i5 and of i2. The input "in" has higher overlap with i1 than in' with i2. Further, since, in the present example, the common P's do not favor i2 to a higher extent than i1, it is obvious that the time to interpret "in" as i1 is smaller than the time which is required to interpret in' as i2. This is confirmed by our simulations (figure s18). The b-values of all items have been put equal to 0.1. In order to guarantee that the input "in" (respectively in') converges to i1 (respectively i2) we put F(i1) (respectively F(i2)) equal to 2F(sat) for the first (respectively the second) interpretation task (else category i0 would attract stronger than its instances; see previous chapter). Then, we obtain that "in" is interpreted as i1 after 1979 updatings (this is a mean value of eight runs of the network; s=91). The input in' is classified as i2 after 3058 updatings (s for eight runs is equal to 211). In conclusion, items which are positively biased by an activated scene are interpreted faster than items which are not or negatively biased by it.

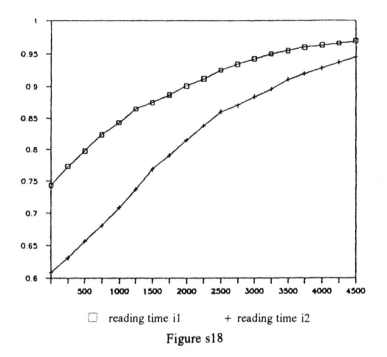

☐ reading time i1 + reading time i2

Figure s18

☐ classification in' + classification in

Figure s19

4.2.2 The effects of contexts on typicalities which are determined by the speed of membership decisions

Also as concerns typicalities which are determined by the speed of membership decisions, our model allows for a straightforward description of the phenomena reported in 3.3. Again, we explain our point by the way of an example. We take the same example as in 4.2.1 (note 3):

i0: 0,1,2
i1: 0,1,2, 3,4,5,6
i2: 0,1,2, 7,8,9,10
i3: 0,1,2, 11,12,13,14
i4: 0,1,2, 15,16,17,18
i5: 2,3,4, 19,20

in: 2,3,4,19,20 / 0,1,2,3,4,5,6
in': 2,3,4,19,20 / 0,1,2,7,8,9,10

Suppose that i1 and the scene i5 are presented simultaneously to the system. This leads to the input "in". In order to verify the category membership of i1, the F-value of i1 itself is temporary put equal to zero. If the b-values of all items are equal to 0.1, then the category membership of i1 is verified after about 4129 neural updatings (s for eight runs is equal to 243). If, on the other hand, the membership of i2 is verified when the scene is activated, it takes about 4472 (s=381) updatings before the network state obtains a correlation of 0.9 with i0 (figure s19). In conclusion, it takes more time to verify the category membership of an item that is negatively biased by an activated scene than to verify the membership of an item that is positively biased by the scene. We notice that the points of 4.2.1 and 4.2.2 can also be explained in a non-connectionist way. If one interprets the P's of our model as "features" of classical feature models, one may explain the considered phenomena in terms of the latter models (e.g. Mc Closkey and Glucksberg, 1979; Smith, Shoben and Rips, 1974). However, chapters VII, XI and X show that our model integrates an explanation for the present phenomenon with explanations for several other facts.

NOTES

Note 1. These results have been extended with regard to false items. Suppose that an item does not belong to a category but that it shares some of its aspects. Then, it takes more time to decide that this item does not belong to the category than in case of a non-category member which shares no aspect with the category. For example, the time which is required to decide that a bat is not a bird is larger than the time required to decide that a chair is not a bird (see for example Collins and Quillian, 1972; Rips, Shoben Smith, 1973; Holoyak and O'Dell, 1974). Now suppose that an item i1 is not a member of a category C but that it is related to items which are typical for the non-contextually biased C. Further, suppose an that item i2 is a non-member of C and that it is not related to items which are typical for the non-contextually biased C but that it is related to items which are typical for the contextually biased C. Then, in case of contextual bias, it takes more time to decide that i2 not a member of C than to decide that i1 is a non-member of C. It is straightforward to extend the formal treatment of 4.2 so as to include this situation.

Note 2. The inputs "in" and in' contain some P's two times - a first time as a component of the instance of i0 and a second time as a component of the scene. Although it is possible to model this by the way of an asymmetric input in which P's that occur twice have higher order parameters, our simulations are made for symmetric M's (i.e. all P's have equal order parameters in the input state). The same qualitative results are obtained for inputs in which components receive more weight when they occur twice.

Note 3. We have chosen the items of the example in such a way that the considered inputs converge to i0 without having to increase $F(i0)$ above $F(sat)$; if one deletes item i4 from the knowledge base, then, for the present b-values, the P's of i0 do not have a sufficiently strong tendency to invade in the network state and i0 will not be retrieved. However, then, one can increase the F-value of i0 or increase the b-values of the items in order to obtain that i0 is retrieved.

IX. THE BASIC LEVEL OF TAXONOMIC ORGANIZATION

1. Introduction

There is substantial empirical evidence that points to the existence of a basic level in conceptual taxonomy (paragraph 2). Intuitively, basic level concepts partition the external world in a way that is optimal for human subjects. The basic level is the highest level of abstraction at which a form can be ascribed to objects. It is also the highest taxonomic level at which motor movements can be associated with objects. It appears that basic level concepts are accessed with more ease than concepts of other levels of abstraction. Further, basic level concepts have ontogenetic primacy. Usually, basic level concepts can be considered as prototypes for their subordinate instances (paragraph 3). In conjunction with our general frame, the model that we have constructed allows to explain the differential ease with which basic level concepts are addressed (paragraph 4). Also the ontogenetic primacy and the evolution of basic level concepts is consonant with our frame (paragraph 5).

Finally, we point out that basic level concepts have some specific properties of orthogonality. These properties are related with the point that part-whole information is centered at the basic level (paragraph 6). Basic level concepts of different superordinate categories are in general at least as orthogonal as the superordinate categories. Two basic level categories are in general more orthogonal than two subordinate concepts that are instances of the same basic level concept. However, basic level concepts of the same superordinate category are in general less orthogonal than two different superordinate concepts. As we will see, this point is tightly related to the failure of the cue validity criterion.

2 Basic level-categories

2.1 The intuition behind the assumption of a basic level

The theory of basic level concepts is largely due to Rosch and colleagues (e.g. Rosch, Mervis, Gray, Johnson and Boyes-Braem, 1976; Rosch, 1978). Intuitively, basic level concepts are the most economic categories to represent the environment.

On the one hand, it is to a subject's advantage to include much information in his categorizations. On the other hand, a superfluously high degree of fine-grainedness in his concept representations would entail that his memory capacity is badly used. Basic level concepts offer a compromise between these two conflicting requirements. In order to formulate this intuition in more exact terms, Rosch, Mervis et al. (1976) proposed the notion "cue-validity". A cue x is a predictor of a concept y with high cue-validity if, when the cue x is given, there is a high chance that a subject will infer or recognize y. The cue-validity of a concept is the sum of the cue-validities of all its cues. Then, basic level categories are defined as the categories with the highest cue-validity. The intuitive idea behind this definition is twofold:

i. Superordinate categories have less properties than basic level categories, so that they have a smaller amount of cues and thus a lower cue-validity.

ii. Subordinate concepts that belong to the same category may resemble each other quite closely, since they may have many properties in common. Hence, the probability that a given cue leads to an activation of a particular subordinate concept is relatively low since it is a cue for several of such concepts.

However, Murphy (1982, p.175) (see also Lakoff 1987, p.52) showed that this definition does not work. The reason is that a cue which allows to infer with probability p that a particular basic level category A is present, allows also to infer with at least probability p that the superordinate category that contains A is present. For example, if "having air brakes" is a cue of high cue-validity for the concept "truck", then it has at least as much cue-validity for the concept "vehicle". In spite of the fact that the cue-validity criterion does not work, it appears possible to define basic level concepts in an experimental way: basic level concepts have a number of experimental properties which differentiate them from other categories. These properties suggest that basic level categories are truly "basic".

2.2 Experimental properties of basic level categories

In the experimental method used by Rosch, Mervis et al. (1976), some concepts are -on intuitive grounds- assumed to be basic level categories. Then, it is verified that they have particular properties, and that more superordinate nor more subordinate categories have these characteristics.

2.2.1 The property of the common attributes of instances

The first property concerns the numerical distribution of properties in a taxonomic tree. It has two aspects:

a. The basic level is the most inclusive (i.e. the most abstract) level at which the instances of a concept have a "relatively" large number of properties in common. Since all instances of such a concept share these properties, they can be attributed to the concept itself.
b. In general, only relatively few properties have to be added in order to arrive at the instances of a basic level concept.

These hypothesises were tested in the following way. First, the experimenters collected some candidates of basic level categories as well as some superordinate and subordinate categories (e.g. "musical instrument" (superordinate category), guitar, piano, drum (basic level categories), folk guitar/classical guitar, grand piano/upright piano, kettle drum/base drum (subordinate concepts)). Then, they gave their subjects pages with one name on the top of each. This name could correspond to a superordinate, a basic level or a subordinate category. Next, the subjects were asked to write down on these pages all properties of the concepts that occurred to them. The results of the experiment supported the hypothesises a. and b. quite well. Subsequently, Rosch, Mervis et al. took the properties that were generated by a first group of subjects and they asked a second group to judge if the first group had given correct properties or not. The resulting "judge-amended" corroborated even more strongly claims a. and b.

2.2.2 The criterion of the common motor movements

A basic level category has the property that a subject makes highly similar motor movements towards each of its instances. Further, the basic level is the highest taxonomic level for which this property holds. Hence, basic level concepts are the most inclusive concepts with which such motor movements can be associated (property a.). Concepts subordinate to the basic level do not differ significantly from basic level ones in the specificity of descriptions of common motor movements nor in the number of common movements that are made to them (property b.). This was corroborated by a similar method as in 2.2.1.

2.2.3 The form-criterion

Property 2.2.1 asserts that the basic level is the highest level at which a relatively high number of concept-properties can be ascribed to objects. The third hypothesis concerns one particular property: it states that the basic level is the highest level of inclusion at which a recognizable form can be associated with the objects. Rosch, Mervis et al. (1976) tested this hypothesis in two ways.

i. For each category and for each level, the form-overlap of couples of instances was calculated. In order to obtain a meaningful result, the shapes of these instances were normalized (this means, first, that the shapes were shown in a "canonical orientation", i.e. an orientation on which most subjects agreed that it was the most "typical" one); second, a scale-normalization was made so that the shape fitted maximally in a particular display). Then, it was examined if basic level categories were the most inclusive ones with the property that the mean overlap of the forms of their instances was significantly larger than the mean form-overlap between instances of the next higher level of abstraction. The evidence appeared to confirm this hypothesis. If one descends the taxonomic tree, one perceives a large increase in similarity in the overall look of the instances when one makes the transition from the superordinate level to the basic level. A significantly smaller increase in similarity is found if one descends below the basic level.

ii. It was tested if the basic level was the most general level at which an average shape of an object allowed to identify the object. This was confirmed. Furthermore, subordinate form averages were not better identifiable than basic level averages.

2.2.4 Basic level concepts as cues in recognition experiments

Property 2.2.3 suggests that form information is integrated in basic level concepts. As another test of this hypothesis, Rosch et al. studied if basic level categories could serve as cues in recognition experiments. The experimenter showed his subjects a noisy pattern in which an object was hidden. Next, the subjects were informed to which basic level category the object belonged. It was studied if this information helped to recognize noisy objects. The results showed indeed that basic level categories were of help in form recognition processes: the knowledge to which basic level concept a hidden object belonged enhanced its detection. The knowledge to which superordinate category the hidden object belonged, on the other hand, did not influence the ease of detection.

In another experiment, subjects were confronted with two stimuli and they were asked to decide if they depicted the same object or not. It was found that knowledge about the relevant basic level categories significantly shortened the required decision time. Knowledge concerning superordinate categories, on the other hand, had no significant influence on performance.

2.2.5 The criterion of classification-speed

Objects are more rapidly classified as members of basic level categories than as members of superordinate or subordinate categories. In the test of this hypothesis, subjects first heard the name of a concept. Then, an object was shown and the subjects were asked to determine if the object belonged to the named concept or not. The experiments showed that the required decision time varied with the taxonomic level to which the concept belonged. The results of this test are summarized in the following table (table IX.1). The first row corresponds to the positive answers and the second one to the negative ones.

Mean reaction time (Msec) for verification of category membership of objects

Response name	Superordinate	Basic level	Subordinate
True	691	535	659
False	630	578	642

Table IX.1 (after Rosch, Simpson et al. 1976)

The table shows that decisions concerning basic level categories were made faster than decisions concerning sub- and superordinate categories. In special, the first part of this result is remarkable: subordinate classifications appear to elicit poorer performance than basic level classifications. The table also shows that more time is required to classify items in subordinate categories than to classify them in superordinate categories.

2.2.6 The dominance of basic level categories in free naming experiments

Point 2.2.5 suggests that basic level concepts are more easily addressed than superordinate and subordinate ones. Hence, one may expect that basic level categories dominate in free-naming situations. Rosch, Mervis et al. (1976) confirmed this hypothesis. In order to test it, pictures of real world objects were shown to a group of subjects. At a total of 540 objects, subjects used (in average) in about 530 cases the name of a basic level concept to describe the picture. About five times, the name of a subordinate category was chosen, and superordinate categories occurred hardly at all. Hence, the names of basic level concepts were overwhelmingly much more used in free naming than words associated with concepts that belonged to other levels.

2.2.7 The genetic primacy of basic level categories

Even quite young children are be able to classify in basic level categories. This could be concluded from two sources of evidence:

i. An analysis of oddity problems and sorting tasks with three year old children showed that the latter were able to classify in basic level categories.
ii. Rosch, Mervis et al. (1976) examined if the first concrete nouns acquired by a child were names at the basic level. A case study (Brown 1974) was considered to test this hypothesis. The result was quite unequivocal: essentially all of the child's first utterances of concrete nouns for the nine most frequently used categories of English were at the basic level of abstraction.

Hence, the traditional claim that children think "complexive" or "associational" (see chapter X) has to be qualified: at least at the basic level of abstraction, young children are able to categorize (note 1).

2.2.8 The primacy of basic level concepts in American Sign Language

Finally, American Sign Language was studied with the aim to determine if the signs used in it corresponded in most cases to basic level objects or not. Again, the evidence was quite unequivocal: signs which denote basic level objects were significantly more frequent than signs referring to concepts at other levels of abstraction.

3 Basic level concepts and prototypes

3.1 A problem concerning the relation between prototypes and basic level categories

We notice that the properties of basic level categories are quite similar with the properties of the prototypes that we considered in V.5. Both prototypes and basic level categories have the property of being retrieved comparably fast. If one measures the speed with which subjects judge category membership, one observes that prototypes are classified with higher speed than non-prototypes. Similarly, basic level categories are retrieved more quickly than other categories. Both prototypes and basic level categories enhance reaction-time in priming experiments. Further, both basic level concepts and prototypes represent the mean of the metric attributes of their instances (e.g. form or size). Rosch herself points to these striking similarities. She owes them to the fact that both special kinds of categories are governed by the same principles of organization (Rosch, 1978, p.36-37):

"For categories of concrete objects (which do not have a physiological basis, as categories such as forms and colors apparently do - Rosch 1974), a reasonable hypothesis is that prototypes develop through the same principles such as maximization of cue-validity and maximization of category resemblance as these principles govern the formation of the categories themselves."

We noticed (see 2.1) that the cue-validity theory does not work. Hence, we have to look for an alternative explanation for the similarities between basic level concepts and prototypes. In Rosch (1978) these topics are treated in different chapters. First, basic level concepts are discussed in the chapter: "The vertical dimension of categories: basic level objects". Next, prototypes are considered in the chapter titled "The horizontal dimension: internal structure of categories: prototypes". A chapter that integrates both dimensions, however, lacks. Actually, a conceptual problem raises when we try to reconcile these results for prototypes with the ones for basic level concepts. At the basic level, several properties hold (see 2.2). These properties are used to demarcate this level. However, some of the instances of the concepts of this level (the prototypical instances) also appear to have these properties. Since the instances belong to a more subordinate level, we conclude that these properties are not able to demarcate a particular level in an unequivocal way. One could try to distinguish between prototypes and basic level categories by a detailed survey of the numerical outcomes of the experiments in which these properties are investigated.

For example, one might compare the speed of processing for basic level categories with the one for prototypes. Apart from the fact that such a systematic study has not been carried out yet, the methodological problems remain:

a. It is methodologically unclear how to differentiate between prototypes and basic level categories by the way of a criterion based on the speed of retrieval. Basic level categories are defined (among others) by the criterion that they are addressed more quickly than other categories, but so are prototypes. Hence, this criterion tends to consider prototypes as basic level concepts rather than to differentiate between them.

b. Since the criteria of speed of retrieval can not differentiate between basic level categories and prototypes, one may make recourse to the criteria related to form. However, one is confronted with the fact that the mean form of the instances of a basic level category are associated with both the prototype and the basic level category. Hence, also this demarcation criterion for basic level categories can not discriminate them from prototypes.

3.2 An alternative view

The previous paragraph suggests the presumption that basic level categories and prototypes are one and the same. They appear to share all experimental properties which have been tested for both of them. Hence, there is no experimental reason not to identify them. This point can be made plausible also from a formal point of view. The representation of a prototype may be a part of the representations of less prototypical items: the set of P's that represents the prototype may be a sub-set of the sets of P's that represent non-prototypical items. It is plausible that the same formal relation holds between the representation of a basic level concept and the representation of its subordinates. The P's that characterize a basic level concept apply also to its instances. In addition to this basic level core, the representations of the instances contain P's which differentiate the instances from each other and from the basic level category. Hence, the formal explanations that we will give in the following paragraphs for properties of basic level categories also hold for the corresponding properties of prototypes. We have to make two remarks with respect to this point.

a. The term "prototype", is used sometimes in a broader sense than the one of the present paragraph: it is used sometimes to refer to instances of subordinate categories. For the sake of example, consider the basic level concept "chair". One can draw a general chair-form which everyone will recognize; one is not committed to draw either a desk chair or a kitchen chair. Now one may call a quite typical kitchen chair a prototype of the subordinate category "kitchen chair". Then, the category "chair" would have prototypes at different taxonomic levels. However, we will see in 5.2 that, in case of familiar contexts, also basic level concepts may be associated with more than one taxonomic level.

b. Prototypes nor basic level concepts always correspond to real world objects. If the mean form of their instances is associated with them, then this form does not necessarily occur in reality (e.g. Posner and Keele, 1968, 1970; Strange, Keeney, Kessel and Jenkins, 1970; Peterson, Meagher, Chait and Gillie 1973; Homa and Voghsburg, 1976).

4 Taxonomic levels and the ease of access of concepts

4.1 The explanation of Rosch

We saw that it takes more time to retrieve a sub- or a superordinate category than to retrieve a basic level category. As a possible explanation of this fact, one may suggest that the way from a perceptual input to a sub- or superordinate category has to pass the basic level. For instance, in order to decide that a certain object in the perceptual field is a piece of furniture, one may have to point out first that it is, for example, a chair. Then, an inference process may be made in order to conclude that the chair is a piece of furniture. If one has to descend to the subordinate level, information may have to be added after a basic level concept has been retrieved. For example, if it has to be pointed out if something is a Louis-XIV-chair or not, then first "chair" may have to be retrieved and next additional information may have to be processed in order to descend to a subordinate level. This stance is adopted by Rosch, Mervis et al. (1976, p.414):

"We may speculate that after identification of the basic class of an object, superordinates are derived by inference from the class membership of the basic object and that subordinates are derived from observation of attributes - additional to those needed to perceive the basic object - which are relevant for subordinate distinctions."

Intuitively, the point that an object is first recognized at a basic level and only afterwards at a superordinate level is quite plausible: the P's involved in abstractions are not readily apparent from perception, whereas the P's of a basic level category partially are (e.g. property 2.2.3). Hence, the recognition of abstract concepts involves an inference process from information which is close to perception to information which is removed from it. Since such an inference may take time, the primacy of basic level concepts seems plausible (see also 4.4). The problem why the recognition of basic level concepts precedes the one of subordinate concepts is of a different nature. The transition from a basic level concept to one of its instances often involves an addition of perceptual information. One may wonder why this information is not taken into account from the start of the processing. In the next sub-paragraph, we suggest an explanation for this problem.

4.2 Basic level concepts and subordinate concepts

As concerns the way in which information is transmitted by the pre-processing system, we can differentiate between two possibilities (see chapter II):

a. The information concerning basic level specifications and the information concerning subordinate specifications enter the non-verbal semantic modules simultaneously.
b. The pre-processing system transmits information corresponding to the basic level of abstraction before it transmits more subordinate information.

Since the evidence shows that a basic level concept is addressed more quickly than a subordinate one, scenario a. is not attractive. If subordinate information would enter before a basic level concept has been addressed, then this information would dissipate during the retrieval of the basic level concept. Hence, the input of the subordinate information would have to be renewed when a subordinate instance would have to be triggered. Further, scenario a. would require the postulation of a mechanism that assures that subordinate information is not destructed again when the input is processed a second time.

According to scenario b., the information required to retrieve a basic level category enters the non-verbal semantic module before the information that allows to specify a subordinate item. This point can be made plausible by our considerations of chapter II. We are reminded of the fact that the pre-processing system has limited capacity. In one moment of attention, only one (relatively small) set of sf's is integrated into an P. When a subject focusses on an object, the first P's which are transmitted stem from the most attention-provoking aspects of the object. It is plausible that, in general, the information concerning the global form of an object as well as the information concerning its global part-whole configuration are especially attention-provoking. Now this is precisely an important kind of information that is integrated in basic level concepts (Tversky and Hemmenway 1984, see 6.1). Hence, when such information is transmitted to the module at issue, the state of the system may be quite close to a basic level concept and the dynamics of the network may lead quickly to the retrieval of a basic level concept. Suppose that the object is scanned for more specific information only when it appears that the patterns which can be retrieved are not sufficiently detailed for the purpose at hand. Then, trivially, a subordinate category can be retrieved only after its corresponding basic level category has been addressed. In conclusion, scenario b. seems to be the more plausible one (see also Biederman, 1987).

From the perspective of our model, we can add the following point. Since basic level concepts are retrieved more frequently than concepts at other levels of abstraction, they may be imprinted with more depth than the latter concepts. According to our model, this entails that their F- and their b-values may be larger than the ones for concepts at other taxonomic levels. The point that their F-value is large relative to the ones of non-familiar concepts entails that they will attract neighboring network states with significantly more force. The fact that they have high b-value entails that, once some of their P's are realized, these P's will have strong tendency to remain in the network state and to draw the other basic level-P's also in the network state. The latter tendency may be strengthened if the P's of the basic level concept participate in different subordinate concepts which have acquired a non-zero b-value.

4.3 An example

Suppose that our model has memorized the following five items:

i0: 0,1,2
i1: 0,1,2, 3,4,5,6
i2: 0,1,2, 7,8,9,10
i3: 0,1,2, 11,12,13,14
i4: 0,1,2, 15,16,17,18

The items i1, i2, i3 and i4 are instances of i0. Suppose that i0 represents a basic level category. The F-values of all items are chosen equal to F(sat). In accordance with the two scenario's considered in paragraph 4.2, we consider two kinds of inputs:

a. According to the first possibility, the input contains specifications which refer to the subordinate level, for instance:

in: 0,1,2,3,4,5,6 + noise

(we assume that the noise consists of two supplementary P's which do not participate in the concepts which are considered).

If the b-values of all items are equal to (or smaller than) 0.2, then the network state does not converge to the basic level concept i0 but to i1 (figure s20). If the b-values of all items are equal to 0.3, however, then the components of i0 are drawn in the network state with sufficient strength and i0 is addressed (figure s21).

b. According to the second possibility, one has that the input contains only information that refers to the basic level of abstraction, for instance

in': 0,1,2 + noise

(again, the noise used in the simulations consists of two supplementary P's which do not participate in the items which are considered)

This time, the input converges to i0 for even for arbitrarily low b-values. Figure s22 illustrates this point for the case in which all b-values are equal to 0.1.

4.4 Superordinate categories and basic level categories

Also superordinate categories are retrieved less quickly than basic level categories. Intuitively, this is quite obvious. After that global shape and part-whole configuration have been transmitted to the non-verbal semantic modules, the P's which characterize the abstract cores of concepts have to be inferred. We illustrate this point with an example:

i0: 0,1,2
i1: 0,1,2, 3,4,5,6
i2: 0,1,2, 3,4,5,6, 7,8,9,10
i3: 0,1,2, 3,4,5,6, 11,12,13,14
i4: 0,1,2, 3,4,5,6, 15,16,17,18

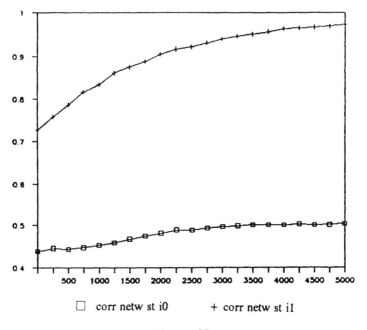

Figure s20

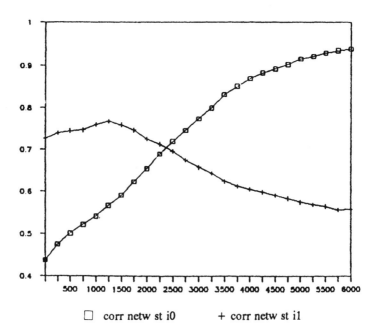

Figure s21

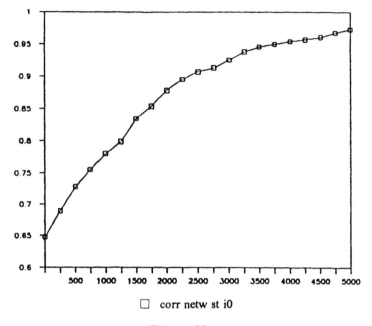

☐   corr netw st i0

Figure s22

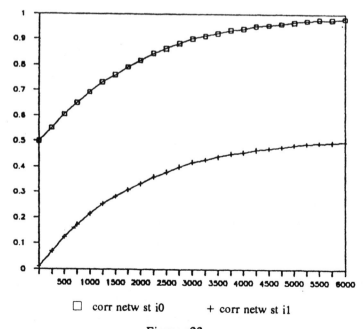

☐   corr netw st i0   + corr netw st i1

Figure s23

Pattern i0 represents a superordinate category; i1 represents one of its basic level concepts. The items i2, i3 and i4 are subordinate instances. We suppose that all concepts have the same, strictly positive b-value and that all F-values are equal to F(sat). Suppose that the network receives input information at the basic level of abstraction; for instance (note 2):

in: 3,4,5,6

Then, the network state quickly converges to i1 (figure s23; all b-values are put equal to 0.1). Once the basic level concept is addressed, the network may be stimulated to retrieve a more subordinate or a more superordinate category. In the latter case, no further input is required. It suffices to destabilize temporary the basic level category (see X,II.8). In the former case, on the other hand, the object has to be scanned for more detailed information. This is compatible with the fact that the retrieval of a subordinate category takes more time than the retrieval of a superordinate category (2.2.5).

5 The development and the differentiation of the basic level

5.1 The ontogenetic primacy of the basic level

The studies in Rosch et al. (1976) suggest that infants and children master basic level categories before categories of other taxonomic levels. This point has to be qualified by the experiments which we described in chapter IV. For instance, Roberts (1988) showed that infants of ten months old are able to memorize and to discriminate subordinate categories. Further, Ross (1980) and Golinkoff and Halperin (1983) show that infants may be aware of superordinate relations. However, these qualifications do not diminish the fact that basic level concepts dominate child language to an overwhelming extent. We give five possible reasons for this fact.

a. First, we are reminded of a point made in the previous paragraph. It is plausible that the pre-processing system transmits information about the global form of objects and about their coarse part-whole configuration before it presents more subordinate information. This entails two points:
a.1. If a subject starts differentiating between the objects of a particular domain, he may in first instance rely on the P's which are transmitted first by the pre-processing system. When such P's express information at the basic level of abstraction, the subject may show a preference to construct basic level concepts.

a.2. For adults as well as for children, basic level categories are addressed with more ease than categories at other levels of abstraction. Further, they are addressed with higher frequency. Since the depth with which a concept is imprinted increases as it is retrieved more often (chapter VI), basic level concepts may achieve a comparatively high amount of consolidation.

b. A second reason may be correlated with instruction: a child's words are largely taught by adults. Since adults access most easily concepts at the basic level, it is conceivable that they have a tendency to learn their children in first instance basic level words. Hence, the latter dominate a child's vocabulary.

The arguments a. and b. concern both the primacy of the basic level over the subordinate one and the primacy of the basic level over the superordinate one. We add some arguments concerning each of these points separately. First, we consider the fact that basic level categories dominate over subordinate categories in the earliest stages of conceptual development.

c. As we have seen, a child's first representations may consist of a few prototypical aspects (chapter IV). Later, the child differentiates between a prototype and other category instances. Now if, by the way of an addition of P's, subordinate differentiations branch off from the representation of a prototype, then the prototype trivially is represented before its instances. To the extent that basic level categories are prototypes (see 3), this point also holds for basic level categories.

Next, we consider the fact that basic level categories have ontogenetic primacy over superordinate categories. We differentiate between two points.

d. The first one is a formal one. If the representations of categories initially consist of a small number of P's, then, in general, initial categories have very few P's in common. Trivially, different concepts which consist of a single component only do not have any P in common. In general, also concepts of a few P's more do not have the internal complexity that would allow them to be organized by the way of an elaborate taxonomic tree. This is possible only from the moment that (subordinate) concepts are represented by a pattern in which several P's participate.

e. Second, we are reminded of the fact that P's common to different concepts may be generated by an application of image schema analysis to concepts. This is possible only after a child has acquired the ability to analyze mental images with help of image schema's and mental image manipulations. Since this ability may be achieved only relatively late (note 3), this source of abstraction is not present at the start of the process of concept genesis.

Finally, we are reminded of the fact that Rosch, Mervis et al. (1976) speculate about the reason why the human processing system developed (philogenetically) in such a way that basic level concepts have become the central representational elements of human conceptual structure.

f. Subjects dispose of a limited vocabulary to communicate about the world. Hence, in the best case, this vocabulary allows to talk about different things of interest with as little redundancies as possible. As we noticed in 2, Rosch, Mervis et al. (1976) suggest that basic level concepts satisfy this constraint.

5.2 The evolution of the basic level

When a subject becomes familiar with a context, he will tend to include an increasing number of P's in his representations of subordinate concepts. One may wonder if this point has implications for basic level concepts. We argue that, when a subject becomes familiar with a context, his basic taxonomic level may branch off into different levels. Each of them has some of the basic level properties described in 2. For the sake of example, consider a subject who is familiar with cars. He may differentiate between sub-groups (e.g. corresponding to different makes) which have the property that their exemplars have significantly more properties in common than two arbitrary instances of "car". For instance, consider the sub-groups of cars "Mercedes" and "Fiat". Suppose that, according to a subject, all instances of "Mercedes" have the properties "high petrol consumption", "large", "solid", "much power", "highly priced", "high weight", "long living", "relatively safe in case of accident", and so on. On the other hand, suppose that, according to the same subject, Fiat-cars have the properties "small", "low fuel consumption", "lowly priced", "low weight", "not much power", "not safe in case of accident", and so on. Further, the subject may also be aware of some motor-movements which are common to the instances of the respective subordinate categories (e.g. related to the position of the back-gear, the position of the buttons for the trafficators and the screenwipers, and so on).

For this subject, the concept "car" does not have the basic level properties b. of 2.2.1 and of 2.2.2: the instances of the more subordinate category "Mercedes" (respectively "Fiat") share significantly more properties than two car instances of different makes. A similar point may hold as concerns motor movements. However, in all other respects, "car" may remain a basic level concept. Rosch, Mervis et al. (1976) arrive at a similar point by consideration of a subject who is familiar with air-planes (p.430):

"His (the former airplane mechanic) taxonomy was interesting. The lists of attributes common to air-planes produced by most subjects were paltry compared to the lengthy lists of additional attributes which he could produce. Furthermore, his motor-programs as a mechanic were quite distinct for the attributes of the engines of different types of planes. "

In general, when a subject becomes highly familiar with a context, he may memorize quite some instances of the subordinate categories. Further, he may recognize that the instances of the latter categories share quite some properties. Then, the old subordinate categories may obtain some basic level properties. When the basic level splits, the old basic level keeps some essential basic level properties. Its instances share significantly more properties (and motor movements) than the superordinate categories. Furthermore, an old basic level concept remains identifiable on the basis of its form (in the example of the airplane expert, the subject could take the role of an average person and list attributes common to all airplanes, and could imagine an average airplane shape from the outside). Consequently, both the new and the old basic level are a kind of "partial" basic level. Hence, as a subject gains experience in a particular field, the concept of "basic level" becomes less sharp. Also from another point of view, this fact is intuitively plausible. The experiments in Rosch, Mervis et al. (1976) all concern categories for which three taxonomic levels are considered: a superordinate one, a basic level one and a subordinate one. Now in situations in which more than three levels are of relevance, the situation must be more complex. It appears that, between the most subordinate and the most superordinate level, different (partial) basic levels may emerge.

6 The orthogonality of basic level categories

6.1 The basic level and partonomic information

We referred in 4.2 to the point that part-whole information may form a central part of basic level concepts. This hypothesis was studied in Tversky and Hemmenway (1984). It was supported substantially by their experimental evidence. More specifically, the following four points were confirmed:

a. It appeared that many attributes of basic level concepts refer to their part-whole configuration. In other terms, the features shared by the instances of the same basic level concept in general concern their parts and the way these parts are assembled.

b. Different basic level categories share hardly any feature that refers to their part-whole configuration.

c. Superordinate categories appear not to contain part-whole information.

d. Finally, discriminations between different subordinate categories do not often depend on part-whole information.

6.2 Orthogonality and the basic level

6.2.1 Introduction

In the present paragraph, we argue that basic level categories have some remarkable properties as concerns orthogonality. The argument makes recourse to 6.1. More specifically, we show the following three points:

i. In general, two basic level categories which belong to different superordinate categories are at least as orthogonal as these superordinate categories themselves.

ii. In general, two basic level categories which belong to different superordinate categories are more orthogonal than two subordinate categories which belong to the same basic level concept.

iii. Often, two basic level concepts which belong to same superordinate category are more orthogonal than two subordinate concepts which belong to the same basic level category.

We notice that the notion "cue validity" can be related intuitively to the conception of orthogonality. Intuitively, an item has high cue-validity if the P's involved in it are highly specific for it. If we assume that all P's of an item have equal weight, then the P's which occur in relatively few other items are highly specific for it. Consequently, an item has high cue-validity if it is quite orthogonal to the other items. We saw that the cue-validity criterion could not furnish a formal differentiation of basic level concepts. Likewise, basic level concepts are not always more orthogonal to one another than concepts at other levels of abstraction: as we will see, basic level concepts that belong to the same superordinate concept are in general less orthogonal than two superordinate concepts.

6.2.2 Superordinate categories and basic level categories

We saw that basic level concepts are dominantly composed by part-whole information and that different basic level categories share few part-whole attributes. Further, part-whole attributes disappear if one makes an abstraction from a basic level concept to a superordinate category. Hence, in general, basic level instances of different superordinate categories do not have more P's in common than the superordinate categories themselves. As a consequence, if two superordinate categories are orthogonal, then the basic level instances of one of them are in general orthogonal with the basic level instances of the other one. Further, if two superordinate categories share some P's, then the overlap between a basic level instance of one of them and a basic level instance of the other one is in general lower than the overlap between the superordinate categories themselves.

We consider a couple of examples. For instance, consider the following items:

i0: 0,1,2
i1: 3,4,5
i2: 0,1,2, 6,7,8,9
i3: 3,4,5, 10,11,12,13

Suppose that the items i0 and i1 represent superordinate categories. Further, suppose that i2, respectively i3, is a basic level instance of i0, respectively i1. In accordance with Tversky and Hemmenway (1984), most of the P's 6, 7, 8 and 9 may be assumed to refer to the part-whole configuration of i2. Similarly, the P's 10, 11, 12 and 13 may express part-whole information of i3. In the present example, we have:

$$Q(i0,i1) = 0$$

so that i0 and i1 are orthogonal. The addition of exclusive sets of P's to these subordinate categories does not change this situation:

$$Q(i2,i3) = 0.$$

Hence, i2 and i3 are orthogonal also. In the next example, the orthogonality of concepts increases as one descends from the superordinate to the basic level:

i0: 0,1,2
i1: 0,3,4
i2: 0,1,2, 5,6,7,8
i3: 0,3,4, 9,10,11,12

Here, one has that the superordinate categories i0 and i1 are not orthogonal (see Appendix I):

$Q(i0,i1) = 0.25$

The same thing holds for the basic level categories i2 and i3. However, since the latter concepts share only one component in seven instead of one component in three, they have lower overlap with each other:

$Q(i2,i3) = 0.098$

The second example is not a fictitious one. As Tversky and Hemmenway notice (1984, pg. 188):

"... superordinate categories can violate ... mutual exclusion. Cars and roller skates may be vehicles as well as toys. A recorder may be a musical instrument as well as a toy."

Hence, it is conceivable that some superordinate categories share a few components. For these superordinate categories, basic level instances that belong to different superordinate concepts are in general more orthogonal than these superordinate categories themselves. Thus far, we confined ourselves to the case of basic level categories which belong to different superordinate classes. Next, we assume that the basic level concepts are members of the same superordinate category. For the sake of concreteness, we consider a simple example:

i0: 0,1,2
i1: 3,4,5
i2: 0,1,2, 6,7,8,9
i3: 0,1,2, 10,1,12,13

The superordinate categories i0 and i1 are perfectly orthogonal since they do not share any P. The basic level categories i2 and i3, on the other hand, share three P's. Hence, they are significantly correlated:

Q(i2,i3) = 0.297

Hence, we perceive that basic level categories may be less orthogonal than superordinate ones. This point is closely related to the observation of Murphy (1982) that basic level concepts do not always have highest cue-validity. Some of the P's of a basic level concept are not really specific for it : the P's which express superordinate properties are in general shared by the representation of the superordinate concept to which it belongs. In case of a hierarchically organized memory structure, other basic level instances of this superordinate category may share these P's.

6.2.3 Basic level categories and subordinate categories

Two different basic level categories are in general more orthogonal than two subordinate categories which are instances of the same basic level concept. This is quite obvious: two subordinate categories which belong to the same basic level category share the P's that characterize the basic level concept. For instance, consider the following knowledge base:

i0: 0,1,2, 3,4,5,6
i1: 0,1,2, 3,4,5,6, 7,8
i2: 0,1,2, 3,4,5,6, 9,10
i3: 0,1,2, 11,12,13,14

Items i0, i3 and i4 represent three different basic level concepts. Items i1 and i2 are subordinate instances of i0. Since the latter items share all components of i0, their overlap is quite high:

Q(i1,i2) = 0.590

The overlap of two different basic level categories which belong to a different superordinate category is in general significantly smaller, because they have a different part-whole configuration and because they share in general no P's that refer to abstract aspects. For instance, in the present example, we have:

Q(i0,i4) = 0

As far as concerns two basic level concepts that belong to the same superordinate category, the situation is more complex. In the present example, more P's are involved in the specification of the basic level than in the specification of the subordinate level. Hence, the basic level concepts i0 and i3 have smaller overlap than two instances of i0:

$Q(i0,i3) = 0.297$

However, if, for some concepts, a subject memorized only a few specifications at the basic level, but many subordinate as well as superordinate specifications, then two subordinate concepts that belong to the same basic level category may be more orthogonal than two basic level concepts that belong to the same superordinate category. For instance, consider the following knowledge base:

i0: 0,1,2,3,4, 5,6
i1: 0,1,2,3,4, 5,6, 7,8,9,10,11,12
i2: 0,1,2,3,4, 5,6, 13,14,15,16,17,18
i3: 0,1,2,3,4, 19,20

Items i1 and i2 are instances of the basic level concept i0; we have:

$Q(i1,i2) = 0.372$

Items i0 and i3 represent basic level concepts that belong to the same superordinate category (characterized by (0,1,2,3,4)). We have:

$Q(i0,i3) = 0.531$

Hence, in the present case, subordinate categories which belong to the same basic level are more orthogonal than basic level concepts that belong to the same superordinate category. We notice, however, that this situation may be expected to be quite exceptional: the number of properties which have to be added to descend from the basic level to the subordinate level is in general significantly smaller than the number of properties which have to be added to descend from the superordinate to the basic level (2.2.1).

NOTES

Note 1. We notice that this result of Rosch et al. can be updated by more recent research that shows that even pre-verbal infants can classify in basic level categories (see e.g. Roberts, 1988). Some studies even suggest that pre-verbal infants can make superordinate differentiations (e.g. Ross, 1980).

Note 2. In addition to these four P's, we added in our simulation one supplementary P that expressed noise; hence, we obtained an input with an odd number of components.

Note 3. For instance, consider the image schema manipulation that has to be carried out in order to examine if fluids in recipients of different forms represent the same volume. As has pointed out by Piaget, this kind of mental manipulation is acquired only around the age of 11-12 (Piaget, 1974).

X. CONCEPTUAL ORGANIZATION AND ITS DEVELOPMENT

X.I. THE EMPIRICAL PSYCHOLOGY OF CONCEPT DEVELOPMENT

1 Introduction

It is generally agreed that children restructure their memory when they grow up. At first, the items which a child has learned are related by unsystematic, complexive associations. We he grows up, part of his memory is restructured and becomes organized in a taxonomic way. Further, in case of young children, concepts are associated mainly by virtue of the fact that they participate in the same scene or by virtue of the fact that they are functionally related. As concerns older children or adults, on the other hand, associative relationships between concepts are based on more abstract, taxonomic principles. This "classical view" has been supported by an impressive amount of evidence (e.g. Vygotski, 1962; Inhelder and Piaget, 1974; Annett, 1959; Anglin, 1970; Sigel, 1953). However, some issues in this domain remained controversial.

For instance, one may wonder if children are unable to classify in a taxonomic way or if this is just a matter of preference. Also, one may wonder if the reorganization of semantic memory is discontinuous or if it is a gradual process. Further, one may consider what is to be understood by a "functionally-based" grouping: it might depend on the storage of temporal sequences or it might involve mainly non-temporal associations. We base our discussions mainly on research that is more recent than the "classical" investigations. The advantage of the more recent methods is that they lead to fairly exact and quantitative data. We select some of the most remarkable results (part I of this chapter) and we relate them to our model (part II of this chapter).

In paragraph 2 and 3, we will see that the free recall method reveals that, as far as concerns young children, slot-filler based relations are more important than categorical and than scene- or script-based relations. The conceptual preference method confirms the fact that young children prefer thematical associations over taxonomic ones. However, the kind of thematic associations that is observed is opposite to the expectation raised by the results of the free recall method. Further, it is evidenced that children can be trained to classify taxonomically. After a short period, however, they spontaneously reverse their classification criterion (paragraph 4). Paragraph 5 summarizes some other more recent experiments that concern the evolution of conceptual structure. They are all in agreement with the classical stance that the organization of knowledge changes form complexive to taxonomic. When a child becomes familiar with a domain, the number of associative links between the items of the domain tends to increase. Also the strength of these links grows. Further, the items tend to group in clusters (paragraph 6).

2 The free recall method and the organization of memory

First, we consider studies which use the free-recall paradigm to asses the structure of semantic memory. In the free-recall method, the experimenter instructs his subjects to memorize a number of items. It is assumed that, if the items cluster in groups during the recall process, these groups reflect the way in which items are clustered in memory. Several studies use this method to examine the organization of semantic memory in children and in adults. The results of these studies agree fairly well with each other. They can be summarized in three points (e.g. Ornstein and Corsale, 1979; Lucariello and Nelson, 1985):

a. If a list contains a number of items which belong to the same category, subjects show a tendency to cluster them in recall.
b. Suppose that a list contains a number of items which belong to the same category. Then, the recall performance for such items is better than the performance for items which are the only instances of their category in the list.
c. These effects are found for both adults and children, but they are significantly stronger for adults than for children. Hence, it appears that taxonomic organization is more manifest in adults than in children. However, to a limited extent, also children can master taxonomic classifications.

For instance, Lucariello and Nelson (1985) used this method to find out if child memory is organized in a taxonomic way or in a thematic way (the ages of their subjects ranged from three years zero months to four years eleven months). They considered two lists. The first one contained items which could be grouped according to taxonomic principles. The second one contained thematically related items. More specifically, their first list included the following nine items: three animals (elephant, dog, cow), three kinds of food (toast, cheese, ice-cream) and three elements of the category "clothes" (pants, coat and pajamas). The thematically organized list contained the three most familiar zoo animals (elephant, tiger, lion), three elements of "lunch food" (peanut butter, cheese, bologna) and three elements of the category "clothes to put on in the morning" (pants, socks, shirt). The results revealed that, for the thematically organized list, recall was significantly better than for the taxonomic list. Moreover, the items of the thematic list clustered to a significantly higher degree. Further, it was found that recall performance increases if a theme is given as a cue. Consequently, this experiment corroborated the hypothesis that script-based concepts offer a closer match to a child's semantic memory than taxonomic categories (note 1).

At this instance, it is useful to make a terminological specification. One may wonder if the "thematic" relations which are considered in Lucariello and Nelson (1985) are, according to the terminology of chapter II, temporal relations or non-temporal relations. It appears that they can be described (at least partially) as non-temporal relations. The fact that, for instance, different animals can be met in a zoo does not entail that they occur in events which are temporally ordered by a script. Similarly, different lunch foods may not occur in memorized events which are temporally ordered. For instance, salad, meat and potatoes may be eaten simultaneously. A similar thing holds for the instances of the sub-category "clothes to put on in the morning". However, although these items do not occur in events which follow one another in a script, they still may be related in a script-based way: it may be that one item can substitute another one in a script. Then, the items have the same function in the script. In more technical terms, they may be fillers of the same slot. However, this kind of relations is called often "slot-filler based relations".

Now we are reminded of the fact that the function of an object can (at least to a certain extent) be expressed by representations that do not invoke explicit temporal relations between different patterns (chapter IV). The fact that two objects have the same function in a script can be described when their representations share the P's which express this function. Further, we are reminded of the fact that functional relations between objects may also be expressed in our type of representation when the objects participate in the same scene. In contradistinction with items which are related by slot-filler based relations, such objects have in general different functions in the scene. We will call this kind of relations "scene-base" relations.

3 The nature of the thematic organization of child-memory

Lucariello and Nelson (1985) examined in a second experiment if slot-filler based relations dominate over scene-based and temporal relations in child memory. Also here, the free recall method was used. Again, two lists were considered. The first one was the slot-filler based list of the first experiment; the second one contained three groups of three items with scene and/or script based relations (elephants, peanuts, cage; sandwich, cup, plate; pants, closet, hanger). The results decided in favor of the slot-filler based associations. In fact, there was no significant difference between the performance on the list with scene and/or script based relations and the performance on the taxonomic list. In the latter two cases, both recall and grouping were significantly less than for the slot-filler list. Hence, the authors concluded (p.280):

"The finding that the slot-filler list was better recalled and organized than was the complementarity-list suggests that slot-filler categories represent a more cohesive organizing structure than do complementarity relations. If spatial/ temporal links were of prime importance in category formation, then memory- performance on the complementary list should have surpassed, or, at least, equaled memory-performance on the slot-filler list. "

This is continuous with the outcomes of other experiments that indicated that spatio-temporal associations among items do not constitute an important source of categorical organization in children (e.g. Bjorklund, 1980; Galbraith and Day, 1978).

4 The conceptual preference method and thematic organization

According to the conceptual preference method, an experimenter presents two items to a subject. Next, the subject receives a third item and he is asked with which of the first two items it has closest relationship. For example, suppose that the experimenter shows a subject a picture of a pin and a picture of a thread. Then, the subject sees a picture of a needle, and he has to decide if the needle is closest related to the pin or if it is closest related to the thread. If he chooses for the pin, the classification has been guided by perceptual similarities or by a criterion in terms of common properties. If, on the other hand, the thread is chosen, the choice is based on functional aspects. In a study that has become famous, Smiley and Brown (1979) showed that a shift in conceptual preference takes place between the age of six and the age of ten; before the shift, children prefer quite consistently thematic grouping; after the shift, taxonomic grouping is preferred (note 2).

Remarkably, however, none of the thematic relations used in Smiley and Brown (1979) concerned items which were substitutable by each other as slot-fillers (along with needle-thread, other examples were: bird-nest, river-boat, sheep-wool, cow-milk, crown-king, spider-web, and so on). Rather, these items were integrated in simple scenes or in simple scripts. We saw that Lucariello and Nelson (1985), on the other hand, argued that, as far as concerns young children, this kind of associations was of rather limited importance; according to their evidence, such relations were not imprinted with more depth than taxonomic relations. We will explain this discrepancy in part II of this chapter by reference to the fact that the respective authors used different experimental methods.

Smiley and Brown (1979) added a second experiment in which they studied if young children were unable to carry out taxonomic classifications or if their thematic classifications were just a matter of preference. Their evidence pointed to the latter possibility. The subjects used in the experiment were kindergartner children of mean age five years and six months. The experimenters tried to teach the children to select the item that was taxonomically related with a given one. More specifically, they gave the children ten examples of taxonomic preferences and they justified their choice. The children were asked to make similar choices for the thirty test-problems that followed. The results showed that the children scored a mean of 24.28 taxonomic choices for thirty problems. Consequently, it is, to a significant extent, possible to teach children to classify in a taxonomic way. In a final experiment, the children were tested again with a one-day delay without repetition of the instruction. It appeared that a significant percentage of subjects returned to their functional mode of classification: only 14 of 24 subjects kept showing a taxonomic preference. Thus, without continued training, children of this age show a tendency to unlearn the taxonomic method of classification.

5 Other methods that evidence the transition from a thematic to a taxonomic organization of memory

Quite recently, different other methods have been used to assess the ontogenetic evolution of the organization of semantic memory. We mention some of the most important ones:

a. In the semantic-priming method, the experimenter shows his subject a noisy item. Then, the subject receives a cue which helps to identify the item. It is studied how the speed of identification varies with the nature of the cue. Mc Cauly, Weil and Sperber (1976) observed that cues which are thematically related to the items facilated recognition in case of children of five and of seven years old. If, on the other hand, a category is given as a cue, then the speed of identification is enhanced only in case of adults. This is consistent with Lucariello and Nelson (1985) (paragraph 2). Here, one observes that, along with recall, also recognition does not benefit from categorical cues before a certain age.

b. Also the Stroop method allows to detect developmental changes in memory organization. This method makes use of couples of written words; the second word of each couple is printed in color. The subjects are asked to name the color of the second word after they have read the first one. It assumed that the strength of association between both words is negatively correlated with the time required to name the second word: the less the subject is concerned with the meaning of the second word, the more quickly it can detect another aspect of it. By a comparison of second, fourth and sixth grade children, Kareev (1980) observed that the strength of association between concepts and their superordinate classes increased with age. The graduality of the effect suggested that semantic memory reorganizes gradually rather than discontinuously.

c. Another method is based on interitem latencies. One assumes that the time between two subsequently mentioned items in a free-recall task decreases as items are associated more tightly. In Bjorklund and Jacobs (1985), different categories were considered, and within these categories, tightly associated items and less tightly associated ones were selected. For example, the category "animal" includes, among others, cow, cat, dog, lion and tiger. In this example, the tightly associated items are (cat,dog) and (tiger,lion). The subjects were children from the grades three, five, seven, nine and college students. For all age-groups, interitem-latencies appeared to be shorter for tightly associated within-category items than for items that belonged to different categories. The results for the loosely associated within-category items, however, differentiated between the age-groups. For seventh- and ninth-graders, the within-category loosely associated items showed shorter interitem latencies than items which belonged to different categories. For the third and fifth-graders, on the other hand, there was no significant difference between the latencies for lowly associated within-category items and inter-category pairs. Hence, for the younger children, category-effects were detectable only for the closely associated pairs. This suggests that they acquired a partial taxonomic organization: some clusters of items could be characterized by taxonomic principles but these principles were not yet sufficiently abstract to include other, less resembling category members.

d. We notice that different studies that we discussed in chapters IV and IX are of relevance for the present discussion. In special, we remind of the following points. Ross (1980) and Golinkoff and Halperin (1983) found that twelve-month-old infants seemed to be able to extract superordinate information. However, in general, children's first concepts are situated at the basic level of abstraction. Only afterwards, superordinate and subordinate categories are formed (Rosch, Mervis et al. 1976). The first verbal concepts often are associated with a single exemplar (Anglin 1977) and they integrate a small number of features (Clark 1973). Later, concepts are enlarged horizontically (i.e. the number of memorized instances increases) and vertically (i.e. the number of taxonomic levels increases).

6 The relation between the organization of memory and the elaborateness of a knowledge base

We saw in chapter V that the background knowledge of a subject may be important for the structure of the categories that he will develop. If items can be organized by reference to background-knowledge, this may result in categories which are centered around prototypes. If a subject does not make recourse to this background knowledge (for instance, because he has no background knowledge in a particular domain), he may structure new items in accordance with exemplar-rules. In the present paragraph, we consider other experiments that concern the relation between the elaborateness of a knowledge base and the structure of categories. Chi (1981) (see also Chi 1976) argued that, if children know more about a particular domain than adults, then their memory performance exceeds the one of adults. This contrasts with "normal" conditions, where adults show a significantly better memory-performance than children (see e.g. Ackerman (1985) for a review of evidence in favor of the latter point).

In normal conditions, the knowledge base of adults is better elaborated than the one of children. Hence, a more elaborated knowledge-base appears to enhance memory performance. The question of relevance, then, is what is to be understood by a "more elaborated" knowledge base. Chi and Koeske (1983) tried to determine the factors which make a knowledge-base "better" elaborated than anotherone by a study of the dinosaur knowledge of a four and a half year old child. The child had been exposed to dinosaur-information for one year and six months. He received a collection of various plastic dinosaurs for use in play and a collection of nine dinosaur books. His parents read these books to him often during this period (with an average of three hours a week). After this period, forty dinosaurs were selected for use in the experiment. They were divided in two groups: one group contained the best known exemplars and the other group consisted of the less known ones (this division was based on the mother's judgement and coincided with the frequency of occurrence in the child's dinosaur books). Then, the authors compared the structure of these two groups in order to obtain information about the differences between a good known collection of items and a less well known one.

The child was tested in two ways. First, he carried out a production task: he was asked to sum up the names of all the dinosaurs that he knew. The production task was repeated six times. In a second task (a clue game), the experimenters determined the properties that the child knew about each dinosaur. It appeared that the best known set differed in three respects from the less known one:

a. The best known set contained a larger number of inter-dinosaur links. These links were determined by the results of the production task: two items which were recalled one after another within a time-interval of ten seconds were supposed to be associatively linked. It appeared that the total number of links between elements of the first set was larger than the total number of links between exemplars of the second set.
b. If one counts the number of times that two items follow each other in the production task, the strength of the link between two exemplars can be expressed by a number between zero and six. It appeared that the strength of the links in the first set was in general higher than the strength of the links in the second set.
c. Finally, subset-clustering was developed to a higher degree in the first set than in the second set. In the first set, it was possible to differentiate subgroups of dinosaur-clusters so that the within-subset links were in general stronger than between-subset links. In the second set, one could also perceive a certain amount of subset-clustering, but to a significantly smaller extent than in the first set.

Chi and Koeske (1983) investigated the effects of these structural differences on recall and on clustering in recall. It appeared that the items of the first set were recalled with more ease. Further, the recalled items of the first set were clustered to a higher degree. The clusters coincided with the subsets that were at issue in point c. The experimenters ensured that, in the course of the year after the experiments, the child could pay only relatively few attention to his dinosaur-books and to his toy-dinosaurs. After this year, the authors studied the retention of the dinosaur-concepts. The results of this study differentiated clearly between the two sets which were considered previously. Eleven of the twenty dinosaurs of the first list were identified correctly. As concerns the second list, on the other hand, only two dinosaurs could be recognized. It is tempting to relate this difference in performance between both sets to the three previously mentioned structural differences a, b and c. Chi and Koeske concluded (1983, p. 37):

"...we offer the ... interpretation that better recall and retention of lists of items may be influenced by how well the composition of the list of items matches the structure of the knowledge base, defined here in terms of the number of direct and indirect links among dinosaur concepts, the strength of linkages, and the particular pattern of intra- and interlinkages, which delineates the cohesion of groupings. "

This study is quite suggestive for the problem how the memory organization of children differs from the one of adults. Adults in general have more elaborate knowledge bases than children, and one may speculate that, also here, "more elaborate" can be specified by the properties a, b and c. One may wonder if the factors a, b and c themselves can be explained. The first two of them seem to be quite natural: as a context is encountered more, more links between the involved items may be observed and each of these links may be observed (or inferred) with higher frequency so that they are imprinted deeper than in case of less frequently realized contexts. However, the third property is intuitively less trivial. Still, it is a crucial one. If it holds, it may offer a schema for the dynamics of conceptual organization: it expresses that the representations of items which belong to a particular context (or to a particular category) cluster more and more as the context (or the category) becomes more familiar. Hence, a cluster/sub-cluster organization is spontaneously created when a domain is often activated. From a formal point of view, such an organization corresponds to the development of taxonomies of concepts. In X,II.7 , we show that our model explains this third property.

X.II. GENERAL DISCUSSION

1 Introduction

In the second part of this chapter, we study how the phenomena considered in the first part can be explained and interpreted by our connectionist model. To start with, we notice that young children often represent taxonomic information in an extensional way. Adults, on the other hand, tend to represent such information in an intrinsic way. This point is suggested by the fact that young children do not use their taxonomic information if this is not required explicitly (paragraph 2 of X.II; see also X.II.5). Our model explains the phenomenon of clustering in free recall (paragraph 3 of X.II); it also shows why the free recall method evidences slot-filler based relations rather than scene-based ones (paragraph 4 of X.II). Further, the model helps to explain why associative preferences are first scene based and later category based. Our analysis sheds light on the seeming contradiction between the free recall method and the associative preference method concerning the kind of thematic relations which are dominant in children (paragraph 5 of X.II).

We show that it is consonant with our view that the number and the strength of the associative relationships between the items of a domain increase as it becomes familiar (paragraph 6 of X.II). Remarkably, the our model predicts the reorganization of a familiar knowledge base (paragraph 7 of X.II). For instance, existing items may become prototypes or new prototypes may be generated. Within a category, sub-categories may be created. The larger the extension of a familiar cluster, the stronger its tendency to reorganize in a taxonomic way. In a familiar domain, the representations of new items are drawn into familiar categories. Our general frame suggests that also mechanisms external to the module at issue enhance clustering. Finally, we point out that our connectionist model allows that abstractions are generated. After their generation, they can be addressed in a straightforward way (paragraph 8 of X.II).

2 The use of categories as cues: evidence for the non-extensional representation of categories

2.1 Extensional representations and cued free recall

In the present paragraph, we point out that the experiments that we considered higher disfavor the stance that taxonomically organized categories are represented extensionally. To start with, we are reminded of the fact that in a free recall experiment, a number of items is presented to a subject; during the next short period, these items remain "highlighted" in memory. In a cued free-recall condition, the subject receives at the beginning of the recall phase the cue that some of the items to be recalled belong to one or more particular categories. For example, he may be informed that some of the items belong to the category "animal". Then, the category "animal" is activated. According to extensional theories, this activation flows" towards the concepts with which "animal" is linked. In special, the memorized instances of "animal" may be stimulated. Now consider the items for which a cue has been given. For these items, two stimulating effects combine: first, they have been active a short time before. Second, activation may have spread from the cue to these items. This explains why they are addressed quite easily and why non-cued items are harder to recall: since the latter have only one source of stimulation, they are harder to access.

So far, an extensional approach can furnish a plausible scenario for cued recall. However, a difficulty raises with respect to some of the other facts considered in the previous paragraphs. We saw that children benefit less or even not at all from category-cues in free recall. In these experiments, children are aware of the category memberships of the items which have to be recalled. For instance, children know that an elephant is an animal. Still, in contradistinction with adults, they do not benefit from this knowledge in cued free recall conditions. Hence, in the semantic graph terminology, children dispose of "arrows" or "links" from the node "animal" to the nodes corresponding to the stored instances of "animal". But for children, the cue "animal" enhances retrieval significantly less than in case of adults. This is the more remarkable since one may expect children to know less animals than adults. Hence, the activation send from the cue to the instances defines a smaller search space in case of children than in case of adults. Actually, performance is opposite to the expectation raised by this consideration.

2.2 Intrinsic representations and cued free recall

At this instance, we are reminded that it is plausible to distinguish different semantic codes, for instance between a verbal one and a non-verbal one (chapter II). In the previous chapters, we discussed processes which were based mainly on non-verbal semantic representations. We will argue in 7 that these non-verbal semantic patterns evolve and that this evolution entails the emergence of taxonomic structures. For instance, P's which participate in the non-verbal representation of "animal" may be formed and they may invade in the representations of their instances. In other words, categories become represented in an intrinsic way. Then, an activation of the non-verbal "animal"-pattern trivially produces a partial activation of the representations of its instances. Schematically, we have:

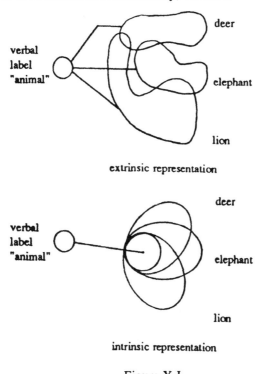

extrinsic representation

intrinsic representation

Figure X.I

As concerns young children, the non-verbal pattern for "animal" (if it exists at all) is not correlated in a systematic way with the non-verbal patterns of memorized instances of "animal". Hence, an activation of the non-verbal semantic "animal"-pattern does not produce a partial activation of the non-verbal semantic patterns for its instances. Consequently, a young child who knows that an elephant is an animal represents this information verbally rather than non-verbally. This suggests to explain the differential cue-benefit of adults relative to children by reference to the non-verbal patterns. In case of an adult, a trigger of the non-verbal pattern of a category results in a partial trigger of the non-verbal semantic representations of the instances of the category, since adults represent categories intrinsically. In case of young children, however, the semantic reorganization that leads to intrinsic representations has not taken place yet. A category is related to its instances only by virtue of relations between verbal labels. Hence, as concerns young children, a cue does not constrain the non-verbal semantic patterns.

Consequently, if cued recall depends in first instance on non-verbal semantic modules, and if children have no intrinsic non-verbal category representations, they do not benefit from cues that correspond to categories. We notice that this scenario emphasizes to the role of non-verbal semantic representations. This is a remarkable point: even in case of free recall and even if the items which have to be remembered are presented exclusively in a verbal way (as is the case in many free recall experiments, e.g. Lucariello and Nelson 1985), non-verbal representations may be of crucial importance.

3 Spontaneous categorical clustering in recall

3.1 A short-term increase of the F-values of patterns

Suppose that some items are presented to a subject. As far as the number of items is not too large, he can memorize these items during a short time period. Since the recall process shows properties which refer to the semantic representations of the items, the items must have been transmitted to semantic modules before recall. The most straightforward hypothesis concerning a short-term memory effect in the module that we describe is that the F-value of a recently activated item increases for a short period (note 3). We denote the increased value by F(st) ("st" stands for "short term"); it must be significantly larger than F(sat). When several items are presented in the context of a free recall experiment, the F-values of all these items temporary increase. This has two consequences:

a. Since the F-values of the presented items are especially high, there is a high chance that they will be triggered in the course of the subsequent recall process.
b. The items which are presented may show effects of interference with each other. If the b-values of the items are strictly positive, then items with common P's tend to be addressed in groups.

Effect b is a direct consequence of the properties of the additive interactions between components (see chapter VI). Suppose, for instance, that four items i0, i1, i2 and i3 are presented and that i0 shares a subset of P's with the items i1 and i2. Suppose that i0 has been triggered during the recall phase. In order retrieve another M, i0 is destabilized. Technically, this means that its F-value is temporary lowered. Then, the recall process goes on: the network state moves from i0 to another M that has been presented. Suppose now that i3 does not contain a subset of P's that participates in i0, i2 and i3. Then, the network state will retrieve i1 or to i2 but not i3. This is a consequence of the fact that the P's that are shared by i0, i1 and i2 have high tendency to remain in the network state. Suppose i1 is retrieved next. Again, in order to retrieve another item, i1 is subsequently temporary destabilized. Suppose that i1 and i3 share only a few P's. Then, the chance that item i2 is recalled next is higher than the chance that i3 is recalled. This time, this is not a consequence of the fact that it shares a subset of P's with i0 and i1: since the F-values of these items are temporary drastically lowered, the P's which are common to i0, i1 and i2 are favored by one highlighted M only. However, if the number of P's which i3 shares with i1 is smaller than the number of P's in the common subset of i0, i1 and i2, then i1 has higher overlap with i2 than with i3. Hence, starting form i1, the network state will address i2 rather than i3.

If one assumes that adults have developed intrinsic representations and that young children have not, then these considerations allow to explain why adults cluster items according to categories in free recall and why children do not: for adults, the effects of interference which are at issue in b. enhance categorical clustering; for young children, this effect is absent. According to this proposal, short term memory effects depend on fields which are induced in long term memory. The limited span of short term memory may be due to two factors (note 4):

i. The number of temporary strong fields F(st) which can be induced in the system may be restricted.
ii. The capacity of the system to maintain fields F(st) may be limited.

3.2 Clusters in recall: an example.

In order to illustrate the argument of 3.1, we consider a simple example. Suppose that, in the context of a free recall experiment, a subject has memorized the following items:

i0: 0,1,2, 3,4
i1: 0,1,2, 5,6
i2: 0,1,2, 7,8
i3: 9,10,11, 12,13
i4: 9,10,11, 14,15
i5: 16,17,18, 19,20

Items i0, i1 and i2 belong to the category which is characterized by the set of P's (0,1,2). Items i3 and i4 belong to the category (9,10,11). Finally, item i5 is the only instance of its category which has been presented. We assume that all b-values are strictly positive. Since F(st) is significantly larger than F(sat), we do not take into account the non-presented items of the long term knowledge base of the network. Suppose that the network recalls a first item. For instance, the first recalled item may be i0 (the issue which item is recalled first is in general dependent on primacy-and recency-effects; see note 4). Then, in order to retrieve another item,

the F-value of i0 is temporary decreased. The network state will move to i1 or i2: the P's 0, 1 and 2 will remain in the network state since they still participate in two M's with especially high F.

Suppose that i1 is recalled next. Subsequently, i1 is destabilized. The network state may move to i2 since it has highest overlap with i1. However, since i3 and i4 share common modes, they may counter this tendency and one of them may eventually attract the network state (notice that, also in psychological experiments, items are not perfectly clustered in recall). Suppose, however, that i2 is retrieved. Then, the issue which item will be retrieved next depends on three factors. First, we notice that i2 has zero overlap with the remaining items. Hence, if it is presented formally as a new input, the values of the consolidations of all items will be quite low. As a consequence, random effects may decide which item will be addressed next. Second, the P's which are shared by i2 and i3 have relatively high tendency to invade in the network state when they are activated slightly by random fluctuations. Third, the recency- and primacy-effects may still play a role. Suppose, for instance, that these factors lead to the retrieval of i3. Then, the next item that is triggered is i4, since it has considerable overlap with i3. Finally, i5 is addressed since the F-values of all other items are temporary significantly lower than F(st). Figure s24 shows a simulation of this example.

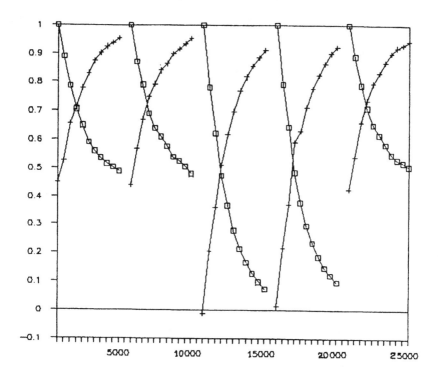

Figure s24. For convenience, each time an item is recognized, we present it as a new input to the network (as a consequence, the correlation of the network state with a recognized item jumps to 1). In the subsequent association process, its F-value is put equal to zero so that the network state keeps on moving. From iteration zero to iteration 5000, item i0 (represented by squares in the picture) decays and i1 (represented by crosses) attracts the network state. Next, i1 is presented formally as a new input (and corresponds to the squares between iteration 5000 and 10000). This leads to the retrieval of i2 (represented by crosses), and so on. See text for further explanation of this picture.

4 Clustering in free recall and thematic associations

We pointed out that the results of the study of Smiley and Brown (1979) and of the study of Lucariello and Nelson (1985) seem to be at odds with each other. In the former study, the preference of children for thematic clusters is evidenced, but these clusters are of the kind that Lucariello and Nelson show to be unimportant. According to the latter authors, the thematic associations which matter in child memory are determined by the criterion that items have to be substitutable for each other in a script. Associations which are based on temporal or a scene-based relationships are significantly less important. Smiley and Brown (1979), on the other hand, show that the latter relations play a relevant role in the organization of child memory. In the present paragraph, we show that slot-filler related items indeed may lead to clustering in free recall. On the other hand, there is no reason to suppose that items which are related in another thematic way cluster in free recall. This is consistent with Lucariello and Nelson (1985). We anticipate that we point out in the next paragraph that also the results of Smiley and Brown can be explained by our model.

Two objects are substitutable by each other in a script if they have a similar function. In agreement with chapters III and IV, we can differentiate between two possibilities as concerns the representation of aspects of function in our representations:

a. According to the first possibility, the function of an object is represented explicitly in the representations. In the present chapter, we met two sub-cases of this possibility: function may be represented in a scene based way or in a slot-filler based way.
b. Second, a subject may not yet have memorized explicitly the function of an object, but he may be able to infer it. More specifically, he may make an image schema analysis of scenes that he memorized and in which the object occurs. He may notice that the object satisfies an image schema that expresses a particular function (after the analysis, he may add the P's that correspond to the detected image schema to the representation of the object; then, case b transforms in case a).

We assume that, as concerns familiar functions of familiar items, function is represented in accordance with possibility a. In case of the slot-filler related items used in Lucariello and Nelson (1985), it is plausible to suppose that the condition of familiarity is fulfilled. Now if the function of objects is represented in accordance with a., and if, more specifically, function is represented in a slot-filler based way, then objects which share a function share one or more P's. Hence, the formal situation is similar to the one of the previous paragraph (in which adult taxonomic categories were considered). Consequently, the same argument can be repeated here to explain that slot-filler related items cluster in free recall.

4.1 Scenes, scripts and free recall

If thematically related items are not fillers of the same slots, then they may occur in the same scene or they may occur in different events of a script. Consider two items which occur in the same scene. Two sub-cases are possible:

i. Suppose that the representation of at least one of both items does not include the skeleton-P of the scene. Then, the fact that they occur in the same scene does not result in common P's. Hence, if the items do not share P's for other reasons, then they will not cluster in free recall.
ii. Suppose that both items are tightly associated with the scene. Then, the skeleton of the scene may participate in the representations of both items. However, this point has to be qualified. Since the items do not fill the same slot, they appear at different places in the scene. Hence, if their representations include P's which refer to the scene, then these P's may refer to different coarse aspects of the scene. In fact, this point is supported by the fact that scene-based associations do not lead to effects of clustering in free recall.

These points explain the evidence collected in Lucariello and Nelson (1985).

5 Preferences in classification tasks

5.1 Judgements of associative relatedness

Smiley and Brown (1979) asked their subjects to choose between alternative association possibilities. For instance, a subject had to decide if a needle was closer to a pin than to a thread. The first kind of associations was based on share of properties, the second kind was based on functional complementarity. It is plausible that "needle" shares (at least for some subjects) one or more P's with "pin": both objects are sharp and thin; one may prick with both of them and hence they are dangerous to play with. In spite of these common P's, children prefer to associate "needle" with thread. This result is obtained quite systematically: children prefer to associate an item with a thematically related one rather than with an item that shares some properties with it.

In case of the stimuli used in Smiley and Brown (1979), it was plausible that, for each couple of thematically related items that was considered, subjects had memorized a simple scene in which it occurred. Although the subjects might have stored also script-based relations (i.e. explicit temporal relations) between the thematically related items, it appears sufficient to consider the scene-based ones in order to explain the evidence. Consider the problem what it may mean for a subject to judge that two items have a close associative relationship. As one possibility, we suggest that a subject may conclude that two items fit with each other if the activation of both of them leads to a trigger of a familiar pattern. In special, this familiar pattern may be a scene in which both items participate. We show that our model predicts that the probability to access a familiar scene can be quite high if two if its participating items are presented.

Consider two objects i0 and i1 and a scene i2 in which they participate. Suppose that both items are presented simultaneously and suppose that the representations of both of them are partially activated. The resulting network state has high correlation with both items. Hence, in case of an ordinary convergence process, it will probably evolve to one of them. However, this process does not furnish an answer to the problem at issue: subject has to examine if the network state leads to a trigger of a familiar scene. Hence, in order to prohibit a quick decay of the network state to i0 or i1, their F-values are temporary put equal to zero. We notice that the representation of the scene i2 shares P's with both items (at least, it includes the skeleton-P of each item). Hence, i2 has high overlap with the initial network state. Consequently, the probability that i2 is addressed may be quite high. We illustrate this with a simple example. Consider the following items:

i0: 0,1,2,3,4,5,12
i1: 6,7,8,9,10,11,12
i2: 0,1,6,7,13,14,15
i3: 2,3,16,17,18,19,20

Suppose that i0 and i1 represent items which participate in the scene represented by i2. We assume that the items i0 and i1 are tightly associated with the scene: the skeleton-P of the scene (component 12) participates in the representations of both items, and, for each of them, two P's that express their respective global configuration are present in the representation of the scene. Now suppose that i0 and i1 are presented simultaneously. Suppose that the resulting input contains the P's of both i0 and i1:

in: 0,1,2,3,4,5,12 / 6,7,8,9,10,11,12

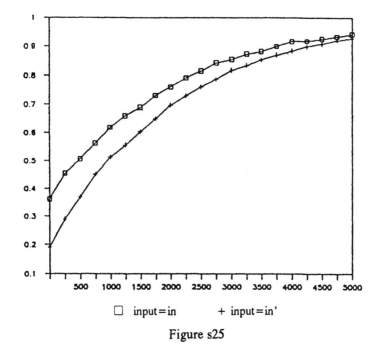

Figure s25

Figure s26

Since a decay of this network state to i0 or to i1 has to be prohibited, the F-values of i0 and of i1 are temporary put equal to zero. Then, for this input, the network will retrieve i2 after about 3795 updatings (this is a mean value for eight runs of the network; the dispersion s is given by $s = 134$). Figure s25 illustrates this point (all b-values are put equal to 0.1). Next, we consider the initial network state in' in which the *P*'s of i0 and of i3 participate:

in': 0,1,2,3,4,5,12 / 2,3,16,17,18,19,20

Again, since a decay of this network state to i0 or to i3 has to be prohibited, the F-values of i0 and i3 are put equal to zero. Then, i2 is retrieved after about 4245 updatings (see figure s25; $s = 150$). Apparently, in' leads to a slower retrieval of a familiar pattern than "in". Hence, we suggest that, as concerns this example, a subject will judge that i0 is more related with i1 than with i3. In the next paragraph, we argue that this situation may be a natural one for young children but not for older ones.

5.2 The reversal of the preferences for older children

The fact that associative preferences reverse when children grow up can be explained in a straightforward way. The explanation depends on two points which we will demonstrate in the next paragraph:

a. When a child becomes more familiar with a context, the memorized patterns of this context reorganize. Categories become organized in a hierarchical, tree-like way. Further, also non-categorically related items tend share sub-groups of *P*'s in a more systematic way.
b. Along with this reorganization, older children have the capacity to address subsets of *P*'s which correspond to abstractions. If they are stimulated to retrieve them, then these subsets themselves may receive consolidation and a verbal label may be attached to them.

We show that these points may cause a reversal of associative preferences. In the previous paragraph, we proposed that a subject concludes that two items are associatively close to each other if a stimulation of both of them leads to a quick trigger of a familiar pattern. Also the present argument is based on this assumption. For the sake of concreteness, we explain our point by the way of an example. Consider the following simple knowledge base:

i0: 0,1,2
i1: 0,1,2, 3,4
i2: 0,1,2, 5,6
i3: 0,1,2, 7,8
i4: 0,1,2, 9,10

i5: 11,12,13
i6: 11,12,13, 14,15
i7: 11,12,13, 16,17

i8: 3,4,14,15,18

We assume that these items are quite familiar so that their F- values are all equal to F(sat) and that their b-values are significantly positive. The items i1, i2, i3 and i4 are instances of the category i0. This situation represents a category with a simple tree-structure: the prototype has invaded its three instances. Further, the prototype itself is consolidated. Similarly, i6 and i7 belong to the category characterized by the prototype i5. Finally, item i8 represents a scene in which both i1 and i6 participate. The scene contains two P's of both items. Suppose now that a subject focusses on two items of the category i0 simultaneously, for instance on i1 and i2. Then, the corresponding initial state of the system may be represented by:

in: 0,1,2,3,4 / 0,1,2,5,6

Suppose that, in order to associate these items with another one, their F-values are temporary lowered. Then, the network state retrieves i0 after about 3036 updatings (the dispersion s for eight runs is given by $s = 128$). This is illustrated in figure s26. Suppose now that the subject focusses on the two items i1 and i6 which participate in the same scene. We propose that the corresponding initial state of the network can be described as:

in: 0,1,2,3,4 / 11,12,13,14,15

Again, the F-values of i1 and i6 are temporary put equal to zero. This time, the network retrieves i0 after 3854 updatings (see figure s26; the dispersion for eight runs is equal to 141; all b-values in this simulation are put equal to 0.1). Hence, the subject will judge that the items i1 and i6 are less tightly related to each other than the items i1 and i2. The present example illustrates the preferences for a subject who has achieved a relatively taxonomically organized knowledge base. Hence, a comparison with the previous paragraph shows that associative preferences reverse when a subject restructures his knowledge base in a tree-like way. The reason for this reversal is that, in the latter case, subsets of relatively abstract *P*'s may exist which are systematically shared by different items. Hence, the categories that contain these subsets have a strong tendency to attract an initial network state. Before the semantic reorganization, there are no such systematically shared subsets of *P*'s. Then, scenes have highest attractivity since they have highest overlap with the initial state.

5.3 The capacity of children to classify in a taxonomic way

We are reminded of the fact that children can be trained to associate items with one another in a taxonomic way instead of on the basis of scenes (Smiley and Brown, 1979). However, when the training is not continued, they spontaneously reverse to their preference for thematic relations. According to our model, this can be explained as follows. As we noticed in 2, children are aware of taxonomic relations. For instance, they know that an elephant is an animal. However, this is memorized only as a relation between verbal labels: the non-verbal representation of a category has in general not yet invaded in the non-verbal representations of its instances. Now in general, mental processes with semantic aspects make recourse to the dynamics of the module that we are describing. In fact, all experiments which are considered in our study confirm this hypothesis. However, non-verbal representations do not reflect all relations between verbal labels. If, in a particular problem situation, the relations which are represented in the non-verbal modules do not suffice to solve the problem, then a subject has to make recourse to the relations between the verbal labels.

For instance, in case of the second experiment in Smiley and Brown (1979), children have to work with memorized relations between verbal labels in order to classify in a taxonomic way. However, in normal conditions, they rely on their non-verbal modules in order to solve the semantic problem of the considered experiment. Hence, when the experimenter stops stimulating the children to classify by virtue of their verbal network, they will rely again on their non-verbal representations. In other terms, according to our interpretation, the tendency of children to reverse their classification preferences to thematic ones is just a special case of the more general tendency to base semantic processes on non-verbal representations rather than on relations between verbal labels.

6 Familiar contexts and associative links between items

The fact that there are more and stronger links in familiar knowledge bases than in less familiar ones (Chi and Koeske 1983) is quite plausible. We are reminded of the fact that associations may be based on the principle of common P's (in case of slot-filler associations and in case of taxonomic relations), on scenes (i.e. an indirect application of the principle of common P's) and on explicit temporal associations.

a. First, we consider scene-based and temporal associations.
i. Consider a set of items which occur in a familiar context. Since the context is often activated, there is a high probability that a subject encounters a scene or a succession of events in which some of these items are involved. Hence, if the depth with which a scene or a temporal association is imprinted increases each time that it is encountered, scenes or temporal associations are in general imprinted with more depth in familiar contexts than in non-familiar ones.
ii. Since a familiar context is often activated, it may be memorized with more detail than a non-familiar one. Hence, the quantity of memorized scenes and of memorized temporal relationships may be larger in case of a familiar context than in case of a non-familiar one.

b. Second, associative links between items may be based on the principle of common P's. We demonstrate in the next paragraph that, in familiar contexts, the representations of items in general share more P's (and in a more systematic way) than in non-familiar ones.

7 The reorganization of the representations of items which belong to familiar contexts

Classical developmental psychology emphasizes that the organization of concepts changes as children grow older. Further, we saw that a subject tends to reorganize his knowledge about a domain if he becomes familiar with it, and we suggested that this may be an important factor behind the ontogenetic evolution of conceptual structure. In the present paragraph, we show how this point is entailed by our model.

7.1 The consequences of an increase of the b-value of one or more memorized patterns

We anticipated in chapter VI that an increase of the b-values of items may necessitate a change of representation. Here, we consider this issue in a more systematic way and we give some additional examples.

7.1.1 An item may become a prototype for other items

7.1.1.1 An increase of the b-value of a single item

If the b-value of a familiar item i0 increases and if its P's participate partially in different other familiar items, then i0 may become a prototype for the latter items. In the present context, this means that it may invade in the latter. Consider the following items:

i0: 0,1,2,3,4
i1: 0,1,2,   5,6
i2:   1,2,3   7,8
i3: 0,   3,4, 9,10
i4: 0,1,   4, 11,12

If the b-value of i0 is 0.6 and if the b-values of the other items are equal to 0.3, then the input

in: 0,1,2,5,6,13,14

converges to i1 (we notice that "in" corresponds to i1 plus noise; the latter is expressed by the P's 13 and 14). If, however, the b-value of i0 has grown to 0.7, the input does not converge to i1 but to an asymmetric mixture which includes the P's 3 and 4. Hence, if B(tr) is smaller than the overlap between i1 and "in", i1 has to change its representation. Since the order parameters of component 3 and component 4 increase quickly (figure s27), they have to be included in the new representation of i1. A similar thing holds for i2 and i3. It follows from the learning rules of our system that the new representations of the items are given by:

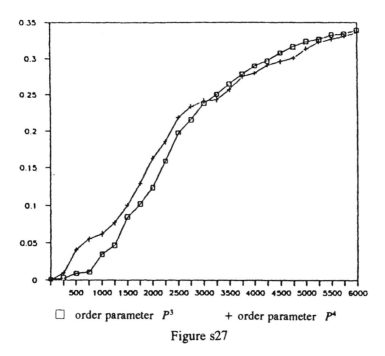

□ order parameter P^3 + order parameter P^4

Figure s27

□ corr netw st j0   + corr netw st j1

Figure s28a

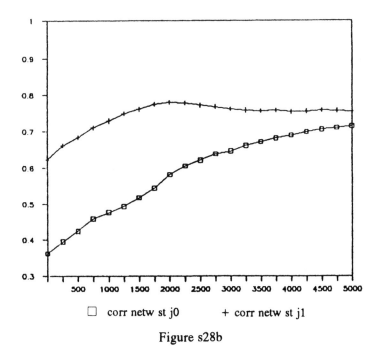

□ corr netw st j0   + corr netw st j1

Figure s28b

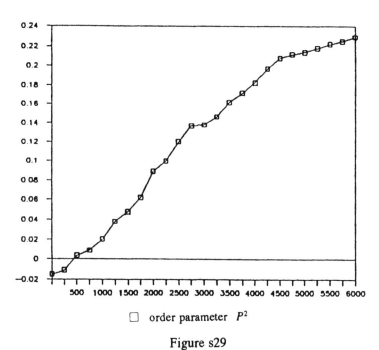

□ order parameter P^2

Figure s29

i'0: 0,1,2,3,4
i'1: 0,1,2,3,4, 5,6
i'2: 0,1,2,3,4, 7,8
i'3: 0,1,2,3,4, 9,10
i'4: 0,1,2,3,4, 11,12

As another simple example, consider the following set of items:

j0: 0,1,2
j1: 0,1,   3
j2:   1,2, 4
j3: 0, 2, 5
j4: 0,1,   6

The input in' with

in': 0,1,3,6,7

converges to j1 if the b-value of j0 is 0.4 and if the b-values of the other items are equal to 0.3. However, if the b-value of j0 exceeds 0.5 (while the other b-values remain constant), then in' converges to an asymmetric mixture (figure s28). Hence, if B(tr) is smaller than the overlap between in' and j1, then j1 has to change its representation. Since the order parameter of component 2 increases quickly, it will have to be included in the new representation of j1 (figure s29).

A similar thing holds for j2 and j3. In accordance with the learning rules of our model (more specifically, learning rule L3), the new representations of the items will be given by:

j'0: 0,1,2
j'1: 0,1,2,3,8
j'2: 0,1,2,4,9
j'3: 0,1,2,5,10

We notice that each of the items j'1, j'2 and j'3 receives, along with a *P* of i0, a supplementary *P* that has to ensure that the representations contain an odd number of components. The latter *P* may result from an attentive scanning of the corresponding object (or scene) or by an image schema analysis of the concept (see chapter VI, rule L9).

7.1.1.2 An increase of the b-values of different items

The reorganization considered in 7.1.1.1 also takes place when the b-values of all items remain equal to each other when they increase (i.e. when the familiarity of each of the involved items increases at the same rate). In case of the first example of 7.1.1.1, the input "in" converges to i1 if all b-values are equal to or smaller than 0.4. If, however, all b-values are equal to (or larger than) 0.5, then the input converges to an asymmetric attractor (figure s30) and i1 has to change its representation. In case of the second example of 7.1.1.1, the input in converges to j1 if all b-values are equal to (or smaller than) 0.4. If, however, all b-values are equal to (or larger than) 0.4, then the input converges to an asymmetric attractor (figure s31) and j1 has to change its representation.

7.1.2 A prototype may emerge from a set of clustered items

The point that a prototype may emerge from a set of clustered items has already been illustrated in example 3 of VI,6. Consider the following items:

```
i0: 0,1,2,     5,6
i1: 0,1,  3,   7,8
i2:   1,2, 4,  9,10
i3:     2,3,4, 11,12
i4: 0,    3,4, 13,14
```

The input "in" with

in: 0,1,3,7,8,15,16

converges to i1 if all b-values are equal to (or smaller than) 0.7. However, if these items become more familiar and if their b-values exceed 0.7, then "in" converges to an asymmetric mixture. If the parameter $B(tr)$ of learning rule L3 is smaller than the overlap between i0 and "in", then i0 has to change its representation. Since component 0 and component 4 have rapidly increasing order parameters, they have to be included in the new representation of i0. A similar thing holds for the other items. In accordance with the learning rule of our model, the items obtain the following new representations:

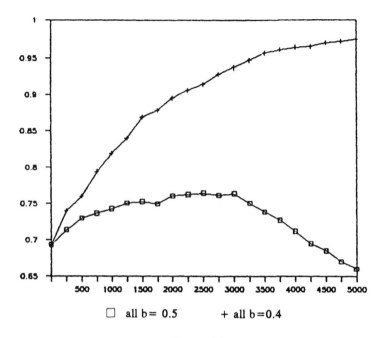

□ all b= 0.5   + all b =0.4

Figure s30

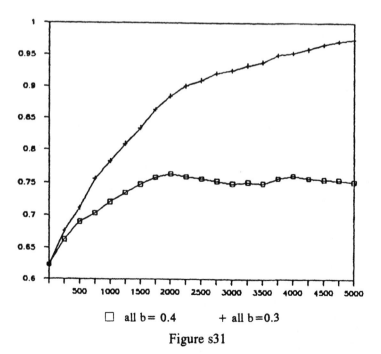

□ all b= 0.4   + all b =0.3

Figure s31

i0: 0,1,2,3,4, 5,6
i1: 0,1,2,3,4, 7,8
i2: 0,1,2,3,4, 9,10
i3: 0,1,2,3,4, 11,12
i4: 0,1,2,3,4, 13,14

As another simple example, consider the following set of items:

j0: 0,1, 3
j1: 1,2, 4
j2: 1,2, 5
j3: 0, 2, 6
j4: 0, 2, 7

The input

in': 0,1,3,8,9

converges to j0 if the b-values of all items are equal to or smaller than 0.4. However, if the items become more familiar and if their b-values become equal to or larger than 0.6, in' converges to an asymmetric mixture (figure s32). The two graphs at the upper side of figure s32 represent the correlation of the network state with i0; for b-values which are equal to 0.6, the network state does not converge to i0, even of the number of updatings that is considered is much larger than in figure s31; if all b-values are equal to 0.5, then the network state converges very slowly to i0 or it converges to an asymmetric mixture with a correlation of more than 0.9 with i0. If B(tr) is smaller than the overlap between in' and j0, then j0 has to change its representation. Since component 2 has a significantly increasing order parameter (figure s32), it has to be included in the new representation of j0. Further, in order to obtain an odd mixture, an additional P has to be included in the new representation of i0 (chapter VI, rule L9). A similar thing holds for the other items. Their new representations are given by:

j'0: 0,1,2, 4, 11
j'1: 0,1,2, 5, 12
j'2: 0,1,2, 6, 13
j'3: 0,1,2, 7, 14
j'4: 0,1,2, 8, 15

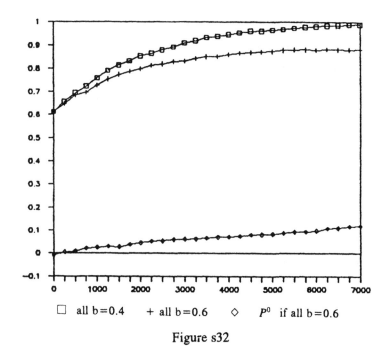

□   all b=0.4   + all b=0.6   ◇ P^0 if all b=0.6

Figure s32

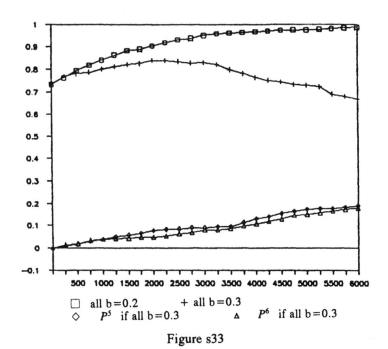

□   all b=0.2   + all b=0.3
◇ P^5 if all b=0.3   ▵ P^6 if all b=0.3

Figure s33

7.1.3 The formation of sub-categories

Consider a set of items which share a subset of P's. This subset may represent, for instance, a superordinate category. The mechanisms of 7.1.1 and 7.1.2 may stimulate the formation of sub-categories. For the sake of concreteness, consider the following items:

i0: 0,1, 2,3,4,5,6
i1: 0,1, 2,3,4,   7,8
i2: 0,1,   3,4,5,   9,10
i3: 0,1, 2,   5,6, 11,12
i4: 0,1, 2,3,   6, 13,14

This set of items is formally equivalent with the items of the first example of 7.1.1.1, except for the fact that the present items share two supplementary P's with each other. Suppose that the b-values of all items are equal to or lower than 0.2. Then, the input

in: 0,1,2,3,4,7,8,13,14

converges to i1 (figure s33). If the items become more familiar, their b-values increase. As soon as the b-values are equal to 0.3, the input does not converge to i1 anymore but to an asymmetric mixture (figure s33; the two upper graphs represent the correlation of the network state with i0). Hence, if B(tr) is lower than the overlap between "in" and i1, then i1 has to change its representation. Figure s33 shows that the order parameters of component 5 and component 6 increase quickly. Hence, they have to be included in the new representation of i0. Similarly, also the representations of i2 and i3 have to change. The new representations are given by:

i'0: 0,1, 2,3,4,5,6
i'1: 0,1, 2,3,4,5,6, 7,8
i'2: 0,1, 2,3,4,5,6, 9,10
i'3: 0,1, 2,3,4,5,6, 11,12

We notice that the change in representation occurs at lower b-values than in the first example of 7.1.1.1. Intuitively, this is plausible. Due to the fact that all items share two supplementary P's, and due to the fact that these P's participate in the network state (note 5), the number of non-zero order parameters of each of the items increases. Hence, the sum-part of their consolidations is larger, so that these sum-parts may contribute the same when they have less weight. Intuitively, this means that category formation has an auto-catalytic property: once a certain amount of categorization has been introduced in a set of items, the formation of sub-categories is facilated. We consider another example. Consider the following items:

```
j0: 0,1,  2,3,4,      7,8
j1: 0,1,  2,3,   5,   9,10
j2: 0,1,    3,4,  6,  11,12
j3: 0,1,      4,5, 6, 13,14
j4: 0,1,  2,   5,6,   15,16
```

Obviously, this set of items is equivalent to the items which have been considered in first example of 7.1.2, except for the fact that the present items share two supplementary P's with each other. Consider, for instance, the following input (that corresponds to j1 plus noise):

```
in':  0,1,2,3,5,9,10,17,18
```

Here, one has that, if all b-values are equal to or lower than 0.3, then the input converges to j1. If the items become more familiar and if their b-values become equal to or larger than 0.4, then the input in converges to an asymmetric mixture rather than to j1 (figure s34; the two upper graphs of the figure represent the correlation of the network state with i1). Hence, if B(tr) is smaller than the overlap between "in" and j1, then j1 has to change its representation. Since components 4 and 6 have quickly increasing order parameters (figure s34), they will participate in the new representation of i1. Similarly, also j0, j2, j3 and j4 have to change their representation if the b-values of all items are equal to or larger than 0.4. The new representations of the items are given by:

```
j'0: 0,1,  2,3,4,5,6,  7,8
j'1: 0,1,  2,3,4,5,6,  9,10
j'2: 0,1,  2,3,4,5,6,  11,12
j'3: 0,1,  2,3,4,5,6,  13,14
j'4: 0,1,  2,3,4,5,6,  15,16
```

Again, we notice that the reorganization takes place at lower b- values than in the first example of 7.1.2.

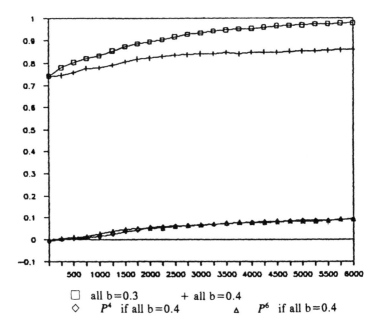

Figure s34

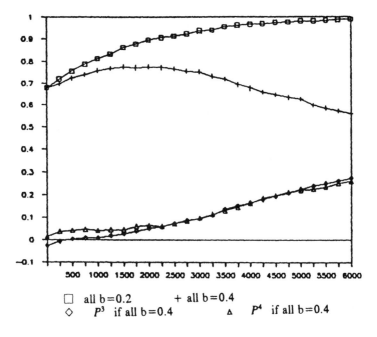

Figure s35

7.2. The effect of the extension of a cluster on the process of clustering

The effects considered in 7.1 occur at lower b-values if the clusters of items contain more elements. In other terms, if a cluster contains many items, then the effects of reorganization will take place at lower degrees of familiarity. The formal reason for this point is that, in case of a large cluster, a larger number of items may contain the P's which are partially shared. Hence, these P's may experience a stronger stimulation to enter in the network state, so that the b-value at which they invade in it may be lower. We illustrate this point with three examples.

a. First, consider the following items:

```
i0: 0,1,2,3,4
i1: 0,1,2,    5,6
i2:   1,2,3   7,8
i3: 0,   3,4, 9,10
i4: 0,   3,4, 11,12
```

This are the same items as in the first example of 7.1.1, except for the fact that the present knowledge base contains the additional item i5. Suppose that all items have the same b-value. Then, the input

in: 0,1,2,5,6,15,16

does not converge to i1 at b-values which are larger than or equal to 0.4 (figure 35). We saw in 7.1.1.2 that, without i5, the critical b-value is about 0.5. Hence, in the present case, the items reorganize at a lower degree of familiarity than in the first example of 7.1.1.2. It is obvious that the new representations will be given by:

```
i'0: 0,1,2,3,4
i'1: 0,1,2,3,4, 5,6
i'2: 0,1,2,3,4, 7,8
i'3: 0,1,2,3,4, 9,10
i'4: 0,1,2,3,4, 11,12
```

b. Second, we consider the items of the first example of 7.1.2. In order to illustrate the present point, we add the items j5 and j6:

j0: 0,1,2,   5,6
j1: 0,1, 3, 7,8
j2:   1,2, 4, 9,10
j3:   2,3,4, 11,12
j4: 0,   3,4, 13,14
j5: 0,1, 3,   15,16
j6:   1,2, 4, 17,18

Suppose that all b-values are equal to each other. Then, in the present case, the input

in: 0,1,3,7,8,19,20

does not lead to a retrieval of i0 anymore for b-values of approximately 0.5 (figure s36; the upper graphs of figure s36 represent the correlation of the network state with i1; the figure illustrates that, for b-values between 0.3 and 0.6, the network shows an intermediate behavior; for instance, for b=0.4, the network state hesitates to converge to i1 but it obtains an overlap higher than 0.9 with i1; for b= 0.5, the network converges to an asymmetric mixture of higher overlap with i1 than in the case b=0.6, but with lower overlap than in the case b=0.4). Hence, in the present case, the change in representation takes place at significantly lower familiarities of the items than in 7.1.2. Obviously, the new representations of the items are given by:

j'0: 0,1,2,3,4, 5,6
j'1: 0,1,2,3,4, 7,8
j'2: 0,1,2,3,4, 9,10
j'3: 0,1,2,3,4, 11,12
j'4: 0,1,2,3,4, 13,14
j'5: 0,1,2,3,4, 15,16
j'6: 0,1,2,3,4, 17,18

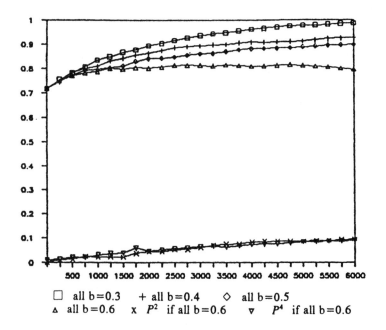

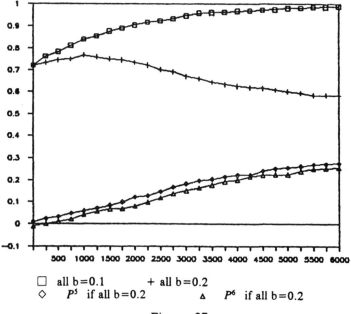

Figure s37

c. We consider the items of the first example of 7.1.3. We extend this knowledge
base with the item k5:

k0: 0,1, 2,3,4,5,6
k1: 0,1, 2,3,4,   7,8
k2: 0,1,   3,4,5,   9,10
k3: 0,1, 2,   5,6, 11,12
k4: 0,1, 2,3,   6, 13,14
k5: 0,1,   4,5,6, 15,16

Then, the input

in'': 0,1,2,3,4,7,9,17,18

does not converge to k1 at b-values which are equal to or larger than 0.2 (figure
s37; the two upper graphs represent the correlation of the network state with i1).
Hence, also here, the reorganization of the representations occurs at lower degrees
of familiarity. We notice that the present point is plausible within the general context
of our model, but that it can also be sustained directly by empirical information (e.g.
Homa and Voghsburg, 1976; Bomba and Siqueland, 1983).

7.3 The representations of new items of a familiar cluster

In the present paragraph, we point out that a cluster of items may influence the
representations of new items. More specifically, if a subset of components is tightly
embedded in the cluster, and if the input corresponding to a new item includes
different P's of this subset, then the representation of the new item will include the
subset entirely. For the sake of concreteness, we consider two examples:

a. First, we consider the items of the first example of 7.1.1.1. Suppose that they
have the same b-values.

i0: 0,1,2,3,4
i1: 0,1,2,   5,6
i2:   1,2,3   7,8
i3: 0,   3,4, 9,10
i4: 0,1,   4, 11,12

Suppose that a new item i4 leads to the following input:

in: 0,1,2,13,14

In accordance with learning rule L1, the first, preliminary representation of the item coincides with in:

i5(prel): 0,1,2,13,14

Suppose that i5(prel) is imprinted with, for instance, an F-value of 0.5 F(sat) and with zero b-value. Now consider the following input:

in': 0,1,2,13,14,15,16

If the b-values of all items (with exclusion of i5) are equal to 0.1, then it converges to i5(prel). However, as soon as the b-values are equal to or exceed 0.2, the input does not converge to i5(prel) anymore (figure s38). Hence, if B(tr) is smaller than the overlap between i5(prel) and in', then item i5 has to change its representation. In accordance with learning rule L3, the new representation of i5 has to include components 3 and 4 because they have rapidly increasing order parameters (figure s38). Hence, the representation of item i5 will be given by:

i5: 0,1,2,3,4, 13,14

b. As a second example, consider the following set of items:

j0: 0,1, 2,3,4, 5,6
j1: 0,1, 2,3,4, 7,8
j2: 0,1, 2,3,4, 9,10
j3: 0,1, 2,3,4, 11,12

Suppose that all b-values are equal to each other. Suppose that a new item j4 has to be learned by the system and that the corresponding input is given by:

in: 2,3,4,13,14

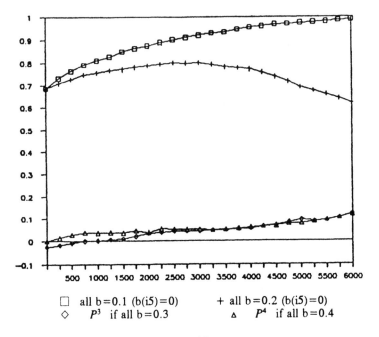

Figure s38

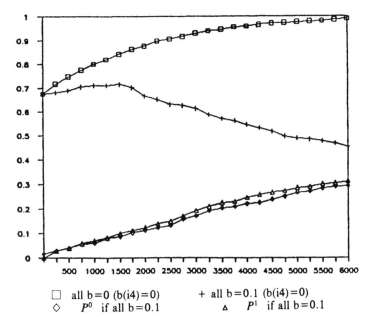

Figure s39

The preliminary representation of j4 coincides with the input:

j4(prel): 2,3,4,13,14

Suppose, for instance, that its F-value equals 0.5 F(sat) and that its b-value is equal to zero. If the b-values of all items are equal to 0, then the input

in': 2,3,4,13,14,15,16

converges to j4(prel). However, as soon as the b-values of the items are larger than 0.1, in' does not converge to j4(prel) anymore (figure s39). Hence, if B(tr) is smaller than the overlap between j4(prel) and in', j4 has to change its representation. Since the order parameters of components 0 and 1 increase quickly, these components have to be included in the new representation of j4 (figure s39). Hence, we obtain:

j4: 0,1, 2,3,4, 13,14

The present example has an interesting interpretation. The components P0 and P1 may express abstract aspects of a concept which are not included in a perceptual input. Still, they may participate immediately in the representation of a new item if the category is sufficiently familiar and elaborated.

7.4 The effects of 7.1, 7.2, 7.3 and cluster formation

7.4.1 The points of 7.1 and 7.2 and clustering

In 7.1 and 7.2, we saw that prototypical subsets of components have the tendency to invade in the representations of the instances of the prototype. As a consequence, these instances tend to share more *P*'s with each other. According to the overlap topology, they become closer to each other. Further, due to the invasion of the prototypical *P*'s, the instances will include a larger number of *P*'s which are not shared by items of other categories. Hence, their overlaps with the latter items decrease. For the sake of illustration, we consider the first example of 7.1.1.1 again:

i0: 0,1,2,3,4
i1: 0,1,2,   5,6
i2:   1,2,3   7,8
i3: 0,   3,4, 9,10
i4: 0,1,   4, 11,12

After reorganization, the new representations of these items are given by:

i'0: 0,1,2,3,4
i'1: 0,1,2,3,4,5,6
i'2: 0,1,2,3,4,7,8
i'3: 0,1,2,3,4,9,10
i'4: 0,1,2,3,4,11,12

The overlap of an arbitrary couple of the latter items is higher than the overlap between the corresponding non-reorganized items. For instance, we have:

$Q(i0,i1) = 0.437$ $Q(i'0,i'1) = 0.687$

$Q(i2,i3) = 0.141$ $Q(i'2,i'3) = 0.531$

Further, consider an item i5 that does not belong to the considered category, but that shares two P's with i1:

i5: 5,6,11,12,13

The overlap between i5 and the items different from i1 is zero before the reorganization and it remains zero after reorganization. The overlap between i'1 and i5, however is smaller than the overlap between i1 and i5:

$Q(i1,i5) = 0.281$ $Q(i'1,i5) = 0.234$

We notice that this point also holds with respect to sub-categories: within a category, items are drawn in their sub-category and they are stimulated to increase their distance to items of other subcategories. Hence, the increase of the b-values of familiar items stimulates them to organize according to a tree-structure.

7.4.2 Point 7.3 and clustering

Also point 7.3 may enhance clustering. If a new item has to incorporate the components of the category or of the context to which it belongs, then it is drawn in the cluster to which other instances of the category or of the context belong. In other terms, in case of a familiar knowledge base, the addition of new items does not lead to a disappearance of the clusters and to homogeneously spread items. On the contrary, the clusters become more elaborate and larger. As a consequence of principle 7.2, the P's which are typical for a cluster increase their tendency to invade in the network state if the number of items of the cluster increases. Intuitively, this means that elaborated clusters have especially high tendency to attract the representations of new items.

7.5 Effects which are external to the system and which enhance conceptual reorganization

7.5.1 Systems external to the system may add P's to the representations of concepts

We are reminded of the fact that our general learning rule includes sub-rules that refer to processes external to the system that we are describing. The representation of a concept may include P's which correspond to simple image schema's. A P that corresponds to an image schema may be shared by the representations of different objects in which this schema can be recognized. Hence, such P's may tie concepts closer to one another. Further, systems external to the module that we are describing may reveal that a particular differentiation between objects does not suffice anymore (e.g. by the production of sensations of dissatisfaction). Then, a subject may scan the corresponding objects in order to include more P's about them. Or, alternatively, he may analyze them with mental image schema's in order to arrive at P's which help to introduce supplementary differentiations.

7.5.2 The interaction of the system with other systems in the ontogenetic process of the redefinition of concepts

Components which are added to the representation of a concept may be suggested by the network itself - due to effects of interference between concepts - or they may be adduced by systems which are external to the network. Sometimes, however, it may be necessary to skip a P from the representation of a concept. In fact, this probably happens quite frequently in conceptual ontogenesis. Children may learn a category after having met a single or a few instances. In first instance, the perceptual attributes of the instances may be associated with the category. Lateron, when the meaning of the concept is adapted to its adult meaning, some of these attributes may have to be skipped from the concept definition. For instance, a young child may memorize that flowers are yellow (Vygotski 1962) or that dogs have spots (Anglin 1977). Then, he ascribes an attribute of the few flowers or dogs that he has met to the entire category of flowers or dogs. In the course of the conceptual learning process, some of these descriptors have to be skipped.

Although our general learning rule does not contain a sub-rule that refers to the possibility to skip P's, it can easily describe this process. For instance, suppose that a child initially only knows his own dog Fido and that Fido has spots. Then, his representation of "dog" may contain a P that corresponds to "spotted fur". Later, he meets more instances of "dog". Probably, some of them do not have spots. Now if he becomes familiar with these instances, the P's which are common to the different instances may form themselves an attractor (learning rule L.4; see 8.1). This way, an attractor appears at a level that is less concrete than the level at which the instances are represented. The interaction with adults stimulates the child to couple this attractor to the verbal label "dog". We notice that this process does not require that P's are skipped from the representation of "Fido". As long as Fido is not forgotten, it may remain represented as a spotted dog. Further, if the concept "dog" changes its representation, the representation of Fido may change accordingly. This is a consequence of the point that the concept "dog" can be a prototypical core of "Fido" and of other instances of dogs. We saw that a prototype has the tendency to invade the representations of its instances. Hence, if, for some or other reason, the prototype gains a P, this may be reflected in the representations of its instances.

The process by which a concept is reduced to a set of P's which are common to different instances may be repeated different times. For instance, this may happen if a prototype for a set of instances of a concept appears not to be a prototype for a new instance. As another possibility, a child may change his representation of a concept if an adult explains that particular perceptual features of a concept are not necessary (note 6). Then, the child may select a subset of P's from the former set of prototypical P's, and the selected subset may be imprinted as an attractor (again, this happens by the way of learning rule L4: see 8.1). The latter may be connected to the verbal label of the category. Since the P's of a prototype must be (at least) partially common to the representations of its instances, and since the number of different instances may increase as a subject gains experience, one might object that, eventually, the prototype may contain only a very few P's. However, here we are reminded again of the fact that P's do not necessarily derive from perception. P's which stem from mental image schema analysis may be especially suited to represent the more abstract aspects of concepts (chapter IV).

Hence, abstract categories and prototypes are subject to a twofold movement. On the one hand, the P's of an instance which do not occur in other instances do not participate in the latest representation of the prototype (old prototypes do not need to be skipped; they may persist as a sub-categories of the new prototype; this way, a hierarchy of prototypes may emerge). Along with this process of "deletion" of P's, prototypes may receive new P's which result from analysis with help of image schema's. Since the latter P's may be less directly linked to perception than the P's which are skipped, one has that prototypes become gradually defined in more abstract terms instead of in terms which are directly apparent from single instances. These points can be sustained with empirical evidence. For instance, in Schwanenflugel, Bjorklund, Guth, Willenborg and Boardman (1984), the concept definitions of children of 5, 7 and 10 year were compared. The authors report a gradual increase with age of children's ability to discriminate between the critical features of a concept, features that are characteristic of several instances and features that are only occasionally associated with a concept. In the same vein, Keil and Batterman (1984) showed that, with age, children give less weight to characteristic features (e.g. a robber uses a gun and is mean) and more weight to defining features (e.g. a robber steals things, regardless of his outlook or of his personality characteristics; see also Bjorklund 1985).

7.6 The general tendency to increase the number of P's in the representations of subordinate concepts

We saw in chapter IV that the mean number of components included in a child's concepts probably increases as the child grows up. This tendency is also found in our model: all principles of 7.1-7.5 illustrate the point that the mean number of P's of the representations of subordinate concepts increases if the corresponding items become more familiar. For the sake of recapitulation, we remember that, according to our theory, there are four ways in which P's may be added. First, the dynamics and the learning rules of the model itself may dictate that particular supplementary P's have to be included in a particular concept. Second, P's may be added to a concept after a mental image schema analysis. Third, P's may be transmitted by the pre-processing system after an object or scene has been scanned attentively. Finally, we are reminded of the point that also P's which correspond to kinesthetic movements as well as P's which correspond to emotions may be included in our frame (chapter IV).

8 The creation and the addressability of abstract concepts

8.1 The creation of abstract concepts

Our general learning rule includes a subrule that specifies how an abstract concept may be extracted from a set of more concrete instances. In the present paragraph, we illustrate this rule with some examples. Further, we show that the possibility to carry out an abstraction operation is included in a natural way in our network (8.2). Consider, for instance, the following knowledge base:

i1: 0,1,2, 3,4,5,6
i2: 0,1,2, 3,4,5,6, 11,12
i3: 0,1,2, 3,4,5,6, 13,14
i4: 0,1,2, 3,4,5,6, 15,16

i5: 0,1,2, 7,8,9,10
i6: 0,1,2, 7,8,9,10, 17,18
i7: 0,1,2, 7,8,9,10, 19,20

Suppose that these items are consolidated and that their F-values are saturated. The item

i0: 0,1,2

can be considered as an abstract category to which all these items belong. Item i1 may interpreted as a basic level category with i2, i3 and i4 as subordinate instances. Similarly, i5 may be interpreted as a basic level concept with i6 and i7 as instances. If i0 is not consolidated yet, the system may decide to start consolidating it. More specifically, learning rule L4 may be applied. We remember that this rule works as follows. First, the network state has to coincide with an instance of i0, for instance, with i1. Subsequently, in order to stimulate the network state to move, the F-value of i1 is decreased for a short while. Next, the b-values of the relevant items are temporary drastically increased (in our simulation, they are put equal to one). Then, the order parameters of the relevant components are considered. Two kinds of P's are candidates for participation in the representation of the abstract category: first, *P*'s with order parameters which are stable and which are significantly positive and, second, *P*'s with order parameters which increase significantly. Components with decreasing order parameters, on the other hand, are excluded from participation in the representation of the abstract concept.

Figure s40 shows indeed that, as concerns the present example, the components of i0 are stable or increase their order parameters. The components of i1 which do not participate in i0, on the other hand, show significantly decreasing order parameters (component 6 behaves like component 3, 4 and 5). Hence, as a consequence of learning rule L4, i0 is consolidated and it starts to play its role as an abstract concept. We consider a second, more complicated example. Consider the following knowledge base:

i2: 0,1,2, 3,4, 7,8,9,10
i3: 0,1,2, 3,4, 7,8,9,10,   23,24
i4: 0,1,2, 3,4, 7,8,9,10,   25,26

i5: 0,1,2, 3,4, 11,12,13,14
i6: 0,1,2, 3,4, 11,12,13,14, 27,28

i7: 0,1,2, 5,6, 15,16,17,18

i8: 0,1,2, 5,6, 19,20,21,22
i9: 0,1,2, 5,6, 19,20,21,22, 29,30

Suppose that i2, i5, i7 and i8 represent basic level concepts. The items i3 and i4 are instances of i2, i6 is an instance of i5 and i9 is an instance of i8. Starting from, for instance, the basic level concept i2, one may try to find a more abstract concept that is not yet consolidated. In order to carry out this search process, the initial network state is put equal to i2. Next, i2 is destabilized and the b-values of all considered items are temporary increased. Then, the order parameters of the relevant *P*'s are considered. If all b-values are temporary put equal to 1, one obtains the evolutions of the order parameters which are depicted in figure s41.

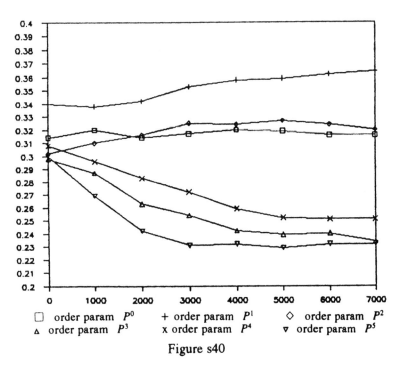

Figure s40

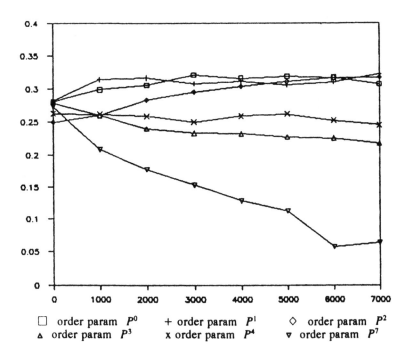

Figure s41

Our simulations show that, within i2, we can differentiate between three groups of
P's (see figure s41). First, components 7, 8, 9 and 10 are no candidates to
participate in the abstract concept(s) to which i2 belongs (in figure s41, this is
illustrated for component 7: its order parameter quickly decays). Second, the
components 0, 2 and 3 will participate in the more abstract concept, since they are
stable (they even slightly increase their order parameters). The abstract concept that
consists of these *P*'s is called i0:

i0: 0,1,2

In the present example, also a second sub-group of *P*'s remains relatively stable,
although these *P*'s have slightly decreasing order parameters. This sub-set is formed
by components 3 and 4. The evolution of these *P*'s differs significantly from the
evolution of components 0, 1 and 2: in the spectrum of possible correlations, they
move to a lower band than the one by which the latter *P*'s are attracted. Hence, in
accordance with learning rule L4, it is possible to introduce a second abstract
concept i1 that is less inclusive than i0:

i1: 0,1,2, 3,4

If we look at the constitution of the items of the present knowledge base, we observe
that i1 can be considered as a (still abstract) sub-category of i0.

8.2 The addressability of abstract concepts

Finally, we point out that an abstraction operation from an instance to a consolidated
superordinate concept can be carried out quite straightforwardly: it suffices to
destabilize the instance. Then, the network state converges to the consolidated item
at the next higher level of abstraction. To illustrate this point, we consider the first
example of 8.1 again and we assume that i0 has been consolidated. We suppose that
the F-values of all items are saturated, and we assume, for instance, the following
b-values:

superordinate concept: $b(i0) = 0$
basic level concepts: $b(i1) = b(i5) = 0.4$
subordinate concepts: $b(i2) = b(i3) = b(i4) = b(i6) = b(i7) = 0.1$

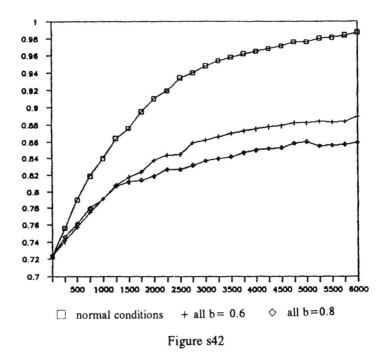

□ normal conditions   + all b= 0.6   ◇ all b=0.8

Figure s42

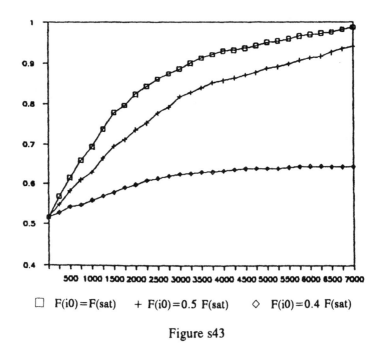

□ F(i0)=F(sat)   + F(i0)=0.5 F(sat)   ◇ F(i0)=0.4 F(sat)

Figure s43

These values express that the basic level concept is more familiar than the concepts at other levels of abstraction and they express that the superordinate concept is not retrieved very often. These values can be considered as "normal conditions" (see chapter IX). For these conditions, an abstraction from the subordinate instance to a basic level concept is made quite quickly. In fact, this point also holds for several other conditions. Only when the b-values of all items of all levels become very high, the classification slows down and becomes problematic. These points are illustrated in figure s42. As long as the b-values of all items are lower than 0.5, i2 is readily classified as an i1. However, if the b-values of all items grow larger than 0.6, the classification becomes more difficult because the P's of i0 tend to participate to a stronger degree in the network state than the P's of i1 which do not belong to i0. Hence, the network state converges to an asymmetric mixture. This effect is strengthened if all b-values become still higher. Figure s42 illustrates this point for all $b = 0.9$.

We consider the transition from the basic level concept i1 to its superordinate category i0. Suppose that the initial network state coincides with i1 and that i1 is destabilized. Then, in normal conditions (i.e. in conditions similar to the ones which are described higher), the network state quickly converges to i0. It is instructive to see what happens if the F-value of i0 is not saturated yet. In other terms, we consider the question how deep i0 has to be imprinted before it can be addressed in an ordinary classification process. Our simulations show that, although the retrieval process slows down gradually when F(i0) decreases, i1 remains classified as an i0 as long as F(i0) is larger than 0.5F(sat). For lower values of F(i0), i0 is not addressed anymore. These points are illustrated in figure s43. We notice that this example suggests an estimate for the initial F-value of a newly learned abstract category.

NOTES

Note 1. In Lucariello and Nelson (1985), category-cues appear not to enhance retrieval. This contrasts with other experiments which show that category-cues bear a significant increase in recall for children (see e.g. Perlmutter and Meyers, 1979; Perlmutter, Sophian, Mitchell and Cavanaugh 1981). Consequently, one has to interpret these experiments with some care. The difference may be due to different factors. One of them is the particular choice of items. Another one is related to the order in which the items are shown to the subjects. If the items are shown in blocked order (as was the case in Lucariello and Nelson, 1985), then categories are salient already during the encoding process, so that the category-cue may be encoded and used in free recall; then, an explicit repetition of the cue by the experimenter may have not much effect (see Perlmutter and Meyers (1979) for evidence in favor of this explanation).

Note 2. Another remarkable point is the non-monotonicity of this trend: elderly adults tend to reverse their preferences towards the one of children. Since this result is in accordance with findings obtained by other authors, (Denney, 1967; Overcast, Murphy, Smiley and Brown, 1975), the suggestion has been made that a thematic or "episodic" organization forms the basic-structure of human knowledge and that a supra-structure of taxonomic organization is superposed on it by formal schooling (e.g. Vygotsky, 1962; Schank, 1976; Brown, 1977; Nelson and Brown, 1978). According to our frame, this point can be interpreted as follows. On the one hand, we will see that familiarity with a domain bears tendencies for cluster formation within this domain (paragraph II,7). This effect is inherent in the dynamics of our model. On the other hand, however, also image schema manipulations may enhance cluster formation (chapter III-IV). If we assume that formal schooling stimulates the use of a relatively complex image schema's, then we have that formal schooling may be a factor that contributes to the taxonomic organization of a knowledge base.

Note 3. Innumerable studies have dealt with the relationship between short-term and long-term memory and a discussion would lead us beyond our scope (see e.g. the review-paper of Dempster, 1985). Our stance agrees, for instance, with Dempster (1985, p.238): *"(In this chapter) I proposed viewing short-term memory as the active portion of long term memory, as many researchers have. "*

Note 4. We notice that the network can model the phenomena of recall only partially: it does not explain how subjects remember the temporal order in which items are presented. There are other interesting phenomena of short term memory which we did not address. For instance, the first items which are mentioned in a free recall test are recalled better than items which are presented afterwards. Also, the items which have been presented lastly are recalled better (e.g. Solso 1988, p.21). These effects can be included in our model if one introduces appropriate time-dependencies in $F(st)$. We will not dwell on this issue.

Note 5. In our example, the components 0 and 1 participate in the input. However, if they would not be present in it, then the dynamics of the network would draw them quickly in the network state. Hence, the argument would still apply.

Note 6. For instance, an adult may stimulate the child to construct mental images in which a concept is accompanied with other perceptual features. If these mental images are imprinted in the memory of the child, it can apply learning rule L8 on his real world instances as well as on the imagined ones. Only the P's which occur with sufficiently high frequency in both kinds of instances are candidates to participate in a new prototype. In special, P's which do not occur in the imagined instances may be skipped from the representation of the prototype.

APPENDIX I

VOTE MIXTURES AND THEIR PROPERTIES

1 Introduction

In this appendix, we study the properties of large binary vectors and of their "vote-mixtures". If a set of large binary patterns is given, one calcluate the order parameters of any other pattern relative to patterns of the given set. Conversely, a set of order parameters does in general not define a unique binary pattern (paragraph 2). However, suppose that a set of verly large randomly generated binary patterns is given (we will refer to these patterns as "groundstates" since they have been used as groundstates in a related context, more specifically in the neural network studied by Amit et al. 1985, 1987a, 1987b). Then, the odd "vote-mixtures" are unequivocally defined by their order parameters (3.2). Our construction schema for vote-mixtures leads to all odd and even symmetric mixture attractors of the Hopfield/Amit network (3.1). We show that the odd as wel as the even vote mixtures are symmetric mixtures of highest overlap with their groundpatters (3.3-3.4). It is possible to derive a general expression for the overlap between two odd vote mixtures (paragraph 4). In paragraph 5, we calculate the fields which are experienced by a groundpattern that occurs in different vote mixtures which are sustained by external fields. Intuitively, a groundpattern is favored to a higher degree if it occurs in more consolidated groundpatterns. We proceed in three steps. First, we consider a groundpattern that occurs in two sustained mixtures. Next, we consider groundpatterns which occur in more than two mixtures. Finally, we calculate the fields experienced by a groundpattern as a function of the number of sustained mixtures in which it occurs. All these case are illustrated by examples.

2 Large binary patterns and order parameters

In many domains of science, the state of a system is decribed as a vector. Consequently, it can be obtained as a sum of its components. In this paper, we consider an alternative representation. It proposes that the components of an object are described by large binary patterns with values +1 and -1. These patterns are generated according to a random schema. More specifically, the i-the value of a pattern P is generated in accordance with the probablity distribution:

$$\rho(P_i) = \frac{1}{2} (\delta(P_i-1)+\delta(P_i+1))$$

(eq.A.1)

If the number of values that participate in these patterns tends to infinity, then two different patterns and tend to be orthogonal (when this number is denoted N, the dispersion of their scalar product decreases like $1/\sqrt{N}$). These patterns are called groundpatterns. The values of a pattern can be interpreted as the activations of neurons of a large, binary network.

For any pattern S , one can calculate the overlap $Q(S,P^\mu)$ with the μ-th groundpattern:

$$Q(S,P^\mu) = \frac{1}{N}\sum_{i=0}^{N} S_i P_i^\mu$$

(eq.A.2)

Hence, if k groundpatterns are given, one can associate a k-tupel with any pattern S . Conversely, a k-tuple of order-parameters does in general not define an unequivocal pattern. Only very special sets of order parameters have this property. In the next paragraph, we show that order parameters that correspond to odd vote-mixtures have this property. These states can be unequivocally defined by the criterion that they are the symmetric states with the largest overlaps with the involved groundpatterns.

3 Vote-mixtures and their order parameters

3.1 Vote-mixtures of an even number of groundpatterns

First, we consider vote-mixtures of n-th order for even n. Since the groundpatterns are generated randomly and since they are supposed to be very large, we can divide the network in 2^n parts of $(1/2^n)N$ neurons so that in each of them, each involved groundpattern is either active in every unit or inactive in every unit. We define an n-th order vote-mixture by the prescription:

a. If, in a part i of the considered partition, at least $n/2 + 1$ groundpatterns are active in all of its units, then the mixture is also active in all of its units.

b. If, in a part i, at least $n/2 + 1$ groundpatterns are inactive in all of its units, then the mixture is also inactive in all of its units.

c. In every part in which exactly $n/2$ groundpatterns are active in all of its units, the mixture has a mean activity equal to a (a is an arbitrary constant between 0 and $+1$).

Consider one such groundpattern. First, we calculate the contributions to Q of the parts involved in points a. and b. of the construction schema. Due to its construction, the vote-mixture is active in

$$a_1 = \frac{1}{2} \sum_{k=0}^{n-1} \binom{n-1}{\frac{n}{2}+k} = \frac{1}{2} 2^{n-1} \qquad \text{(eq.A.3)}$$

parts in which the considered groundpattern is also active, and it is active in

$$a_2 = \frac{1}{2} \sum_{k=0}^{n-1} \left[\binom{n-1}{\frac{n}{2}+k} - \binom{n-1}{\frac{n}{2}} \right] = \frac{1}{2} 2^{n-1} - \binom{n-1}{\frac{n}{2}} \qquad \text{(eq.A.4)}$$

parts in which the considered groundpattern is non-active. For reasons of symmetry, the vote-mixture is inactive in a_1 parts in which the groundpattern is inactive and it is inactive in a_2 parts in which the groundpattern is active. Hence, the contribution of these parts to the overlap between the groundpattern and the vote-mixture is equal to:

$$\frac{1}{N} \frac{N}{2^n} (2a_1 - 2a_2) = \frac{1}{2^{n-1}} \binom{n-1}{\frac{n}{2}} = \frac{1}{2^n} \binom{n}{\frac{n}{2}} \qquad \text{(eq.A.5)}$$

Next, we consider the parts which are involved in point c. of the construction procedure.

i. First, the contribution to Q of a part in which $n/2$ participating groundstates are active and in which the considered groundstate is active is equal to:

$$\frac{1}{N} (\frac{N}{2^n})(2a-1)$$

ii. Second, the contribution to Q of a part in which $n/2$ participating groundstates are active and in which the considered one is inactive is equal to:

$$-\frac{1}{N}(\frac{N}{2^n})(2a-1)$$

Now we notice that there are as many parts in which c. applies and in which the considered groundstate is active as there are parts in which c. applies and in which the considered groundstate is inactive. Hence, these contributions cancel and the overlap between the vote-mixture and its groundstate is equal to:

$$m^{Am}(n) = \frac{1}{2^n}\begin{bmatrix} n \\ n/2 \end{bmatrix} \tag{eq. A.6}$$

3.2 Vote mixtures of an odd number of groundpatterns

Next, we consider the case of an n-th order mixture with n odd. Again, we divide the network in 2^n parts so that in each of them, each involved groundpattern has either mean activation one or mean activation zero. The prescription to obtain a vote mixture is as follows (note 1):

a. In each part of the considered partition in which at least $n/2 + 1/2$ of the groundpatterns are active in every unit, the vote-mixture is also active in every unit.

b. In the units of all other parts, the vote-mixture is inactive.

We notice that this prescription corresponds to a kind of "vote"- operation: if more than half of the groundpatterns vote positive, then the mixture takes a positive value; if more than half of the groundpatterns votes negative, then the mixture pattern is inactive. Consider such a groundstate. In

$$a_1 = \sum_{k=0}^{\frac{n-1}{2}}\begin{bmatrix} n-1 \\ \frac{n-1}{2}+k \end{bmatrix} = \frac{1}{2}2^{n-1} \tag{eq. A.7}$$

parts of the partition, the considered groundstate as well as the mixture are active.

In

$$a_2 = \sum_{k=1}^{\frac{n-1}{2}} \left(\begin{array}{c} n-1 \\ \frac{n-1}{2}+k \end{array} \right) = \frac{1}{2}2^{n-1} - \left(\begin{array}{c} n-1 \\ \frac{n-1}{2} \end{array} \right) \qquad \text{(eq.A.8)}$$

parts, the mixture is in active and the groundstate is active. For reasons of symmetry, both the considered groundstate and the mixture are inactive in a_1 parts, in a_2 parts, the mixture is active and the considered groundstate is inactive. Hence, the overlap between the considered groundstate and the mixture is given by:

$$2(\frac{1}{N})N\frac{1}{2^n}(a_1 - a_2) = \frac{1}{2^{n-1}}\left(\begin{array}{c} n-1 \\ \frac{n-1}{2} \end{array} \right) = m^*(n)$$

$$\text{(eq.A.9)}$$

This number is equal to the overlap of an odd symmetric attractor of the Hopfield/Amit-network with its groundpatterns (Amit et al. 1985). We point out that the odd vote-mixture of order n coincides with one of the even vote-mixtures of n-1 of the involved groundpatterns. It is selected by the constraint that the additional groundpattern must have the same overlap with the vote mixture. We notice that the present argument does not guarantee that an odd vote-mixture of order n is the only pattern that has overlaps with its groundpatterns which are given by formula (eq.A.9): it might be that a construction schema different form the present one would lead to other odd symmetric mixtures with similar overlaps. In the next paragraph, however, we show that this is not possible.

3.3 The odd vote-mixtures represent a unique network state

Consider an odd mixture M of the groundpatterns $P^1,...,P^n$; suppose that M is obtained in accordance with the construction schema of 3.1.4. Suppose that an alternative construction schema leads to a symmetric mixture M' that has also Amit-overlaps (eq.A.9) with the same groundpatterns. We show that M' must be equal to M and, hence, that the odd vote-mixtures represent a unique network state. Consider the network partition introduced in the previous paragraph and that corresponds to M . We proceed in three steps.

i. First, we suppose that M' differs from M in only a single part P of the partition. Further, we suppose that M is active in every unit of P. In other terms, in part P, the mean activity of M is one and the mean activity of M' is lower than one. In the parts where M is always inactive, M and M' do not differ. Since M is active in P, one has that at least $n/2 + 1/2$ groundpatterns are active in all of its units. We call the set of these groundpatterns G. Then, the fact that M' is not active in every unit of P entails that it has lower overlap with the groundpatterns of G than M. Hence, the overlap of M' with these groundpatterns is lower than the Amit-overlap (eq. A.9). Further, we notice that the sum of the overlaps between M' and the groundpatterns is lower than the sum of the overlaps between M and the groundpatterns. If we denote the present M' by M^1, we have:

$$\sum_{\nu=1}^{n} Q(M^1, P^\nu) < \sum_{\nu=1}^{n} Q(M, P^\nu) = n.m^*(n) \qquad \text{(eq.A.10)}$$

Since the right hand expression depends only on the order parameters, this quantity is the same for each symmetric mixture with Amit-overlaps with its components. Hence, every pattern M^1 that appears in the left side of the inequality (eq.A.10) can not be a mixture with Amit-overlaps with its groundpatterns.

ii. Second, we suppose that M' differs from M in more than one part in which M is always active but that it is equal to M in the parts where M is always inactive. Suppose, more specifically, that M' differs from M in the parts P^1 and P^2. We will refer to this M' as M^2. Consider the state M^1 which is equal to M except in P^1 where it is equal to M^2. It is easy to see that:

$$\sum_{\nu=1}^{n} Q(M^2, P^\nu) < \sum_{\nu=1}^{n} Q(M^1, P^\nu) \qquad \text{(eq.A.11)}$$

Suppose the mean activation of M^2 in P^2 is a with $a < 1$. Then, the contribution of P^2 to the considered sum in case of M^2 is equal to:

$$\frac{1}{2^n}(\sum_{V+} (2a-1) \; - \; \sum_{V-} (2a-1) \;)$$

$$= p(2a-1) \; - \; (n-p)(2a-1) \; = \; (2p-n)(2a-1)$$

(eq.A.12)

$V+$ denotes the set of groundpatterns which are always active in P^2 ; its number of elements is denoted p
$V-$ denotes the set of groundpatterns which are always inactive in P^2 ; it has n-p elements

On the other hand, the contribution of P^2 to the considered sum in case of M^1 is equal to:

$$\frac{1}{2^n}(\sum_{V+} 1 \; - \; \sum_{V-} 1) \; = \; 2p-n$$

Since for part P^2 one has $p > n/2$, and since M^1 and M^2 differ only in this part, we conclude that expression (eq.A.11) holds indeed. Hence, due to (eq.A.10) and (eq.A.11), M^2 can not be a mixture with Amit-overlaps with its groundpatterns. This point is easily generalized for M^2 's which differ from M in more than two parts in which M is positive.

iii. Consider a state M^3 which differs from M in parts where M is active in every unit as well as in parts in which M is inactive in every unit. Consider the state M^2 which is identical to M^3 in all parts where M is active and which is identical to M in all parts where M is inactive. M^2 is a state of the kind considered in ii. We show that

$$\sum_{\nu=1}^{n} Q(M^3,P^\nu) \; < \; \sum_{i=1}^{n} Q(M^2,P^\nu)$$

(eq.A.13)

Consider a part R in which M^2 is inactive in every unit and in which M^3 has a mean activity $a > 0$. The contribution of R to the sum of overlaps between M^3 and the groundpatterns is equal to:

$$\sum_{P^{\nu} \in P+} Q(M^3, P^{\nu}) + \sum_{P^{\nu} \in P-} Q(M^3, P^{\nu}) = (2p'-n)(1-2a)$$

(eq.A.14)

P- is the set of groundpatterns which are inactive everywhere in R
P+ is the set of groundpatterns which are active everywhere in R
p' is the number of elements of P-

Similarily, the contribution of R to the sum of overlaps between M^2 and the groundpatterns is equal to:

$$\sum_{P^{\nu} \in P+} Q(M^2, P^{\nu}) + \sum_{P^{\nu} \in P-} Q(M^2, P^{\nu}) = 2p'-n$$

(eq.A.15)

Due to the definitions of the respective mixture states, we have that the number p' of groundpatterns which are inactive everywhere in R is striclty larger than the number of groundpatterns which are active everywhere in R. Hence, for each part R in which M^2 and M^3 differ and in which M is inactive, the sum of overlaps between M^3 and the groundpatterns is smaller than the sum of overlaps between M^2 and the groundpatterns. Consequently, as concerns M^3, this sum can never obtain the value which is typical for Amit-overlaps. Hence, it is demonstrated that also an alternative M' of the kind considered in iii. can not be a mixture with Amit-overlaps with its groundpatterns. This demonstrates the theorem.

3.4 The odd vote-mixtures are odd symmetric mixtures of maximal overlap with the participating groundstates

Consider an odd symmetric n-th order mixture M' that has no Amit-overlaps with its groundpatterns. Then, the argument of the previous paragraph shows that its overlaps with its groundpatterns are lower than in case of the vote-mixture. Indeed, if it is different from the vote-mixture, then it differs from it in at least one part of the partition introduced in 3.1.4. Then, the demonstration of the theorem 3.2 shows that the sum of overlaps with its groundpatterns is necessarily smaller than in case of the vote-mixture. Since M' is supposed to be symmetric, this entails that its overlap with each of the involved groundpatterns is smaller than the Amit-overlap $m^*(n)$.

3.5 The even vote-mixtures are even symmetric mixtures with highest overlap with their groundpatterns

Next, we consider the even symmetric mixtures. We show that the even mixtures which are generated by the procedure of 3.1.3 are the even symmetric mixtures which have highest overlap with their groundpatterns. In fact, the argument is quite similar to the one of 3.3. Again, we consider the partition introduced in 3.1.3. Consider a mixture M' which differs from any mixture M that is generated according to the construction schema of 3.1.3. We use the notation N' to refer to the restriction of the original network N to the parts where not exactly $n/2$ groundpatterns of M are active.

I. First, we consider the case in which M' differs from M in at least one of the parts of N'. Like in 3.3, we differentiate between three subcases.

i. First, we suppose that the alternative symmetric mixture M' differs from the Amit mixture M in exactly one of the parts of N' and that M is active in this part. Then, the same argument as in 3.3 shows that, as far as concerns the network N' (and as far as concerns the restriction of all patterns to this network), the sum of the overlaps of M' with its groundpatterns is smaller than the sum of the overlaps of M with its groundpatterns.

ii. As far as concerns the network N', point i. can generalized like in 3.3 to the case in which M' differs from M in more than one part in which M is active.

iii. Similarily, it can be shown like in 3.3 that, as far as concerns the restriction of all patterns to N', if M' differs from M in a part where M is inactive, then the sum of the overlaps of   with the groundpatterns is striclty smaller than the sum of the overlaps of M with the groundpatterns.

It follows from these points that, if a mixture M' differs from M in N', then the sum

$$\sum_{\nu=1}^{n} Q(M'/N, V^\nu/N')$$

is smaller than the sum

$$\sum_{\nu=1}^{n} Q(M/N', V^\nu/N')$$

("/" denotes the restriction operator)

Hence, if M' must have Amit-overlaps with its groundpatterns, then the sum of the overlaps of M' with its groundpatterns in the part N\N'must be strictly positive. However, this is impossible for reasons of symmetry. For every groundpattern P^ν that contributes a positive amount s to this sum, one can find another groundpattern P^μ that contributes the amount -s. The latter groundpattern is active in every part of N\N' where P^ν is inactive and it is inactive in every part of N\N' where P^ν is active. Hence, the sum of the overlaps of M' with the groundpatterns in N\N' is equal to zero. Hence, when taken over the entire network N, the sum of the overlaps of M' with its groundpatterns is always smaller than $n.m^{Am}(n)$.

II. Second, consider a mixture M' that is in accordance with the construction schema of 3.1.3 in N' but not in the parts of N in which exactly n/2 patterns are active. Suppose that the mean activities of M' in these parts are given by:

$$a_1,...,a_{\binom{n}{\frac{n}{2}}}$$

We suppose that, by an appropriate choice of the indices, the considered parts are arranged in such a way that the mean activities of M' in them decrease:

$$a_1 \geq ... \geq a_{\binom{n}{\frac{n}{2}}}$$

Since M' differs from M , at least two numbers in this sequence are different form each other. Now due to the nature of the network partition, one can find a groundpattern P^ν which is always inactive in the first

$$\frac{1}{2}\binom{n}{\frac{n}{2}}$$

of these parts and which is active in the remaining ones. Obviously, the overlap of M' with this groundpattern is lower than $m^*(n)$. Hence, also case II is excluded. This proves the theorem.

4 Calculation of the overlaps between odd vote-mixtures

4.1 Derivation of the general formula

We show that the overlap between two odd vote-mixtures of can be expressed in terms of:

i. the number of groundpatterns which they share.
ii. the orders of the vote-mixtures

Consider a vote-mixture M^1 of order p and a vote-mixture M^2 of order q (p and q are supposed to be odd). Suppose that they share r groundpatterns. Then, their overlap can be calculated as follows.

1. First, we notice that, after a rearrangement of the indices, the r common groundpatterns can be partitioned in 2^r parts so that each of the groundpatterns is either always active or always inactive in these parts (this point is obvious from the argument of 3.1). Likewise, the p-r remaining groundpatterns of M^1 can be partitioned in 2^{p-r} parts so that a similar property holds. Finally, the same point holds for the q-r non-common groundpatterns of M^2 .

2. We calculate the probability p(+ +) that both M^1 and M^2 are positive in a unit i of the network (eq.A.16):

$$p(M_i^1 = +1 \wedge M_i^2 = +1) =$$

$$= p(((0+(i)) \vee (1+(i)) \vee ... \vee (r+(i))) \wedge M_i^1 = +1 \wedge M_i^2 = +1)$$

$$= p((0+(i)) \wedge M_i^1 = +1 \wedge M_i^2 = +1) + ... + p((r+(i)) \wedge M_i^1 = +1 \wedge M_i^2 = +1)$$

The abbreviation "s+(i)" stands for "s common groundpatterns are positive in i". The first term of (eq.A.16) is equal to:

$$\frac{1}{2^r} \binom{r}{0} \cdot \frac{1}{2^{p-r}} \sum_{\substack{x-1 > \frac{p}{2} \\ x=0,...,p-r}} \binom{p-r}{x} \cdot \frac{1}{2^{q-r}} \sum_{\substack{y-1 > \frac{p}{2} \\ y=0,...,q-r}} \binom{q-r}{y}$$

More general, the s-th term is equal to:

$$\frac{1}{2^r}\binom{r}{s}\cdot\frac{1}{2^{p-r}}\sum_{\substack{x+s>\frac{p}{2}\\x=1,\ldots,p-r}}\binom{p-r}{x}\cdot\frac{1}{2^{q-r}}\sum_{\substack{y+s>\frac{q}{2}\\y=1,\ldots,q-r}}\binom{q-r}{y}$$

The probability $p(++)$ is obtained as a sum over this expression for s going from zero to r. Since the probability $p(++)$ and the overlap Q are related by:

$$Q = 4p(++) - 1$$

we obtain for the overlap between M^1 and M^2 (eq.A.17):

$$Q = -1 + \frac{1}{2^{p+q-r-2}}\sum_{s=0}^{r}\binom{r}{s}\sum_{\substack{x+s>\frac{p}{2}\\x=0,\ldots,p-r}}\binom{p-r}{x}\sum_{\substack{y+s>\frac{q}{2}\\y=0,\ldots,q-r}}\binom{q-r}{y}$$

4.2 Some examples

We give some examples to illustrate the formula of the previous paragraph. Several of these examples have been used in the course of the psychological part of our text (chapters X, XII and XIII). First, we consider some examples for which p=q (4.2.1); subsequently, we give some examples in which p and q are different (4.2.2).

4.2.1 Examples in which p=q

1. Suppose that p=3 and q=3. We obtain:

	r=1	r=2
Q	.25	.5

2. Suppose that p=5 and q=5. We obtain:

	r=1	r=2	r=3	r=4
Q	.14	.281	.437	.625

3. Suppose that $p=7$ and $q=7$. We obtain:

	$r=1$	$r=2$	$r=3$	$r=4$	$r=5$
Q	.098	.196	.297	.406	.531

	$r=6$
Q	.687

4. Suppose that $p=9$ and $q=9$. We obtain:

	$r=1$	$r=2$	$r=3$	$r=4$	$r=5$
Q	.075	.15	.226	.305	.39

	$r=6$	$r=7$	$r=8$
Q	.482	.59	.727

5. Suppose that $p=11$ and $q=11$. We obtain:

	$r=1$	$r=2$	$r=3$	$r=4$	$r=5$
Q	.061	.121	.182	.245	.31

	$r=6$	$r=7$	$r=8$	$r=9$	$r=10$
Q	.379	.453	.535	.631	.754

6. Suppose that $p=13$ and $q=13$. We obtain:

	$r=1$	$r=2$	$r=3$	$r=4$	$r=5$
Q	.051	.102	.153	.205	.259

	$r=6$	$r=7$	$r=8$	$r=9$	$r=10$
Q	.314	.372	.433	.5	.574

	$r=11$	$r=12$
Q	.661	.774

4.2.2 Examples in which p is different from q

1. Suppose that p=5 and q=3. We obtain:

	r=1	r=2	r=3
Q	.187	.375	.625

2. Suppose that p=7 and q=3. We obtain:

	r=1	r=2	r=3
Q	.156	.312	.5

3. Suppose that p=9 and q=5. We obtain:

	r=1	r=2	r=3	r=4	r=5
Q	.102	.205	.312	.430	.570

4. Suppose that p=11 and q=5. We obtain:

	r=1	r=2	r=3	r=4	r=5
Q	.092	.185	.280	.383	.5

5. Suppose that p=11 and q=5. We obtain:

	r=1	r=2	r=3	r=4	r=5
Q	.085	.169	.256	.349	.451

6. Suppose that p=15 and q=5. We obtain:

	r=1	r=2	r=3	r=4	r=5
Q	.079	.157	.283	.322	.415

4.3 Properties of overlaps between vote mixtures

We use vote-mixtures in order to represent multi-component states. This entails that it is desirable that vote-mixtures have particular metric properties. For instance, we would want that the overlap between vote mixtures increases as they share more components. Further, we would want that the overlap between vote mixtures decreases when the number of non-shared groundpatterns increases. These properties are considered in the present paragraph.

4.3.1 Property 1

Consider three vote mixtures M^1 , M^2 and M^3 . Suppose that M^1 and M^2 are composed of p components and that M^3 contains q components. Further, suppose that M^1 shares r components with M^3 and that M^2 shares r' components with M^3 , and suppose that $r > r'$. Then, the overlap Q_1 between M^1 and M^3 is larger than the overlap Q_2 between M^2 and M^3 .

We write down the overlaps which are considered in this proposition (eq. A. 18a,b):

$$Q_1 = -1 + \frac{1}{2^{p+q-r-2}} \sum_{s=0}^{r} \begin{bmatrix} r \\ s \end{bmatrix} \sum_{\substack{x+s > \frac{p}{2} \\ x=0,\ldots,p-r}} \begin{bmatrix} p-r \\ x \end{bmatrix} \sum_{\substack{y+s > \frac{q}{2} \\ y=0,\ldots,q-r}} \begin{bmatrix} q-r \\ y \end{bmatrix}$$

$$Q_2 = -1 + \frac{1}{2^{p+q-r'-2}} \sum_{s=0}^{r'} \begin{bmatrix} r' \\ s \end{bmatrix} \sum_{\substack{x+s > \frac{p}{2} \\ x=0,\ldots,p-r'}} \begin{bmatrix} p-r' \\ x \end{bmatrix} \sum_{\substack{y+s > \frac{q}{2} \\ y=0,\ldots,q-r'}} \begin{bmatrix} q-r' \\ y \end{bmatrix}$$

This proposition can be demonstrated straightforwardly if $q=r$ and if $r'=q-1$. A similar point holds for concrete values of p, q and r which are relatively small. For larger values of these variables, we have to make recourse to numerical computations. The numerous computations that we have made (note 2) were all in agreement with this proposition (this is illustrated in the tables of 4.2).

4.3.2 Property 2

Consider three mixtures M^1, M^2 and M^3. The mixture levels of these concepts are respectively p, q and r. Suppose that all components of M^3 participate in M^1 and in M^2, and suppose that q is larger than p. Then, the overlap Q_1 between M^1 and M^3 is larger than the overlap Q_2 between M^2 and M^3.

This property can be demonstrated. Obviously, it is demonstrated if we show that it holds for q=p+2 (notice that that the smallest difference between p and q is two since these numbers are bound to be odd). We consider the expression that gives the overlap between M^1 and M^3. An argument similar to the one of 4.1 leads to the following expression:

$$Q_1 = -1 + \frac{4}{2^p} \sum_{\substack{s=0,\dots,r \\ s>\frac{r}{2}}} \binom{r}{s} \sum_{\substack{x+s>\frac{p}{2} \\ x=0,\dots,p-r}} \binom{p-r}{x}$$

(eq.A.19)

Similarly, for Q_2, we have:

$$Q_2 = -1 + \frac{4}{2^{p+2}} \sum_{\substack{s=0,\dots,r \\ s>\frac{r}{2}}} \binom{r}{s} \sum_{\substack{x+s>\frac{p+2}{2} \\ x=0,\dots,p+2-r}} \binom{p+2-r}{x}$$

(eq.A.20)

We are reminded of the fact that the second factor of these equations expresses the number of cases (for the partition introduced in 4.1) in which the first mixture state is positive for a given value of s. We point out a relation between the parts in (eq.A.19) and in (eq.A.20) which are at issue in the second summation. In (eq.A.19), each of the 2^r parts which are at issue in the first summation are divided in 2^{p-r} parts by the partition from which the second term is derived. We call the latter partition P1. In (eq.A.20), each part of the first term is divided in 2^{p+2-r} parts by the partition P2 which is involved in the second term.

We assume that all groundstates of M^1 participate in M^2. If the theorem is proved for this case, the it holds for the case in which the assumption does not hold, since (eq.A.19) and (eq.A.20) do not depend on it. If the assumption of inclusion is accepted, then, each part of P1 includes four parts of P2: a part in which the two additional groundpatterns of M^2 are positive, a part in which the first one is positive and the second one negative, a part in which the first one is negative and in which the second one is postive, and, finally, a part in which both additional groundpatterns are negative. These four parts are of equal size.

Equations (eq.A.19) and (eq.A.20) contain the same number of terms in the first summation ($s=0,..., r$). We differentiate between four cases for s:

a. $s > (p+1)/2$

In the parts P1 of the network where this relation holds, M^1 as well as M^2 are always positive. Hence, for these values of s, the second summations in (eq.A.19) and (eq.A.20) are equal to each other (we pointed out that the number of parts of P2 is four times the number of parts of P1; however, the normalizing factor in (eq.A.19) is four times smaller than the normalizing factor in (eq.A.20); this bears equal values for the second summations).

b. $s = (p+1)/2$

In the parts (according to P1) of the network where this relation holds, M^1 is always positive, but M^2 is not. To see the latter point, consider such a part of P1. We pointed out that it corresponds to four parts of P2. In one of them, M^2 is negative: if the two additional groundpatterns of M^2 are negative, then the number of groundpatterns of M^2 which are positive in this part is smaller than half of the mixture level of M^2. In the three other P2-parts, M^2 is positive. Hence, the considered term s gives a larger contribution to Q_1 than to Q_2.

c. $r/2 < s < (p+1)/2$

In the parts P1 where this relation holds, four further sub-cases have to be considered

c.1. x satisfies the relation $s+x > \dfrac{n_1}{2} + \dfrac{1}{2}$

If a part of the partition P1 satisfies this condition, then both M^1 and M^2 are positive in it. Hence, in these parts, the contributions to the respective overlaps are equal to each other.

c.2. x satisfies the relation $s + x = \dfrac{n_1}{2} + \dfrac{1}{2}$

Consider a P1-part in which this condition is satisfied. In such a part, M^1 is positive but M^2 is not always positive. Consider the four P2-parts which are associated with this P1-part. In the P2-part that corresponds to the addition of two negative groundpatterns, M^2 is negative. In the three other P2-parts, M^2 is positive.

c.3 x satisfies the relation $s + x = \dfrac{n_1}{2} - \dfrac{1}{2}$

If this relation holds for a P1-part in which this relation holds, then M^1 is negative in it. However, in one of the P2-parts which are associated with this P1-part, M^2 is positive: if the two additional patterns of M^2 are positive, then M^2 is positive.

c.4 x satisfies the relation $s + x < \dfrac{n_1}{2} - \dfrac{1}{2}$

In P1-parts that correspond to these values of s and x, both M^1 and M^2 are negative. Hence, these parts give a zero contribution to the respective overlaps.

Consider the cases c.2 and c.3. Supose that d denotes the value of x for which c.2 applies $d = ((n_1 + 1)/2) - s$. Then, the number of P2-parts in which M^1 is positive in case c.2 is given by:

$$a = 4 \begin{pmatrix} n_1 - r \\ d \end{pmatrix}$$

The number of P2-parts in which M^2 is positive in case c.2 is equal to:

$$b = 3 \begin{pmatrix} n_1 - r \\ x \end{pmatrix}$$

The number of P2-parts in which M^2 is positive in case c.3 is given by:

$$c = \begin{pmatrix} n_1 - r \\ d - 1 \end{pmatrix}$$

Now we have that $a > b + c$. In order to see this, we notice that:

$$\begin{pmatrix} n_1 - r \\ d \end{pmatrix} > \begin{pmatrix} n_1 - r \\ d-1 \end{pmatrix}$$

since, as a condition on the first summation, $s > r/2$. Hence, case c leads to a strictly larger contribution to Q_1 than to Q_2. This proves the theorem.

It is tempting to suggest the following generalization of the present theorem:

Consider three mixtures M^1, M^2 and M^3. The mixture levels of these groundpatterns are respectively n_1, n_2 and n_3. Suppose that M^1 as well as M^2 share r groundpatterns with M^3, and suppose that n_2 is larger than n_1. Then, the overlap Q_1 between M^1 and M^3 is larger than the overlap Q_2 between M^2 and M^3.

The validity of this proposition has been tested for several examples. This point is illustrated in the following table. Two mixtures of level p and q are considered. The number of common groundpatterns is equal to r.

p	q	Q (r=1)	Q (r=2)
3	3	.25	.5
5	3	.185	.375
7	3	.156	.312
9	3	.136	.273
11	3	.123	.246
13	3	.112	.225

p	q	Q (r=1)	Q (r=2)	Q (r=3)	Q(r=4)
5	5	.140	.281	.437	.625
7	5	.117	.234	.359	.5
9	5	.102	.205	.312	.429
11	5	.092	.184	.280	.382
13	5	.084	.163	.256	.348
15	5	.078	.157	.237	.322

p	q	Q (r=1)	Q (r=2)	Q (r=3)	Q(r=4)
7	7	.097	.195	.296	.406
9	7	.085	.170	.258	.351
11	7	.076	.153	.232	.314
13	7	.070	.140	.212	.287
15	7	.065	.130	.197	.265
17	7	.061	.122	.184	.248

p	q	Q (r=5)	Q (r=6)
7	7	.531	.687
9	7	.453	.570
11	7	.402	.5
13	7	.365	.451
15	7	.337	.414
17	7	.315	.385

p	q	Q (r=1)	Q (r=2)	Q (r=3)	Q(r=4)
9	9	.074	.149	.225	.305
11	9	.067	.134	.202	.273
13	9	.061	.123	.185	.249
15	9	.057	.114	.172	.231
17	9	.053	.107	.161	.216
19	9	.050	.101	.152	.204

p	q	Q (r=5)	Q (r=6)	Q (r=7)	Q(r=8)
9	9	.389	.482	.589	.726
11	9	.347	.426	.514	.617
13	9	.316	.387	.463	.548
15	9	.292	.356	.425	.5
17	9	.273	.332	.395	.462
19	9	.257	.313	.371	.432

5 Calculation of the fields experienced by components which occur in different mixtures

A pattern may experience a field h^ν. This means that a scalar is defined in each unit of the network over which the pattern is ranged. If, in each unit, this scalar has the sign of the activation value of the pattern, then we say that the pattern is "sustained" by the field. As a special case, a vote-mixture may be sustained by a field of constant magnitude (i.e.: for all i and j, $h_i^\nu = h_j^\nu$). Different fields may be superposed on each other. For instance, suppose that two vote-mixtures M^1 and M^2 are sustained by a field h^1 and h^2, respectively. Then, we can define a total field by the prescription $h = h^1 + h^2$.

In the network model that we propose, each learned pattern experiences a consolidating field, and each pattern tends to become realized to the extent that it experiences a sustaining field. In the present paragraph, we show that, if a groundpattern occurs in different consolidated patterns, then it shows a relatively high tendency to become realized. This property is used to describe the fact that prototypical cores of properties may have higher tendency to become realized than groundpatterns which occur in a single learned pattern only.

5.1 The case of components which occur in two sustained vote-mixtures

Consider a groundpattern P^1 that occurs in two vote-mixtures M^1 and M^2. Suppose that these vote-mixtures have r groundmodes in common and that M^1 is of order p and M^2 of order q (p and q are odd numbers). Further, suppose that both mixtures M^k (k = 1,2) are sustained by external fields h^k with

$$h^k = h^k M^k$$

For a neuron i of the network, there are four possibilities as concerns the way these fields combine their effects:

a. $M_i^1 = +1$ and $M_i^1 = +1$; then neuron i experiences an external field equal to $h^1 + h^2$ (possibility (+ +))

b. $M_i^1 = +1$ and $M_i^2 = -1$; then neuron i experiences an external field equal to $h^1 - h^2$ (possibility (+ -))

c. $M_i^1 = -1$ and $M_i^2 = +1$; then neuron i experiences an external field equal to $-h^1 + h^2$ (possibility (-+))

d. $M_i^1 = -1$ and $M_i^2 = -1$; then neuron i experiences an external field equal to $-h^1 - h^2$ (possiblity (--))

Now we argue that, if P^1 participates in M^1 as well as in M^2 , then the external fields have a higher tendency to stimulate P^1 than to inhibit it. More specifically, we point out that:

1. If P^1 is positive in neuron i, then the chance that i experiences a parallel field $h^1 + h^2$ is higher than the chance that it experiences an antiparallel field $-h^1 - h^2$.

2. If P^1 is negative in neuron i, then the chance that i experiences a parallel field $-h^1 - h^2$ is higher than the chance that it experiences an antiparallel field $h^1 + h^2$.

We will demonstrate point 1. Point 2 follows from this demonstration due to the symmetry of the problem. Consider a unit i in which P^1 is active.

i. First, we calculate the probability of case $p(++)$. We have:

$$p(++) = p \{ [((0+(i)) \lor ... \lor ((r-1)+(i))] \land M_i^2 = +1 \land M_i^2 = +1 \}$$

The abbreviation "$s+(i)$" denotes that, along with P^1 , exactly s other common groundpatterns are active in neuron. A calculation similar to the one of 4.1 gives (eq.A.21):

$$p(++) = \frac{1}{2^{p+q+r-1}} \sum_{s=0}^{r-1} \binom{r-1}{s} \sum_{\substack{x+s+1 > \frac{p}{2} \\ x=0,...,p-r}} \binom{p-r}{x} \sum_{\substack{q+s+1 > \frac{q}{2} \\ y=0,...,q-r}} \binom{q-r}{y}$$

ii. Second, we calculate the probablity of case (--). We have:

$$p(--) = p \{[(0-(i)) \lor ... \lor ((r-1)-(i))] \land M_i^1 = -1 \land M_i^2 = -1 \}$$

The abbreviation "s-(i)" denotes that exactly s common groundpatterns (which are different from P^1) are inactive in neuron i. A calculation similar to the one of 4.1 gives (eq.A.22):

$$p(--) = \frac{1}{2^{p-q-r-1}} \sum_{s=0}^{r-1} \binom{r-1}{s} \sum_{\substack{x+s > \frac{p}{2} \\ x=0,\dots,p-r}} \binom{p-r}{x} \sum_{\substack{y+s > \frac{q}{2} \\ y=0,\dots,q-r}} \binom{q-r}{y}$$

Obviously, p(--) is smaller than p(+ +). Hence, we conclude that, if $P_i^1 = +1$, then there is a higher probablity that i will experience a parallel field $h_i^1 + h_i^2$ than an antiparallel field $-h_i^1 - h_i^2$. The probability that such a unit i experiences external fields which are in conflict with each other can be obtained from:

$$p(+ -) + p(- +) = 1 - p(++) - p(--)$$

If $h_i^1 = h_i^2$, then the expression in the left side of this equation gives the probablity that a unit i with $P_i^1 = +1$ experiences a zero external field.

5.2 Some examples

We give some examples which illustrate the formulas of the previous sub-paragraph.

1. Suppose p=3 and q=3. We obtain:

	r=1	r=2
p(+ +)	.562	.625
p(+ -)	.187	.125
p(- +)	.187	.125
p(--)	.062	.125

2. Suppose p=5 and q=5. We obtain:

	r=1	r=2	r=3	r=4
p(+ +)	.473	.508	.547	.549
p(+ -)	.215	.18	.14	.094
p(- +)	.215	.18	.14	.094
p(--)	.098	.133	.172	.219

3. Suppose p=7 and q=7. We obtain:

	r=1	r=2	r=3	r=4	r=5
p(++)	.431	.455	.48	.508	.539
p(+-)	.226	.201	.176	.148	.117
p(-+)	.226	.201	.176	.148	.117
p(--)	.118	.143	.168	.195.	.227

	r=6
p(++)	.578
p(+-)	.078
p(-+)	.078
p(--)	.266

4. Suppose p=9 and q=9. We obtain:

	r=1	r=2	r=3	r=4	r=5
p(++)	.405	.424	.443	.463	.484
p(+-)	.231	.212	.193	.174	.153
p(-+)	.231	.212	.193	.174	.153
p(--)	.132	.151	.17	.19	
.211					

	r=6	r=7	r=8
p(++)	.507	.534	.568
p(+-)	.129	.103	.068
p(-+)	.129	.103	.068
p(--)	.234	.261	.295

5.3 Components which occur in more than two vote-mixtures

The argument of 5.1 can be generalized to the case in which a groundpattern participates in several vote-mixtures which are sustained by external fields. For instance, suppose that a groundpattern P^1 participates in three vote-mixtures M^1, M^2 and M^3. The orders of these vote-mixtures are respectively n_1, n_2 and n_3. Suppose that they share r groundpatterns; further, for the sake of simplicity, suppose that these groundpatterns are the only ones which are shared by any couple of considered mixtures. The external field that sustains M^i (i=1,2,3) is denoted h^i. Again, we suppose that:

$$h^i = h^i M^i$$

Consider a unit i in which $P_i^1 = +1$. There are eight possibilities as concerns the way in which the external fields may combine in i:

a. i may experience a field equal to $h^1 + h^2 + h^3$ (possibility $(+++)$)
b. i may experience a field equal to $h^1 + h^2 - h^3$ (possibility $(++-)$)
c. i may experience a field equal to $h^1 - h^2 + h^3$ (possibility $(+-+)$)
d. i may experience a field equal to $-h^1 + h^2 + h^3$ (possibility $(-++)$)
e. i may experience a field equal to $h^1 - h^2 - h^3$ (possibility $(+--)$)
f. i may experience a field equal to $-h^1 + h^2 - h^3$ (possibility $(-+-)$)
g. i may experience a field equal to $-h^1 - h^2 + h^3$ (possibility $(--+)$)
h. i may experience a field equal to $-h^1 - h^2 - h^3$ (possibility $(---)$)

The probability of each of these cases can be calculated in a way similar to the cases of 5.1. For instance, we have (eq.A.23,a,b,c,d):

$$p(+++) = \frac{1}{2^{n_1 + n_2 + n_3 + 2r - 1}} \cdot$$

$$\sum_{s=0}^{r-1} \binom{r-1}{s} \sum_{\substack{x+s+1 > \frac{n_1}{2} \\ x=0,\dots,n_1-r}} \binom{n_1-r}{x} \sum_{\substack{y+s+1 > \frac{n_2}{2} \\ y=0,\dots,n_2-r}} \binom{n_2-r}{y} \sum_{\substack{z+s+s > \frac{n_3}{2} \\ z=0,\dots,n_3-r}} \binom{n_3-r}{z}$$

$$p(++-) = \frac{1}{2^{n_1 + n_2 + n_3 - 2r - 1}} \cdot$$

$$\sum_{s=0}^{r-1} \binom{r-1}{s} \sum_{\substack{x+s+1 > \frac{n_1}{2} \\ x=0,\dots,n_1-r}} \binom{n_1-r}{x} \sum_{\substack{y+s+1 > \frac{n_2}{2} \\ y=0,\dots,n_2-r}} \binom{n_2-r}{y} \sum_{\substack{z-s-1+r > \frac{n_3}{2} \\ z=0,\dots,n_3-r}} \binom{n_3-r}{z}$$

$$p(+--) = \frac{1}{2^{n_1+n_2+n_3-2r-1}} \cdot$$

$$\sum_{s=0}^{r-1} \binom{r-1}{s} \sum_{\substack{x+s+1>\frac{n_1}{2} \\ x=0,\ldots,n_1-r}} \binom{n_1-r}{x} \sum_{\substack{y-s-1+r>\frac{n_2}{2} \\ y=0,\ldots n_2-r}} \binom{n_2-r}{y} \sum_{\substack{z-s-1+r>\frac{n_3}{2} \\ z=0,\ldots,n_3-r}} \binom{n_3-r}{z}$$

$$p(---) = \frac{1}{2^{n_1+n_2+n_3-2r-1}} \cdot$$

$$\sum_{s=0}^{r-1} \binom{r-1}{s} \sum_{\substack{x+s>\frac{n_1}{2} \\ x=0,\ldots,n_1-r}} \binom{n_1-r}{x} \sum_{\substack{y+s>\frac{n_2}{2} \\ y=0,\ldots,n_2-r}} \binom{n_2-r}{y} \sum_{\substack{z+s>\frac{n_3}{2} \\ z=0,\ldots,n_3-r}} \binom{n_3-r}{z}$$

Obviously, $p(+++)$ is larger than $p(---)$. Further, as is illustrated in the examples of the next sub-paragraph, $p(++-)$ is in general strictly larger than $p(+--)$.

5.4 Examples

5.4.1 Vote-mixtures of the same order

First, we consider the case in which the vote-mixtures have the same order n. Then, we have $p(++-)=p(+-+)=p(-++)$, and $p(+--)=p(-+-)=p(--+)$. The formulas of 5.3 lead to the following quantities:

1. n=3:

	r=1	r=2
p(+++)	.421	.562
p(++-)	.141	.062
p(+--)	.047	.062
p(---)	.016	.062
T+	.843	.75
T-	.157	.25

2. n=5:

	r=1	r=2	r=3	r=4
p(+++)	.325	.397	.465	.547
p(++-)	.148	.110	.082	.047
p(+--)	.067	.069	.059	.047
p(---)	.031	.035	.113	.172
T+	.768	.728	.711	.688
T-	.232	.272	.289	.312

3. n=7:

	r=1	r=2	r=3	r=4	r=5
p(+++)	.286	.331	.377	.423	.475
p(++-)	.148	.124	.104	.084	.064
p(+--)	.077	.077	.071	.064	.052
p(---)	.041	.066	.097	.131	.174
T+	.73	.704	.689	.677	.668
T-	.27	.296	.311	.323	.332

	r=6
p(+++)	.540
p(++-)	.039
p(+--)	.039
p(---)	.227
T+	.656
T-	.344

4. n=9

	r=1	r=2	r=3	r=4	r=5
p(+++)	.258	.294	.328	.362	.389
p(++-)	.147	.13	.115	.101	.086
p(+--)	.084	.082	.078	.073	.066
p(---)	.048	.068	.091	.116	.144
T+	.7	.685	.673	.664	.656
T-	.3	.315	.327	.336	.344

	r=6	r=7	r=8
p(+++)	.436	.479	.534
p(++-)	.071	.055	.034
p(+--)	.058	.048	.034
p(---)	.176	.213	.261
T+	.65	.644	.637
T-	.35	.356	.363

T+ denotes the chance that the field exprienced in a unit i with $P_i^1 = +1$ is positive:
T+ $= p(+++) + 3p(++-)$
T- denotes the chance that the field exprienced in a unit i with $V_i^1 = +1$ is negative:
T- $= p(---) + 3p(+--)$

We notive that, for reasons of symmetry, $p(+++)$ is also the chance that a field $-h^1 - h^2 - h^3$ is experienced in a unit i for which $P_i^1 = -1$. Likewise, $p(++-)$ is also equal to the chance that a unit i with $P_i^1 = -1$ experiences a field $-h^1 - h^2 + h^3$, and so on. Hence, T+ expresses the chance that the total external field in a unit is parallel with the activation value of the groundpattern P^1. Similarly, T- gives the chance that the total external field in a unit is anti-parallel with the activation value of the groundpattern P^1. The previous table shows several points which are intuitively plausible. For instance, up to the case in which r+1=n, $p(++-)$ is larger than $p(+--)$ (if r+1=n, then $p(++-)$ = $p(+--)$). Further, the quantity T+ is always significantly larger than T- (note 4).

5.4.2 Some examples for mixtures of different order

For the sake of illustration, we consider also a few examples for mixtures of different order.

1. $n_1 = 7$; $n_2 = 5$; $n_3 = 3$

	r=1	r=2
p(+++)	.338	.418
p(++-)	.113	.062
p(+-+)	.154	.113
p(-++)	.177	.145
p(+--)	.051	.062
p(-+-)	.059	.062
p(--+)	.081	.074
p(---)	.027	.062
T+	.782	.739
T-	.218	.261

2. $n_1 = 9$; $n_2 = 7$; $n_3 = 5$

	r=1	r=2	r=3	r=4
p(+++)	.287	.337	.385	.435
p(++-)	.131	.102	.077	.05
p(+-+)	.15	.126	.106	.085
p(-++)	.164	.143	.127	.112
p(+--)	.068	.072	.07	.067
p(-+-)	.075	.074	.068	.06
p(--+)	.086	.81	.07	.056
p(---)	.039	.065	.098	.136
T+	.732	.708	.695	.682
T-	.268	.292	.305	.318

5.5 The fields experienced by a component as a function of the number of sustained vote-mixtures in which it occurs

5.5.1 Derivation of the formulas

Suppose that different vote-mixtures are sustained by external fields, and suppose that these vote-mixtures share a varying number of groundstates. For the sake of simplicity, we confine ourselves to three vote-mixtures M^1 , M^2 and M^3 which obey the following four specifications:

i. There are exactly r groundstates which participate in the three vote-mixtures M^1 , M^2 and M^3 .

ii. M^1 is of order n_1 ; it shares $r+1$ groundpatterns with M^1 and r groundpatterns with M^3 .

iii. M^2 is of order n_2 ; it shares $r+1$ groundpatterns with M^1 and r groundpatterns with M^3 .

iv. M^3 is of order n_3 ; it shares r groundpatterns with M^1 and r groundpatterns with M^2 .

Mixture M^μ (μ $=1,2,3,4$) experiences a sustaining field h^μ given by:

$$h^\mu = h^\mu M^\mu$$

Then, the higher the number of mixtures in which a particular groundpattern participates, the higher the extent to which this groundpattern is stimulated by the external fields. The formulas which specify the fields which are experienced in a particular groundpattern can be derived in a way which is highly similar to the method of 5.4. Furthermore, it is straightforward to generalize them for sitations which are more complex than the one which is presently considered. For such situations, however, the formulas may become rather tedious.

First, we consider a groundpattern P^1 that is shared by the three mixtures. Consider a unit i in which P^1 is positive. As usual, the chance that i experiences an external field $h^1+h^2+h^3$ is denoted $p(+++)$. By a method similar to the one of 5.4, we obtain (eq.A.24a):

$$p(+++) = \frac{1}{2^{n_1+n_2+n_3-2r-2}} \cdot$$

$$\sum_{s=0}^{r-1} \binom{r-1}{s} \sum_{\substack{b=0,1 \\ 1+s+b+x>\frac{n_1}{2} \\ x=0,\ldots,n_1-r-1}} \binom{n_1-r-1}{x} \sum_{\substack{1+s+b+y>\frac{n_2}{2} \\ y=0,\ldots,n_2-r-1}} \binom{n_2-r-1}{y} \sum_{\substack{1+s+z>\frac{n_3}{2} \\ z=0,\ldots,n_3-r}} \binom{n_3-r}{z}$$

Let $p(>><)$ denote the expression $p(+++)$ but with a reversed inequality in the last summation. Similarily, $p(<>>)$ denotes the expression $p(+++)$ but with a reversed inequality in condition on the summation over x. Likewise, $p(<<>)$ denotes $p(+++)$ but with a reversed inequality in the summation over x and in the summation over y; $p(<<<)$ denotes $p(+++)$ with reversed inequalities in the conditions on the summations over x,y and z. The quantities p ($>><$), $p(><$ $<)$, and $p(<><)$ are defined in a similar way. Then, we have:

$$p(++\text{-}) = p(>><)$$
$$p(+\text{-}+) = p(><>) = p(\text{-}++) = p(<>>)$$
$$p(+\text{--}) = p(><<) = p(\text{-}+\text{-}) = p(<><)$$
$$p(\text{--}+) = p(<<>)$$
$$p(\text{---}) = p(<<<)$$

Second, we calculate the same probablities for the pattern P^2 that participates in M^1 and in M^2 but not in M^3 . Suppose that P^2 is positive in a unit i. Again, the chance that i experiences a parallel field $h^1+h^2+h^3$ is denoted $p(+++)$. Likewise, the chance that i experiences an external field $h^1+h^2-h^3$ is denoted $p(++\text{-})$, and so on. A calculation similar to the ones of 5.4 leads to (eq.A.24.b):

$$p(+++) = \frac{1}{2^{n_1+n_2+n_3-2r-2}}.$$

$$\sum_{s=0}^{r}\binom{r}{s} \sum_{\substack{s+1+x>\frac{n_1}{2} \\ x=0,\ldots,n_1-r-1}} \binom{n_1-r-1}{x} \sum_{\substack{s+1+y>\frac{n_2}{2} \\ y=0,\ldots,n_2-r-1}} \binom{n_2-r-1}{y} \sum_{\substack{s+z>\frac{n_3}{2} \\ z=0,\ldots,n_3-r}} \binom{n_3-z}{z}$$

Also for this expression, the quantities $p(> > <)$, $p(> < >)$, and so on can be defined. They are related with the probabilities $p(++-)$, $p(+-+)$, and so on, in the same way as in case of P^1 :

$$p(++-) = p(> > <)$$
$$p(+-+) = p(> < >) = p(-++) = p(< > >)$$
$$p(+--) = p(> < <) = p(-+-) = p(< > <)$$
$$p(--+) = p(< < >)$$
$$p(---) = p(< < <)$$

Third, we consider a pattern P^3 that participates in M^1 only. The probabilities $p(+++)$, $p(++-)$, and so on, can be calculated in a similar way as in the two previous cases. For instance, we have (eq.A.24c)

$$p(+++) = \frac{1}{2^{n_1+n_2+n_3-2r-2}}.$$

$$\sum_{s=0}^{r}\binom{r}{s} \sum_{b=0,1} \sum_{\substack{s+b+1+x>\frac{n_1}{2} \\ x=0,\ldots,n_1-r-2}} \binom{n_1-r-2}{x} \sum_{\substack{s+b+y>\frac{n_2}{2} \\ y=0,\ldots n_2-r-1}} \binom{n_2-r-1}{y} \sum_{\substack{s+z>\frac{n_3}{2} \\ z=0,\ldots,n_3-r}} \binom{n_3-r}{z}$$

Like in the two previous cases, the probabilities $p(++-)$, $p(+-+)$, and so on, can be obtained as $p(> > <)$, $p(> < >)$, and so on. For reasons of symmetry, the same expressions hold for a groundpattern that participates in M^2 only. Finally, we consider a groundpattern P^4 that participates in M^3 only. Remarkably, the probablities $p(+++)$, $p(++-)$, and so on, are different from the corresponding probabilities in case of P^3 . This time, we obtain (eq.A.24c)

$$p(+++) = \frac{1}{2^{n_1+n_2+n_3-2r-2}}.$$

$$\sum_{s=0}^{r} \binom{r}{s} \sum_{b=0,1} \sum_{\substack{s+b+x>\frac{n_1}{2} \\ x=0,\ldots,n_1-r-1}} \begin{bmatrix} n_1-r-1 \\ x \end{bmatrix} \sum_{\substack{s+b+y>\frac{n_2}{2} \\ y=0,\ldots,n_2-r-1}} \begin{bmatrix} n_2-r-1 \\ y \end{bmatrix} \sum_{\substack{s+1+z>\frac{n_3}{2} \\ z=1,\ldots,n_3-r-1}} \begin{bmatrix} n_3-r-1 \\ z \end{bmatrix}$$

The relations between $p(++-)$ and the quantities $p(> > <)$, between $p(> < >)$ and $p(+-+)$, and so on, are the same as in the three previous cases. We notice that, for reasons of symmetry, in each of the cases, $p(+++)$ gives the probability that the field experienced in i is equal to $-h^1-h^2-h^3$ if $P_1^\nu=-1$ ($\nu = 1,\ldots,4$). Similarily, $p(++-)$ gives the probability that the field experienced in i is equal to $-h^1-h^2+h^3$ if $P_i^\nu=-1$, and so on.

5.5.2 Some examples

We consider two examples in order to illustrate the formulas of the previous paragraph:

1. $n_1 = 7$; $n_2 = 7$; $n_3 = 7$; $r=3$

	P^1	P^2	P^3	P^4
$p(+++)$	.392	.344	.294	.302
$p(++-)$	.116	.164	.137	.50
$p(+-+)$	.089	.058	.107	.100
$p(-++)$	.089	.058	.029	.100
$p(+--)$	.060	.090	.119	.048
$p(-+-)$	.060	.090	.041	.048
$p(--+)$	.087	.039	.068	.154
$p(---)$	.108	.156	.255	.198
T+	.685	.625	.567	.552
T-	.315	.375	.433	.448

2. $n_1 = 11$; $n_2 = 9$; $n_3 = 7$; $r = 4$

	P^1	P^2	P^3	P^4
p(+ + +)	.378	.332	.290	.300
p(+ +-)	.089	.135	.109	.037
p(+ -+)	.090	.058	.100	.107
p(-+ +)	.106	.074	.048	.116
p(+--)	.066	.098	.124	.133
p(-+-)	.064	.096	.053	.047
p(--+)	.082	.036	.062	.056
p(---)	.125	.171	.214	.204
T+	.663	.599	.547	.560
T-	.337	.401	.453	.440

NOTES

Note 1. Also the mirror images (the negatives) of the groundstates are stable attractors of the Hopfield/Amit network. An odd mixture that includes one or more mirror images of groundstates is also a stable attractor. If a groundstate represents a particular component, then its mirror image might be used to represent the opposite of this component. We will not dwell on this issue.

Note 2. Vote-mixtures have several remarkable mathematical properties; they are studied in Van Loocke (1991b).

Note 3. Apparently, this prescription can be formulated without reference to the considered partition of the network. The partition is essential, however, for the argument that follows.

Note 4. One has to be cautious, however, with general statements. For instance, it is intuitively plausible that the quantity $p(+--)$ decreases if the number of shared groundstates increases. The table shows that this property holds for all considered cases but one: for $n = 5$, $p(+ +-)$ equals 0.67 if $r = 1$, and it is equal to 0.69 if $r = 2$. Although this violation of the intuition at issue is small and although it appears to be highly exceptional, it entails that it is impossible to give a mathematical proof of the intuition.

APPENDIX II

SOME CONVERGENT PROPERTIES OF THE CONCEPTUAL DATA-BASE OF THE RIGHT HEMISPHERE

1 Introduction

Several experiments have been performed in order to determine the properties of the conceptual databases of the left and the right hemisphere. These experiments bear a cluster of related properties as far as concerns right hemisphere concepts (paragraph 2). For instance, it appears that the conceptual database of the right hemisphere allows that more than one representation is active during a relatively long time interval, whereas the left hemisphere depends more on focal activation. Also, the type of associations stored in or generated by the respective hemispheres appears to be different. The right hemisphere contains associations that may relate semantically distant concepts; the left hemisphere, on the other hand, has a preference for associative relations between semantically tightly related concepts. Further, inter-conceptual relations appear to be more prominent in the right hemisphere, whereas the left hemisphere has a preference for inner-conceptual relations. However, the right hemisphere does represent inner-conceptual relations, at least as far as typical concepts are concerned. Remarkably, the typicalities of concepts are reflected in decision latencies in case of the right hemisphere, but not in case of the left hemisphere.

These properties fit the properties that one may expect of a module that stores non-specific associations (paragraph 3). Subsequently, in order to discuss supplementary characteristics of the conceptual database of the right hemisphere, we consider a more general view on lateralization (paragraph 4). This general view suggests some points concerning the nature of the components of the concepts of the right hemisphere (paragraph 5). This, in turn, sheds some light on the question if particular evidence concerning the interactions between components may refer to the right hemisphere (paragraph 6). Finally, we point out that the resulting cluster of properties can be described by the connectionist model that we proposed in chapter VI (paragraph 7).

2 Properties of the conceptual database of the right hemisphere

2.1 Focal and non-focal representations

The dichotomy between focal and non-focal representations has been put forward a number of times in the context of discussions concerning lateralization (e.g. Zaidel, 1983, 1986; Burgess and Simpson, 1988; note 1). If a representation is focal, then priming effects must occur only to a limited extent. According to the usual interpretation, if a concept A is a prime for a concept B, then the activation of A causes a partial activation of B. Since a situation in which several concepts are partially active is antithetic to focal activation, automatic priming must be limited when a focal activation has to be maintained. Most authors agree on the fact that, in particular experimental contexts, both hemispheres show priming effects (e.g. Underwood, Rusted and Thwaites, 1983; Marcel and Patterson, 1978; Walker and Ceci, 1985; note 2). These experiments usually involve one or other variation of a lexical or a semantic decision task (see e.g. Joanette, Goulet and Hannequin, 1990 for a review).

Two such experiments, which had a more detailed scope, are of special interest for our discussion. Burgess and Simpson (1988) varied the time intervals between the presentation of a prime and the appearance of the target. As concerns the left hemisphere, the presentation of the hint speeded up the decision task for short intervals (35 milliseconds). For longer intervals (750 milliseconds), however, this effect disappeared: priming effects were no longer observable. In the right hemisphere, on the other hand, priming effects took more time to appear, but they remained during the longer intervals. We notice that, in general, these longer intervals correspond to realistic conversational circumstances. In most sentences, the time between the pronunciation of a prime and of a word that is primed is significantly larger than 35 milliseconds. The suggestion that priming spreads out more significantly in the right hemisphere is also made in Zaidel (1983,1986).

Chiarello (1985,1988) points out another qualitative difference between priming in the left and in the right hemisphere. When a hint is false, this has a negative effect on the lexical decision times of the left hemisphere, but no effect on the decision times of the right one. One possible interpretation is that, when a false hint is activated in the left hemisphere, it must be deactivated before the target item can be fully activated. On the other hand, when the right hemisphere depends less on focal patterns, it may tolerate that an unrelevant hint remains partially active while the target item is processed (note 3). This is consistent with the outcomes of a series of experiments concerning lateralized Stroop-effects (Tsao, Feustel and Soseos, 1979; Franzon and Hugdahl, 1986; Schmit and Davis, 1974). When a word that denotes a color is printed in another color, effects of interference between color and meaning may occur. These effects of interference are stronger in the left hemisphere than in the right one. This can be interpreted if one assumes that, in the left hemisphere, the meaning of a word that has been read has to be suppressed before a rival word with a rival meaning can become activate. These points suggest that, although the left hemisphere obviously shows spread of activation in certain circumstances, it has a tendency to rely on focal representations. The right hemisphere seems to be more apt to keep more than one meaning active during longer time intervals.

2.2 Associations between concepts and semantic distance: close versus remote associative transitions

We will argue below that the components of a concept of the right hemisphere do not correspond to categorical relations. Hence, as far as concerns this hemisphere, categorical relations between parts may not play a dominant role as concerns the associative topology. Then, two concepts are associatively related when they share one or more component parts or one or more properties, but structural similarity is no requirement for associative proximity. Consequently, one may expect that, when compared to the left hemisphere, the associative topology of the right hemisphere relates concepts which are semantically more distant from each other. It is possible to adduce evidence for this point. Rodel, Landis and Regard (1989) analyzed paralexias produced when a word was presented briefly in lateralized vision. It appeared that the right hemisphere generated paralexias that were semantically more remote from the target word than did the left hemisphere. Further, in a lateralized semantic judgement task, their subjects were asked to estimate the link between two words. It appeared that the right hemisphere assumed more often a strong link between semantically distant words than did the left hemisphere.

2.3 Associations between concepts: intra-conceptual versus inter-conceptual

The right hemisphere apparently masters category-membership relations (see below). However, when compared to the left hemisphere, criteria like share of properties or appearance in the same scene seem to play a relatively large role in its associative topology. Drews (1987) used a semantic decision task to examine if there was an inter-hemispheric difference concerning the relative prominency of inter- versus intra-categoric relationships. His evidence suggested that inner-categoric relations are more prominent in the left hemisphere, whereas the converse holds for the right hemisphere. A similar point was made by Zaidel (1982, 1985). Zaidel compared paradigmatic relations (more or less comparable to intraconceptual relations) with syntagmatic relations (more or less comparable to inter-conceptual relations). Split brain patients had to carry out a reading test with distractors. Analysis of the errors showed that the errors made by the left hemisphere were led more often by paradigmatic relations, whereas the ones made by the left hemisphere were guided by syntagmatic relations.

Brownell and colleagues report findings which can be interpreted along similar lines (Brownell, 1988; Brownell, Potter and Michelow, 1984). They worked with three groups of subjects: a normal control group, a group of persons with damage to the left hemisphere and a group with right-sided brain damage. The subjects had to carry out a semantic choice task. Sets of three words were shown. For each such set, they had to select the two words that were most strongly related. Each set of three words was chosen in such a way that two of the words had a denotative relation (reminiscent of intra-conceptual relations) and that two of the words had a connotative relation (more or less reminiscent of inter-conceptual relations). It appeared that subjects with damage to their left hemisphere showed a preference for connotative relations, whereas subjects with damage to their right hemisphere choose most often for connotative relations. The choice-behavior of the normal subjects was in between the choice behavior of the two groups with brain damaged subjects. In a similar vein, Brownell, Bihrle et al. (1985; quoted in Joanette, Goulet et al. 1990) suggest that the left hemisphere has a more dictionary-like character, whereas the right hemisphere plays an important role as far as concerns finding connotations.

2.4 Typicalities and lateralization

Another remarkable difference between the hemispheres as far as concerns conceptual organization has been pointed out in Zaidel (1990). It concerns the internal structure of concepts. For a long while, concepts were thought off as classes defined in terms of necessary and sufficient conditions. According to this view, an exemplar belongs to a concept if the corresponding conditions are fulfilled; else, it does not belong to it (Katz and Postal, 1964; Trabasso and Bower, 1968; Winston, 1970; Bourne, 1970). Nowadays, however, it is generally accepted that category-membership is not an all or nothing-issue. Rather, concept membership has a wide range of gradations (Rosch, 1973; Rosch and Mervis, 1975; Smith, Shoben and Rips, 1974; Mc Closkey and Glucksberg, 1978). The "typicality" of a concept can be experimentally assessed by measuring decision latencies: the more typical an item is for its category, the more quickly it is classified as a member of this category

(Rosch and Mervis, 1975; Rosch, Simpson and Miller, 1976). Typicalities have a number of properties. For instance, items which share more characteristics with a prototype of a category are more typical. Items that have more additional characteristics relative to a prototype are less typical. Items of a category which resemble the ones of another category are less typical.

Zaidel (1990) examined if the differences between decision latencies for typical and non-typical items were the same in both hemispheres. Remarkably, only the right hemisphere showed the pattern that was observed in Rosch and Mervis (1975). The right hemisphere classified typical items more quickly than non-typical ones. The left hemisphere, on the other hand, classified typical and non-typical items with equal speed. This is consistent with the suggestion that the left hemisphere stores its concepts more like a dictionary, at least if compared with the right hemisphere. In a dictionary, a difficult word is looked up with equal speed as a non-difficult word. The pattern of the right hemisphere, on the other hand, is more reminiscent of distributed representations. If the representation of an activated item has some characteristics in common with the representation of a prototype of a category, then the representation of this prototype is also partially active when distributed representations are used. To the extent that a category is represented by its prototypes, this will be expressed in decision latencies (note 4). We notice that the fact that the right hemisphere gives the patterns of latencies observed in non-lateralized experiments suggests that the right hemisphere plays a role in non-lateralized classification tasks, at least as far as relatively typical items are concerned (note 5).

3 Modules for non-specific associations and modules for specific relations

Since the conceptual database of the right hemisphere shows spread of activation and maintains priming effects during longer intervals, its type of activation is of the non-focal kind. If a concept is active, the mechanism of spread of activation may trigger a large number of connotatively related concepts, of which some are semantically close and of which some are semantically more distant. This type of associations has been addressed in chapter IV, where we called them "non-specific associations", in contradistinction with "specific relations". For the sake of clarity, we notice that a module that stores unspecific associations may be able to make associative transitions between concepts of the same category, between a category and its instance, or the reverse. Indeed, since concepts of the same category often share a number of components, an associative transition between them is perfectly possible in a module that stores unspecific associations. If, in addition, a cue is provided that gives a bias to one of the instances of a concept, the association process may go from a concept to one of its instances. Also the reverse process is perfectly possible. As is apparent from Zaidel (1990), the right hemisphere even plays an important role in category membership judgements, at least as far as typical members of a category are concerned. The compatibility between the storage of unspecific associations and the possibility of concept membership decisions can be illustrated also by the point that the model to which the present monograph refers includes both features.

If the conceptual database of the right hemisphere stores non-specific associations, it must have the properties that we considered in chapter III.3. For instance, we remember that modules that store unspecific associations include the representations of the components of concepts. In this elementary sense, the module at issue has to rely on distributed representations: a concept is represented together with its properties. Distributed representations inevitably lead to the phenomenon of spread of activation and hence to non-focal patterns of activation. In effect, the model that we constructed relies on distributed representations.

We must keep in mind, however, that the distributedness at issue is on the level of the psychological model, and that current connectionist models are usually not intended as physiological models (note 6). In effect, physiological neurons are far more complicated than the neurons of connectionist models, and the nature of the relation between both units remains unclear. Still, one may wonder if there is some physiological evidence for the fact that the right brain uses representations that distributed to a higher extent than the representations of the left brain. At the present moment, there is only indirect evidence for such point. Goldberg and Costa (1981) combine evidence suggesting that the ratio of grey matter to white matter is larger in the right hemisphere (Gur, Packer et al., 1980) with evidence that the right hemisphere contains more tissue (Whitaker and Ojeman 1977). They conclude that there is relatively more white matter in the right hemisphere, and hence that there are more interregional an connections in this hemisphere. They suggest to interpret this as evidence for the fact that the right hemisphere relies more on distributed representations than the left one. On a more functional level, an argument concerning differences in distributedness has also been developed in Woodward (1988) (note 7).

Further, we noticed in III.3 that concepts of non-verbal modules must adapt their structure when a subject becomes familiar with a domain. This point was met again in chapter X; we documented that, as a context becomes more familiar, the associations present in it tend to evolve from loose associations to more taxonomically organized ones (e.g. Chi and Koeske, 1983; Ornstein and Corsale, 1979; Lucariello and Nelson, 1985; Smiley and Brown, 1979; Vygotsky, 1962;

Inhelder and Piaget, 1964; Annet, 1959; Anglin, 1970; Sigel, 1953). It is of relevance to notice that to a substantial extent, the studies referred to address relations which are, according to our terminology, non-specific (e.g. Chi and Koeske, 1983; Vygotsky, 1962; Inhelder and Piaget, 1964, and so on; see also Van Loocke 1993). Hence, we suggest that the processes at issue may take place in at least some of the modules that store non-specific associations. Due to the prominence of this kind of associations for the conceptual data-base of the right hemisphere, this is an additional argument for the point that such processes take place in this database (see paragraph 6).

Also as concerns other experimental results, the question can be asked if they refer to modules that store non-specific associations or to modules that store specific relations. It would be desirable to have some criterion that decides to which type of module a given property of concepts refers, but it is not easy to give such a criterion. As concerns one particular property, this question is of special importance. This property describes how the components of concepts interact. The experimental results concerning this interaction, together with the properties ascribed higher to the conceptual database of the right hemisphere, were described by a connectionist model in previous research (Van Loocke, 1990, 1991a, 1991b, 1993). In the following paragraphs, we develop an argument that suggests that the experiments at issue may indeed refer at least to the database of concepts of the right hemisphere. In order to develop this argument, we start with a general point concerning the process of lateralization.

4 A more general view on the process of lateralization

Particular clusters of mental capacities tend to develop in a lateralized way. One explanation for this point refers to a snowball process (Kosslyn, 1987). It is based on three assumptions. First, the argument states that some processes have an innate tendency for lateralization. The processes at issue require a high speed coordination of several subprocesses. If such processes would be guided by control centers in both hemispheres, serious problems of coordination between these centers would result, since an interhemispheric transfer of information costs time. More specifically, there appears to be an innate bias to localize the speech-controller in the left hemisphere (Molfese and Molfese, 1979, 1983; Crowell, Jones, Kapuniai and Nakagawa, 1973; Davis and Wada, 1977; Day and Ulatovska, 1979; Dennis and Whitaker, 1976) and to localize the controller for rapid visual search in the right one (De Renzi, 1982; Kohn and Dennis, 1974). The second premise states that learning processes within a module depend on feedback from modules with which they interact. The goal of the learning processes within a module is the amelioration of its outputs. In order to be informed about the quality of its outputs, a module has to receive feedback from the modules to which these outputs are send (note 8). According to the third assumption, a process of transhemispheric degradation takes place as a stimulus is transferred from one hemisphere to the other one.

As a consequence of the third premise, modules tend to receive stronger feedback from modules in the same hemisphere. Hence, due to the second premise, modules of the same hemisphere become more adapted to each other than to modules of the other hemisphere. Consequently, innately lateralized cores may stimulate the lateralized development of related modules, for instance of modules that give regularly input to them. For a similar reason, the input modules of the latter modules may show a tendency to develop in a lateralized way, and so on: a kind of snowball effect results (Kosslyn, 1987).

An elaboration of this general point suggests to differentiate between two kinds of imagery. Each kind appears to be associated with one hemisphere, in contrast with the more simple, popular notion that the right hemisphere is dominant as concerns imagery processes. Images that are suited for association with verbal concepts are developed in the left hemisphere. Such images must not contain irrelevant shape variations. For instance, an image that corresponds to the verbal category "cup" must not contain information about its color, or about details of the shape of its ear. Rather, it must represent a cavity of the order of magnitude of a hand, possibly with an ear of the magnitude of some fingers. Schematic images can be specified in terms of their part-whole structure. The relations between parts may be expressed in a not quite specific or "categorical" way; hence the term "categorical representations". Such representations are organized in a modular way: a part of an object may itself be represented in terms of its part-whole structure, and so on. These representations are object-centered, since it would be redundant to associate a single verbal concept with an image for each possible perspective of the corresponding object. The usefulness of this kind of representations has been suggested regularly in cognitive psychology and in artificial intelligence (e.g. Marr, 1982; Ballard and Brown, 1982; Latto, Mumford and Shah, 1984).

The right hemisphere specializes in another kind of visual representation (Kosslyn, 1987). For spatial orientation purposes, it is necessary to take into account the specific position and orientation of the objects in the environment. Rather than a representation in terms of categorical part-whole relations, a coordinate representation that does not filter out such information is of relevance here. Such a representation may also be used for recognition purposes: a categorical part-whole representation may be too coarse for this end, for instance if variations of expressions on a face are at issue. Recognition processes may require quite exact spatial information, such as second order metric information (e.g. ratios of distances among pairs of parts; see e.g. Diamond and Carey, 1986), and this kind of representation allows for the computation of such information.

5 A supplementary hypothesis

The coordinate representations stored in the right hemisphere can serve as a basis for the derivation of structural information: they can be mentally inspected in order to determine the relative locations of the parts of a memorized scene or object. However, one may wonder if the right hemisphere mechanism that analyzes the relative locations of parts is identical to the corresponding mechanism in the left hemisphere. Some empirical facts suggest that the processes that give structure to right hemisphere images have significant limitations. For instance, D. Zaidel (1990) examined the capacity of the right hemisphere to retrieve relations between details of parts of a memorized scene. Subjects were shown pictures featuring, for instance, a boy fishing with his dog at his side. The dog was a main part of the scene; its relation to other main parts could be retrieved from memory. However, when questions concerning the details of the dog were asked (e.g. "Was his head turned to the left or to the right?"), the right hemisphere of split brain patients did not score higher than chance, whereas the left hemisphere did. This suggests that the right hemisphere is able to give structure at one level of detail, but that for more specific analysis, left hemisphere processes may be required.

Other evidence that is discussed in Zaidel (1990) is congruent with this point. Subjects were shown pictures that contained a global, familiar shape filled in a highly non-typical way with details. Hence, the recognition of the details had to rely on information stemming from the visual input image, not on memorized information concerning parts that are typically present at a particular place in a certain global shape. In such a situation, the right hemisphere of split brain patients appeared to be able to recognize the global shape, but it could not recognize the details. Several other authors suggested that the right hemisphere lacks the mechanisms required to work generatively with parts or that it lacks descriptive tools to analyze objects in elementary parts at different levels of detail (e.g. Corballis, 1987; Goldberg and Costa, 1981; Levy, 1974; Levine, 1982; Kosslyn, 1988).

Although it can be argued that the structure of the mental images of the right hemisphere is different from the structure of the modular and categorical images of the left hemisphere, the right hemisphere must be able to extract object-centered shape information about images and their parts. This is suggested by the fact that both the left as well as the right hemisphere dispose of a memory for concepts. As we noticed higher, it is much more economic to associate an object-centered image with a concept. Hence, it is plausible that the right hemisphere disposes of the capacity to extract perspective-independent form information. Consequently, if it is assumed that the right hemisphere uses coordinate representations (Kosslyn, 1987), then this hemisphere must master perspective dependent as well as perspective independent coordinate representations.

In a coordinate representation, the relations between different parts of an image are stored implicitly. Parts can be assembled on a kind of display in accordance with their coordinates. Then, the resulting image may be scanned and relational information may be obtained. Also categorical representations allow for the derivation of implicit relational information. According to Kosslyn (e.g. Kosslyn, 1980, 1987), also this type of representations can be retrieved on a kind of mental screen, and also in this case, scanning processes may extract relational information. In case of categorical representations, however, part of the relational information is memorized in an explicit way. To make this point more clear, let us consider an example. The information that the tail of a dog has a particular form and that it is at the back of its trunk may be represented in a categorical representation (i) or in a coordinate representation (ii).

(i). tail: "form specification", "categorical relation to anchor"
(ii). tail: coordinates of intensity values in a picture of a prototypical dog.

In principle, a "form specification" in case (i) may be in terms of coordinates or in terms of a code that is more apt for higher level visual processing, such as volumetric primitives (Marr 1982; Biederman, 1987). According to the theory of Kosslyn (e.g. Kosslyn, 1975, 1980, 1987; Kosslyn, Pinker, Smith and Schwartz, 1979), the points on a mental display or "surface matrix" are defined in terms of coordinates. If an image is retrieved and loaded on this structure, each of its points receives an intensity value in accordance with the long term representation of the image. Hence, if categorical image representations are defined in terms of, for instance, volumetric primitives, then these primitives are translated in intensity values and coordinates when the image is retrieved on the surface matrix.

The part of specification (i) that is termed "categorical relation to anchor" defines the place of the tail in an image of a dog. The anchor may be a "skeleton" of a dog (Marr 1982) or some other very rough outline of a typical dog. Possibly, also a main part like a trunk may serve as a reference place on which other parts are anchored by the way of categorical relations. In the latter case, the second part of (i) may denote "at the back of the trunk". Apparently, in case (i), categorical information is partially explicit: the long term representation of "tail" includes a categorical relation. When the image is retrieved, additional relational information may be derived, such as "the ears are higher and shorter than the tail". In case of coordinate representations (ii), in contrast, all relational information is implicit: only when a part is retrieved on the surface matrix, relations with other parts or with the whole can be inferred.

This is of importance for our discussion since it suggests a point concerning the components of the concepts stored in the right hemisphere. If the concepts of this hemisphere are represented in a distributed way (in other terms, if the components of a concept participate in the representation of the concept), their representations may include some components referring to perceptual properties. If these components are borrowed from the representations of the images associated with the concepts, then these components do not refer to categorical relations between parts of the image. This point holds for the representations of concepts of the right hemisphere only. Further, if the representations of the concepts of the right hemisphere borrow some of their components from the images associated with them, then these components are probably not hierarchically organized at successive levels of detail, as may hold for the left hemisphere (see higher). However, we have seen that the right hemisphere appears to be able to structure memory images at one level of detail. This suggests that components of concepts derived from a right hemisphere image may correspond to some general outline of the image and to its main parts, but not to more fine-grained details.

6 The interaction between the components of concepts and its consequences

As we have pointed out in chapter V, there is an extensive literature concerning the way in which the components of concepts interact. According to the "prototype" classification model, the chance that a concept is retrieved is proportional to the sum of the extents to which its components are activated (e.g. Reed, 1972, 1973). The exemplar model, on the other hand, assumes that the chance that a concept is retrieved is proportional to the product of the extents to which its components are activated (e.g. Medin and Schaffer, 1978; Medin, Dewey, Murphy, 1983). In general, a multiplicative interaction entails that similarities to the individual items of a category will be most important in membership decisions. An additive interaction may put emphasis on the overall similarity with a particular item, for instance a prototype. Initially, these models were considered to be rivals, but it was later acknowledged that they correspond to different stages of familiarity with a context of concepts. The exemplar model appears to be adequate for new and unfamiliar concepts, whereas the prototype model becomes more adequate as concepts get more familiar (Medin, Altom, Murphy, 1984; Medin, Wattenmaker, Hampson, 1987). This point is consistent with other research. If a context becomes familiar, the organization of concepts tends evolve to clusters of more typical cores around which less typical items are located (e.g. Rosch, 1978, Chi and Koeske, 1983). Along with familiarity, also the number of acquired concepts is of significance for this tendency (Homa and Voghsburg 1976; Bomba and Siqueland 1983).

The question of importance in the present context is if these facts reflect the organization of the conceptual data-base of the right hemisphere, of the left hemisphere or of both hemispheres. We put forward three arguments for the stance that they reflect properties of at least the conceptual database of the right hemisphere. First, consider the emergence of prototypes. We saw that, as concerns the right hemisphere, items are organized around prototypes, and typicality gradients can be defined in terms of decision latencies (Zaidel, 1990). Consequently, the process by which prototypes are generated must be reflected in the right hemisphere. We saw that this process is in part a consequence of an evolution of the interactions between the components of concepts. Hence, the studies that describe the evolution of these interactions may refer (at least) to the right hemisphere. Second, one can examine the components of concepts that were considered in the experiments at issue. Such an examination shows that different kinds of components were used (Van Loocke, 1993). However, in no such experiment, a component corresponded to a categorical relation. Also from this point of view, the experiments may have reflected properties of the conceptual database of the right hemisphere. A third point concerns the nature of the associations that are generated by the conceptual database of the right hemisphere. Higher, we differentiated between specific and non-specific associations (paragraph 3). A substantial portion of the evidence used to argue that clusters and hierarchies of clusters emerge in familiar contexts refers to non-specific association. We saw that this type of associations is prominent in the conceptual database of the right hemisphere.

Hence, to the set of properties that we ascribed higher to the right hemisphere, we add that the interaction between the components of concepts may evolve in such a way that concepts become organized around prototypes, and that hierarchical clusters of concepts may emerge. We have to keep in mind, however, that the present argument does not exclude that some modules of the left hemisphere have some of the properties that belong to this cluster. For instance, it is plausible that also the conceptual database of the left hemisphere evolves towards a more taxonomic organization as a child grows up, since formal schooling appears to create an environment in which such kind of organization is favored (Schank, 1976; Brown, 1977; Nelson and Brown, 1978; note 9).

7. The relation of these properties with the connectionist model of chapter VI.

Let us briefly recapitulate. We considered a cluster of properties that we ascribed to a module that is specialized in non-specific associations. Throughout this appendix, we have put forward the connection between these properties and the conceptual database of the right hemisphere. Non-specific associations may be guided by constraints in terms of components that are stimulated or inhibited, but not by constraints in terms of specific relations. They may occasionally lead to associative transitions from a concept to semantically distant concepts. The representations used by the module are non-focal and they show automatic spread of activation. Inter-conceptual associations occur frequently, but also inner-conceptual relations are mastered, especially as far as typical members category are concerned. Typicalities are reflected in decision latencies. Our discussion suggests that the module at issue uses distributed representations, and that the interactions between the components of the concepts may evolve as familiarity increases. As a result, prototypes may emerge, as well as more or less hierarchically organized clusters of concepts.

The connectionist model that we described in chapter VI has all these properties (see also Van Loocke, 1990, 1991a, 1991b, 1993). In addition, it has also other properties to which we referred in the course of this appendix. For instance, it predicts the specific properties of typicality arrangements which we mentioned in 2.4. Also, it predicts that a new concept is drawn in its context or in its category. The fact that all these properties can be described by a single model can be seen as an additional argument for the attribution of these properties to the same module.

NOTES

Note 1. For the sake of simplicity, we restrict ourselves in discussions concerning issues of lateralization to right handed subjects.

Note 2. There is quite some discussion as concerns the nature and the extension of the conceptual database of the right hemisphere. For instance, it is debated if right hemisphere concepts are necessarily concrete or imageable (e.g. Lambert and Beaumont, 1983; Patterson and Besner, 1984; Bryer and Stripstein, 1985; Mc Mullen and Bryden, 1987), or if verbs are fully represented in the right hemisphere (Day, 1979; Sidtis and Gazzaniga, 1983; Zaidel, 1978; Zaidel, 1982). That the right hemisphere has a memory for concepts, however, is widely accepted, as is testified the by numerous authors who try to attribute characteristics to it.

Note 3. If the pattern of activation is bound to be focal, then also when a correct hint is shown to the left hemisphere, the hint possibly must to be suppressed to some extent before the target word can become active. However, in case of a correct hint, the target can become partially active by spread of activation so that the time required to activate the target fully may be shortened.

Note 4. Distributed representations do not necessarily entail that, if an item shares properties with other categories as well, that this affects its classification time. However, as concerns the connectionist model to which the present text refers, this is a straightforward property.

Note 5. The point that the right hemisphere is important for typicality judgements has been suggested also in another context. Wapner, Hamby et al. (1981) proposed that the right hemisphere judges if a scene is plausible in a context: it contains a "plausibility metric" that the left hemisphere lacks to some extent (see also Gardner, Brownell, Wapner and Michelow, 1983).

Note 6. A connectionist stance that is often put forward is that present connectionist models are at an "intermediate level" (e.g. Smolensky, 1988a) between physiological models and classical psychological models. They contain some terms that may, in the long run, become related to physiological objects. At present, however, the merits of these terms are that they allow to formulate models that are psychologically more interesting than models without such terms.

Note 7. On a more general level, Semmes (1968) made a related point. For a long time, the right hemisphere was considered as the "minor" or "inferior" hemisphere. Semmes (1968) noticed that this was due to the fact that right hemisphere lesions result less often in apparent behavioral deficits than left hemisphere lesions. However, this may be due to the point that the right hemisphere depends more on distributed representations, rather than due to its "inferiority".

Note 8. The importance of feedback in learning processes is abundantly illustrated in connectionist models (see e.g. Rumelhart and Mc Clelland, 1986).

Note 9. The present argument does also not exclude that the right hemisphere contains other modules that store concepts and which have characteristics different from the ones considered here. For instance, to a certain extent, the right hemisphere seems to be able to deal antonymic relations (Joanette, Goulet and Hannequin, 1990). It is not obvious how to represent such relations in a system that stores non-specific associations.

APPENDIX III

SOME NOTES CONCERNING SIMULATIONS

This appendix contains some specifications about the simulations which are presented in chapters VI-X.

1 The finite size of the network and its implications: pseudo-orthogonal P's

The network that is used in our simulations has 2048 neurons in its basis-layer. Since the theory about the network is concerned with the thermodynamic limit (i.e. with networks with an infinite number of units, see Van Loocke, 1991a), our simulations contain some finite-size effects which do not agree with the theory. However, these effects are small. The finite size effects are basically due by the fact that, for finite networks, the P's are not perfectly uncorrelated. This is due to the point that P's must not only be mutually orthogonal with each other: they must be generated randomly in order to show the topological properties of the vote-mixtures that we considered in Appendix I. For instance, a third order mixture M of three P's must not be correlated with a P that does not participate in the mixture. This property does not hold automatically for orthogonal P's. Consider, for example, the following four P's of a network with 8 units:

$$P^1 \quad : (+1,+1,+1,+1,-1,-1,-1,-1)$$
$$P^2 \quad : (+1,+1,-1,-1,+1,+1,-1,-1)$$
$$P^3 \quad : (+1,-1,+1,-1,+1,-1,+1,-1)$$
$$P^4 \quad : (+1,-1,-1,+1,-1,+1,+1,-1)$$

It is readily verified that these P's are orthogonal to each other. However, if one considers the mixture M of the first three P's:

$$M: (+1,+1,+1,-1,+1,-1,-1,-1)$$

then it is readily verified that M is not orthogonal with P^4 (the overlap between M and P^4 is equal to -0.5). At closer sight, one observes that M is not randomly related with P^1 , P^2 and P^3 : the i-th value of M is equal to the product of the i-th value of P^1 , P^2 and P^3 . In practice, one can approximate the requirement of random relatedness of P's in finite networks as follows. One starts with an arbitrary pattern P^0 with mean activation value zero. Then, one generates randomly other patterns (with mean activation value zero) until a random pattern with an overlap of less than Q(tr) with the first pattern is found. This is the second P. Next, one generates other random patterns (with mean activation value zero) until one obtains a pattern with an overlap with P^0 and P^1 that is lower than Q(tr). This pattern is the third P.

From the fourth P on, the constraint of pseudo-orthogonality with the previous patterns is supplemented with another constraint: an additional P must have on overlap of at most Q'(tr) with the odd mixtures of the P's which are already obtained. In practice, it appears to suffice to verify if the overlap of the new P with the with the highest order odd vote-mixture(s) of the previous P's is less than Q'(tr) (if an odd number of P's has been generated before the new P, the vote-mixture of all previous P's is taken and it is controlled if the overlap of the new P with this mixture is lower than Q'(tr); if an even number of P's has been generated before the k-th P is generated, one has to control the overlap of the new P with all sets of k-1 previously generated P's). In case of our network with N=2048, we took Q(tr)=0.25 and Q'(tr)=0.005. As concerns the examples that we consider, the fluctuations which result from this pseudo-orthogonality are harmless as concerns the basic properties of the system.

2 The fluctuations produced by the random order in the updating rule

Different runs of the same input and for the same memories may produce different results. This is due to the fact that the units of the network update asynchronously and in random order. In general, different runs do not differ very much from each other, and they differ only as concerns the speed with which a recognition or an association is made. However, in special conditions, different runs may lead to the retrieval of different patterns. This possible if different concepts attract an input with approximately the same strength. Then, a small fluctuation may decide which association is actually made. This situation is illustrated, for instance, in example 2 of chapter VI: for b-values equal to 0.2 for i1, i2, i3 and i4, and for a b-value of 0.7 for i0, the system "doubts" and it may answer differently in different runs. Usually, however, the dispersions for different runs are relatively small. This fact is illustrated in paragraph 3 of this appendix, were the dispersions for the examples of chapter VI are shown. The curves which are shown in the chapter VI systematically represent the mean values of eight runs. The subsequent chapters contain illustrations in which single runs are depicted.

3 The dispersions produced by the random updating schema

We give the dispersions for each of the simulations which are described in chapter VI. We notice that the mean values of the relevant correlations as well as the dispersions on these correlations are slightly dependent on the particular set of pseudo-orthogonal components with which the system operates (see 1). However, these dependencies do not damage the basic properties of the model. The first row of each of the following tables shows the number of neural updatings of the system. The second row contains the correlations of the network state with the item at issue. Finally, the third row shows the dispersion on these correlations.

Example 1 (figure s1; correlation of the network state with i0 and dispersion on this correlation)

updat.	0	1000	2000	3000	4000
correl.	.281	.160	.088	.040	.012
dispers.	.0	.010	.011	.006	.007

updat.	5000	6000
correl	.006	-.009
dispers.	.006	.004

Example 1 (figure s1; correlation of the network state with i4 and dispersion on this correlation)

updat.	0	1000	2000	3000	4000
correl.	.437	.657	.787	.873	.924
dispers.	.0	.010	.005	.011	.008

updat.	5000	6000
correl.	.954	.970
dispers.	.006	.004

Example 1 (figure s2; correlation of the network state with i0 and dispersion on this correlation)

updat.	0	1000	2000	3000	4000
correl.	.281	.455	.625	.734	.801
dispers.	.0	.010	.012	.008	.007

updat.	5000	6000
correl.	.840	.866
dispers.	.007	.010

Example 1 (figure s2; correlation of the network state with i0 and dispersion on this correlation)

updat.	0	1000	2000	3000	4000
correl.	.437	.354	.235	.164	.120
dispers.	.0	.017	.011	.009	.007

updat.	5000	6000
correl.	.094	.078
dispers.	.006	.007

Example 1 (figure s3; correlation of the network state with i0 and dispersion on this correlation)

updat.	0	1000	2000	3000	4000
correl.	.281	.429	.624	.775	.860
dispers.	.0	.005	.008	.009	.007

updat.	5000	6000
correl.	.912	.944
dispers.	.006	.005

Example 1 (figure s3; correlation of the network state with i4 and dispersion on this correlation)

updat.	0	1000	2000	3000	4000
correl.	.437	.402	.268	.146	.080
dispers.	.0	.007	.007	.008	.007

updat.	5000	6000
correl.	.037	.010
dispers.	.006	.004

Example 2 (figure s4; correlation of the network state with i0 and dispersion on this correlation)

updat.	0	1000	2000	3000	4000
correl.	.352	.470	.605	.746	.845
dispers.	.0	.018	.023	.026	.017

updat.	5000	6000
correl.	.903	.941
dispers.	.012	.008

Example 2 (figure s4; correlation of the network state with i1 and dispersion on this correlation)

updat.	0	1000	2000	3000	4000
correl.	.693	.733	.697	.613	.549
dispers.	.015	.024	.026	.018	.016

updat.	5000	6000
correl.	.515	.488
dispers.	.016	.009

Example 2 (figure s5; correlation of the network state with i0 and dispersion on this correlation)

updat.	0	1000	2000	3000	4000
correl.	.352	.390	.413	.430	.438
dispers.	.0	.006	.005	.004	.005

updat.	5000	6000
correl.	.444	.448
dispers.	.004	.003

Example 2 (figure s5; correlation of the network state with i1 and dispersion on this correlation)

updat.	0	1000	2000	3000	4000
correl.	.693	.813	.886	.932	.958
dispers.	.0	.010	.008	.008	.005

updat.	5000	6000
correl.	.973	.985
dispers.	.006	.006

Example 2 (figure s6; correlation of the network state with i1 and dispersion on this correlation)

updat.	0	1000	2000	3000	4000
correl.	.352	.388	.409	.425	.435
dispers.	.0	.007	.006	.004	.005

updat.	5000	6000
correl.	.442	.445
dispers.	.004	.003

Example 2 (figure s6; correlation of the network state with i1 and dispersion on this correlation)

updat.	0	1000	2000	3000	4000
correl.	.693	.807	.881	.927	.956
dispers.	.0	.007	.009	.007	.007

updat.	5000	6000
correl.	.974	.985
dispers.	.004	.003

Example 3 (figure s7; correlation of the network state with i0 and dispersion on this correlation)

updat.	0	1000	2000	3000	4000
correl.	.370	.334	.305	.293	.285
dispers	.0	.008	.005	.004	.005

updat.	5000	6000
correl.	.280	.280
dispers.	.006	.005

Example 3 (figure s7; correlation of the network state with i1 and dispersion on this correlation)

updat.	0	1000	2000	3000	4000
correl.	.507	.695	.809	.885	.927
dispers.	.0	.004	.010	.010	.008

updat.	5000	6000
correl.	.954	.972
dispers.	.008	.005

Example 3 (figure s8; correlation of the network state with i0 and dispersion on this correlation)

updat.	0	1000	2000	3000	4000
correl.	.370	.454	.520	.562	.584
dispers.	.0	.009	.006	.007	.007

updat.	5000	6000
correl.	.601	.593
dispers.	.007	.018

Example 3 (figure s8; correlation of the network state with i1 and dispersion on this correlation)

updat.	0	1000	2000	3000	4000
correl.	.507	.577	.600	.620	.630
dispers.	.0	.010	.010	.014	.012

updat.	5000	6000
correl.	.632	.619
dispers.	.011	.019

The two final tables show the order parameters of the groundstates of picture s9; the dispersions on the order parameters are given in the third row.

Example 3 (figure s9; order parameter of $P2$ and dispersion on this order parameter)

updat.	0	1000	2000	3000	4000
or. par.	-.020	.025	.057	.075	.084
dispers.	.0	.010	.010	.007	.005

updat.	5000	6000
or. par.	.090	.094
dispers.	.004	.005

Example 3 (figure s9; order parameter of *P4* and dispersion on this order parameter)

updat.	0	1000	2000	3000	4000
or. par.	.006	.050	.077	.090	.098
dispers.	.0	.011	.010	.010	.007

updat.	5000	6000
or. par.	.104	.108
dispers.	.007	.003

BIBLIOGRAPHY

Ackerman, B. (1985), Children's retrieval deficit, in: C. Brainerd, M. Pressley (Eds.), *Progress in cognitive development research* (pp. 1-46), New York: Springer Verlag

Allman, J., Baker, J., Newsome, W., Petersen, S. (1981), Visual topography and function: Cortical-visual areas in the owlmonkey, in: C. Woolsey (Ed.), *Multiple visual areas*, vol.2, Cortical sensory organization, Humana Press

Ament, W. (1899), *Die Entwicklung von Sprechen und Denken beim Kinde*, Leipzig: Barth

Amit, D. (1987), The properties of models of simple neural networks, in: I. Morgenstern, L. Van Hemmen (Eds.), *Heidelberg Symposium on Glassy Dynamics* (pp. 121-167), Berlin: Springer Verlag

Amit, D. (1988), Neural networks: achievements, prospects, difficulties, in: W. Guttinger, G. Dangelmayr (Ed.), *The physics of structure formation* (pp. 5-23), Berlin: Springer Verlag

Amit, D., Gutfreund, H., Sompolinsky, H. (1985), Spin-glass models of neural networks, *Physical Review A*, 32, 1007-1018

Amit, D., Gutfreund, H., Sompolinsky, H. (1987), Statistical mechanics of neural networks near saturation, *Annals of Physics*, 173, 30-67

Anderson, J.R., Kline, P., Beasly, C. (1979), A general theory and its application to schema abstraction, in: G. Bower (Ed.), *The psychology of learning and motivation*, New York: Academic Press

Anderson, R.C., Mc Gaw, B. (1973), On the representation of the meaning of general terms, *Journal of Experimental Psychology*, 101, 301-306

Anderson, R.C., Ortony, A. (1975), On putting apples into bottles -A problem of polysemy, *Cognitive Psychology*, 7, 167-180

Anderson, R.C., Pichert, J. Goetz, Schallert, D., Stevens, K., Trollip, S. (1976), Instantiation of general terms, *Journal of Verbal Learning and Verbal Behavior*, 15, 667-679

Anderson, R.C., Shifrin, Z. (1980), The meaning of words in context, in: R. Spiro, B. Bruice, W. Brewer (Eds.), *Theoretical issues in reading comprehension* (pp. 331-348), Hillsdale: Erlbaum

Anglin, J. (1970), *The growth of word meaning*, Cambridge: MIT Press

Anglin, J. (1977), *Word, object and conceptual development*, New York: Norton

Annett, M. (1959), *The classification of instances of four common class concepts by children and adults*, British Journal of Psychology, 29, 233-236

Anooshian, L., Siegel, A. (1985), From cognitive to procedural mapping, in: C. Brainerd, M. Pressley (Eds.), *Progress in cognitive development research* (pp. 47-101), Springer Verlag

Arbib, M. (1972), *The metaphorical brain*, Wiley-Interscience

Arbib, M. (1982), Perceptual-motor processes and the neural basis of language, in: M. Arbib (Ed.), *Perspectives in neurolinguistics, neuropsychology and psycholinguistics*, London: Academic Press

Armstrong, J., Gleitman, L., Gleitman, H. (1983), *What some concepts might not be*, Cognition, 13, 263-308

Ashby, W. (1952), *Design for a brain*, Chapman and Hall

Attneave, F. (1968), Triangles as ambiguous figures, *American Journal of Psychology*, 81, 447-453

Bacci, S., Mato, G., Parga, N. (1990), Dynamics of a neural network with hierarchically stored patterns, *Journal of Physics, A: Mathematical and general*, 23, 1801-1810

Ballard, D. (1986), Cortical connections and parallel processing: Structure and function, *Behavioral and Brain Sciences*, 9, 67-120

Ballard, D., & Brown, C. (1982), *Computer vision*. New York: Prentice-Hall.

Barsalou, L. (1983), Ad hoc categories, *Memory and Cognition*, 11, 211-227

Barsalou, L. (1985), Ideals, central tendency, and frequency of instantiation as determinants of graded structure in categories, *Journal of Experimental Psychology: Learning, Memory and Cognition*, 11, 629-654

Barr, R., Caplan, L. (1987), Category representations and their implications for category structure, *Memory and Cognition*, 15, 397-418

Battig, W., Montague, W. (1969), Category norms for verbal items in 56 categories: A replication and extension of the Connecticut category norms, *Journal of Experimental Psychology*, Monograph, 80

Beach, L. (1964), Cue probabilism and inference behavior, *Psychological Monographs*, 78 (Whole No.582)

Bierwisch, M. (1969), On certain problems of semantic representations, *Foundations of Language*, 5, 153-184

Bierwisch, M. (1970), On semantics, in: J. Lyons (Ed.), *New horizons in linguistics* (pp.178-194), London, Penguin

Binder, K., Young, A. (1986), Spin-glasses: experimental facts, theoretical concepts, and open questions, *Review of Modern Physics*, 58, 801-976

Bjorklund, D. (1980), Developmental differences in the timing of children's awareness of category relations in free recall, *International Journal of Behavioral Development*, 3, 61-70

Bjorklund, D. (1985), The role of conceptual knowledge in the development of organization in children's memory, in: C. Brainerd, M. Pressley (Eds.), *Progress in cognitive development research* (pp. 103-142), New York: Springer Verlag

Bomba, P., Siqueland, E. (1983), The nature of infant form categories, *Journal of Experimental Child Psychology*, 35, 294-328

Bobrow, D., Norman, D. (1975), Some principles of memory schemata, in: D. Bobrow, A. Collins (Eds.), *Representations and understanding: Studies in cognitive science* (pp. 131-149), New York: Academic Press.

Bourne, L. (1970), Knowing and using concepts, *Psychological Review*, 77, 546-556

Bower, T. (1974), *Aspects of development in infancy*, San Fransisco: Freeman

Brown, A. (1977), Development, schooling and the acquisition of knowledge about knowledge, R. Anderson, J. Spiro, W. Montague. (Eds.), *Schooling and the acquisition of knowledge* (pp.42-71), Hillsdale: Erlbaum

Brownell, H. (1988). Appreciation of metaphoric and connotative word meaning by brain-damaged patients. In C. Chiarello (Ed.), *Right hemisphere contributions to lexical semantics* (pp. 19-32), New York: Springer Verlag.

Brownell, H., Potter, H., & Michelow, D. (1984). Sensitivity to lexical denotation and connotation in brain damaged patients: A double dissociation? *Brain and language*, 22, 253-265.

Bruner, J., Goodnow, J., Austin, G. (1956), *A study of thinking*, New York: Wiley

Bryer, R., & Stripstein, E. (1985). Concreteness and imageability in lateral differences in word perception. *Cahiers de psychologie cognitive*, 5, 111-125.

Burgess, C., & Simpson, G. (1988). Cerebral hemisphere mechanisms in the retrieval of ambiguous word meanings, *Brain and Language*, 33, 86-103.

Caelli, T., Julesz, B., Gilbert, E., (1978), On perceptual analyzers underlying visual texture discrimination: Part II, *Biological Cybernetics*, 29, 201-214

Caron, R., Caron, A., Meyers, R. (1982), Abstraction of invariant facial expressions in infancy, *Child Development*, 53, 1008-1015

Cassirer, E. (1923/1953), *Structure and function and Einstein's theory of relativity*, New York: Dover publications

Chi, M (1976), Short-term limitations in children: Capacity or processing deficits? *Memory and Cognition*, 4, 559-572

Chi, M. (1978), Knowledge structure and memory development, In: Siegler, R. (Ed.), *Children's thinking: What develops?* Thirteenth Annual Carnegie Symposium on Cognition, Hillsdale: Erlbaum

Chi, M. (1981), Knowledge development and memory performance, in: M. Friedman, J. Das, N. O'Connor (Eds.), *Intelligence and learning*, New York, Plenum Press

Chi, M., Feltovich, P. Glaser, R. (1981), Categorization and representation of physics knowledge by experts and novices, *Cognitive Science*, 5, 121-152

Chi, M., Koeske, R. (1983), Network representation of a child's dinosaur knowledge, *Developmental Psychology*, 19, 29-39

Chiarello, C. (1985). Hemisphere dynamics in lexical access: automatic and controlled priming. *Brain and Language*, 26, 146-172.

Chiarello, C. (1988). Semantic priming in the intact brain: separate roles for the left and the right hemispheres? In C. Chiarello, (Ed.), *Right hemisphere contributions to lexical semantics* (pp. 59-69), New York: Springer Verlag.

Chomsky, N. (1969), *The acquisition in syntax in children form 5 to 10*, Cambridge: MIT Press

Clark, E. (1973), What's in a word? On the child's acquisition of semantics in his first language, in: T. Moore, (Ed.), *Cognitive development and the acquisition of language* (pp. 111-144), New York: Academic Press

Clark, H., Chase, W. (1972), On the process of comparing sentences against pictures, *Cognitive Psychology*, 3, 472-517

Cohen, L., Strauss, M. (1979), Concept acquisition in the human infant, *Child Development*, 50, 419-424

Collins, A., Quillian, M. (1969), Retrieval time from semantic memory, *Journal of Verbal Learning and of Verbal Behavior*, 8, 240-248

Conrad, C. (1974), Context effects in sentence comprehension: A study of the subjective lexicon, *Memory and Cognition*, 2, 130-138

Cooper, L., Shepard, R. (1973), Chronometric studies of the rotation of mental images, in: W. Chase (Ed.), *Visual information processing*, New York: Academic press

Corballis, M. (1989). Laterality and human evolution, *Psychological Review*, 96, 3, 492-505.

Cornell, E. (1974), Infants' discrimination of photographs of faces following redundant presentations, *Journal of experimental Child Psychology*, 18, 98-106

Crowell, D., Jones, R., Kapuniai, L., & Nakagawa, J. (1973). Unilateral cortical activity in newborn humans: An early index of cerebral dominance, *Science*, 180, 205-208.

Davis, A., & Wada, J. (1977). Hemispheric asymmetries inhuman infants: spectral analysis of flash and click evoked potentials, *Brain and language*, 4, 23-31.

Day, J. (1979). Visual half-life recognition as a function of syntactic class and imageability, *Neuropsychologia*, 17, 515-519.

Day, J., & Ulatowska, H. (1979). Perceptual, cognitive and linguistic development after early hemispherectomy: Two case studies, *Brain and language*, 7, 17-33.

Dempster, F. (1985), Short-term memory development in childhood and adolescence, in: C. Brainerd, M. Pressley (Eds.), *Progress in cognitive development research* (pp. 209-248), Springer Verlag

Denis, M. (1982), On figurative components of mental representations, in: F. Klix, J. Hoffman, E. van der Meer, (Eds.), *Cognitive research in psychology*, Berlin: Verlag der Wissenschaften

Denney, N., Ziobrowsk, M. (1972), Developmental changes in clustering criteria, *Journal of Experimental Child Psychology*, 13, 275-282

Denney, D., Moulton, P. (1976), Conceptual preferences among preschool children, *Developmental Psychology*, 12, 509-513

De Renzi, E. (1982), *Disorders of space exploration and cognition*, New York: Wiley.

Diamond, R., & Carey, S. (1986). Why faces are not special: an effect of expertise. *Journal of experimental psychology: General*, 115, 107-117.

Drews, E. (1987). Qualitatively different organizational structures of lexical knowledge in the left and right hemisphere, *Neuropsychologia*, 25, 419-427.

Effron, R., Yund, E. (1974), Dichotic competition of simultaneous tone bursts of different frequency, I: Dissociation of pitch from lateralization and loudness, *Neuropsychologia*, 12, 278-286

Fagan, J (1976), Infants' recognition of invariant features of faces, *Infant Behavior and Development*, 47, 627-638

Franzon, M., & Hugdahl, K. (1986). Visual half-field presentations of incongruent color words: Effects of gender and handedness. *Cortex*, 22, 433-445.

Galbraith, R., Day, R. (1978), Developmental changes in clustering criteria? A closer look at Denny and Ziobrowski, *Child Development*, 49, 889-891,

Gardner, H., Brownell, H., Wapner, W., & Michelow, D. (1983). Missing the point: The role of the right hemisphere in the processing of complex materials. In E. Perecman, (Ed.), *Cognitive processing in the right hemisphere* (pp. 169-191). New York: Academic Press.

Garrod, S., Sanford, A. (1977), Interpreting anaphoric relations: the integration of semantic information while reading, *Journal of Verbal Learing and of Verbal Behavior*, 16, 77-90

Gibson, E. (1969), *Principles of perceptual learning and development*, New York: Appleton-Century-Crofts

Gibson, E., Owsley, J., Johnson, C. (1978), Perception of invariance by five-month-old infants: differentiation of two types of motion, *Developmental Psychology*, 14, 407-415

Gibson, E., Spelke, E. (1983), The development of perception, in: J. Flavell, J. Markman (Eds.), *Cognitive development* (Vol 3 of P. Mussen (ed.), Carmichael's manual of child psychology) Wiley: New York

Goldberg, E., & Costa, L. (1981). Hemispheric differences in the acquisition and use of descriptive systems, *Brain and Language*, 14, 144-173.

Goldman, D., Homa, D. (1977), Integrative and metric properties of abstracted information as a function of category discriminability, instance variability, and experience, *Journal of Experimental Psychology: Human Learning and Memory*, 3, 375-385

Golinkoff, M., Halperin, M. (1983), The concept of animal: one infant's view, *Infant Behavior and Development*, 6, 229-233

Goodglass, H., Kaplan, E. (1963), Distrbance of gesture and pantominme in aphasia, *Brain*, 86, 703-720

Greenfield, M., Smith, J. (1976), *The structure of communication in early language development*, New York: Academic Press

Grossberg, S. (1976), Adaptive pattern classification and universal recoding: Part I. Parallel development and coding of neural feature detectors, *Biological Cybernetics*, 23, 121-134

Grossberg, S. (1980), How does the brain build a cogntitive code, *Psychological Review*, 87, 1-51

Grossberg, S. (1982), *Studies of mind and brain*, Dordrecht, Holland: Reidel

Grossberg, S., (Ed.), (1987a), *The adaptive brain I: Cognition, learning, reinforcement and rythm*, North Holland

Grossberg, S., (Ed.), (1987b), *The adaptive brain II: Vision, speech, language and motor control*, North holland

Grossberg, S., Mingolla, E. (1985), Neural dynamics of form perception: Boundary completion, illusary figures, and neon color spreading, *Psychological Review*, 92, 173-211

Grossberg, S., Stone, G. (1986), Neural dynamics of word recognition and recall: Attentional priming, learning, and resonance, *Psychological Review*, 93, 46-74

Guillaume, P. (1927), Les débuts de la phrase dans le langage de l'enfant, *Journal de Psychologie*, 24, 1-25

Gumenik, W. (1979), The advantage of specific terms over general terms as cues for sentence recall: Instantiation or retrieval? *Memory and Cognition*, 7, 240-244

Gur, R., Packer, I., Hungerbuhler, J., Reivich, M., Obrist, W., Amarnek, W., & Sackheim, H. (1980). Differences in the distribution of gray and white matter in human cerebral hemispheres, *Science*, 207, 1226-1228.

Gursney, R., Browse, R. (1988), Aspects of visual texture discrimination, in: Z. Pylyshyn (ed.), *Computational processes in vision: an interdisciplinary perspective*, Norwood: Ablex Publishing Corporation

Gutfreund, H. (1988), Neural networks with hierarchically correlated patterns. *Physical Review A*, 39, 6365-6372.

Hampton, J., Gardiner, M. (1983), Measures of internal category structure: A correlational analysis of normative data, *British journal of psychology*, 74, 491-516

Hayes-Roth, F. (1979), Understanding mental imagery: interpretative metaphors versus explanatory models, *The Behavioral and Brain Sciences*, 2, 553-554

Hayes-Roth, B., Hayes Roth, F. (1977), Concept learning and the recognition and classification of exemplars, *Journal of verbal Learning and Verbal Behavior*, 16, 321-338

Hebb, D (1949), *The organization of behavior*, New York: Wiley

Heider, E. (1972), Universals in color naming and memory, *Journal of Experimental Psychology*, 93, 10-20

Hinton, G. (1979), Imagery without arrays, *The Behavioral and Brain Sciences*, 2, 555-556

Hinton, (1990). Mapping part-whole hierarchies in connectionist networks. *Artificial Intelligence*, 46 (1-2), p. 47-76.

Hinton, G., Mc Clelland, J., Rumelhart, D. (1986), Distributed representations, in: D. Rumelhart, D., J. Mc Clelland (Eds.), *Parallel distributed processing: Explorations in the microstructure of cognition*, Volume 1: Foundations, Cambridge: Bradford Books/MIT Press

Hoffman, R., Denis, M., Ziesler, M. (1983), Figurative features and the construction of visual images, *Psychological Research*, 45, 39-54

Holland, J., Holoyak, K., Nisbett, R., Thagard, P. (1986), *Induction: processes of inference, learning, and discovery*, MIT Press

Homa, D., Cross, J., Cornell, D., Goldman, D., Schwartz, S. (1973), Prototype abstraction and classification of new instnaces as a function of number of instances defining the prototype, *Journal of Experimental Psychology*, 101, 116-122

Homa, D., Chambliss, D. (1975), The relative contributions of common and distinctive information on the abstraction from ill-defined cateogires, *Journal of Experimental Psychology: Human Learning and Memory*, 1, 351-359

Homa, D., Vosburgh, R. (1976), Category breadth and the abstraction of prototypical information, *Journal of Experimental psychology: Human Learning and Memory*, 2, 322-330

Hopfield, J. (1982), Neural networks and physical systems with emergent collective computational abilites, *Proceedings of the National Academy of Sciences of the USA*, 79, 2554-2558

Hubel, D., Wiesel, T. (1962), Receptive fields, binocular interaction, and the functional architecture in the cat's visual cortex, *Journal of Physiology*, 160, 106-154

Hubel, D., Wiesel, T. (1968), Receptive fields and functional characteristics of monkey striate cortex, *Journal of Physiology*, 195, 215-243

Hubel, D., Wiesel, T. (1977), Functional architecture of macaque monkey visual cortex, *Proceedings of the Royal Society of London*, Series B, 198, 1-59

Huttenlocher, J. (1968), Constructing spatial images: a strategy in reasoning, *Psychological Review*, 75, 550-560

Inhelder, B., Piaget, J. (1964), *The early growth of logic in the child*, New York: Norton

Jackson, J (1958), *On localization*, In: Selected writings (Vol. 2) New York: Basic Books (Original work published in 1869)

Joanette, Y., Goulet, P., & Hannequin, D. (1990). *Right hemisphere and verbal communication*, New York: Springer Verlag.

Johnson, M., *The body in the mind: The bodily basis of reason and imagination*, Chicago: University of Chicago Press

Johnson-Liard, P. (1979), "The thoughtless imagery" controversy, *Behavioral and Brain Sciences*, 2, 557-558

Johnson-Liard, P. (1982), Propositional representations, procedural semantics, and mental models, in: J. Mehler, E. Walker, M. Garret (Eds.), *Perspectives on mental representation* (pp. 11-131), Hillsdale: Erlbaum

Julesz, B. (1981), Textons, the elements of texture discrimination, a,d their interactions, *Nature*, 290, 91-97

Julesz, B. (1984), Toward an axiomatic theory of preattentive vision, in: Edelman, G., Cowan, M., Gall, E. (Eds), *Dynamic aspects of neocortical function*, New York: Wiley

Katz, J., Fodor, J. (1963), The structure of a semantic theory, *Language*, 39, 170-211

Katz, J., Postal, P. (1964), *An integrated theory of linguistic descriptions*, Cambridge: MIT Press

Keenan, J., Moore, R. (1979), Memory for images of concealed objects: a reexamination of Neisser and Kerr, *Journal of Experimental Psychology: Human Learning and Memory*, 5, 374-358

Keil, F., Batterman, (1984), A characteristic-to-defining shift in the development of word meaning, *Journal of verbal Learning and Verbal Behavior*, 23, 221-236

Kenyeres, E. (1926), Les premiers mots de l'enfant, *Archives de Psychologie*, 20, 191-218

Kohn, B., & Dennis, M. (1974). Selective impairment of visuo-spatial abilities in infantile hemiplegics after right cerebral hemidecortication, *Neuropsychologia*, 12, 505-512.

Kosslyn, S. (1973), Scanning visual images: some structural implications, *Perception and Psychophysics*, 14, 90-94

Kosslyn, S. (1975), Information representation in visual images, *Cognitive Psychology*, 7, 341-370

Kosslyn, S. (1976), Can imagery be distinguished from other forms of internal representation? Evidence from studies of information retrieval time, *Memory and Cognition*, 4, 291-297

Kosslyn, S. (1980), *Image and mind*, Cambridge, Harvard University Press

Kosslyn, S., (1987). Seeing and imaging in the cerebral hemispheres: a computational approach, *Psychological Review*, 94, 148-175.

Kosslyn, S. (1988), Aspects of a cognitive neuroscience of mental imagery, *Science*, 240, 1621-1626.

Kosslyn, S., Holoyak, K., Huffman, C. (1976), A processing approach to the dual coding hypothesis, *Journal of Experimental Psychology: Human Learning and Memory*, 2, 223-233

Kosslyn, S., Alper, S. (1977), On the pictorial properties of visual images: effects of image size on memory for words, *Canadian Journal of Psychology*, 31, 32-40

Kosslyn, S., Pomerantz, J. (1977), Imagery, propositions, and the form of internal representations, *Cognitive Psychology*, 9, 52-76

Kosslyn, S. Schwartz (1977), S., A simulation of visual imagery, *Cognitive Science*, 1, 265-298

Kosslyn, S., Ball, T., Reiser, B. (1978), Visual images preserve metric spatial information: Evidence from studies of image scanning, *Journal of Experimental Psychology: Human Perception and Performance*, 4, 47-60

Kosslyn, S., Pinker, S., Smith, G., Schwartz, S. (1979), On the demystification of mental imagery, *The Behavioral and Brain Sciences*, 2, 535-581

Lakoff, G. (1973), Hedges: A study in meaning criteria and the logic of fuzzy concepts, *Journal of Philosophical Logic*, 2, 458-508

Lakoff, G. (1987), *Women, fire, and dangerous things*, University of Chicago Press

Lambert, A., & Beaumont, J. (1983). Imageability does not interact with visual field in lateral word recognition with oral report, *Brain and Language*, 20, 115-142.

Latto, A., Mumford, D., & Shah, J. (1984), The representation of shape. In *Proceedings of IEEE workshop on computer vision*, Annapolis, MD (pp. 183-191), Washington DC: Institute of Electrical and Electronics Engineers.

Lawrence, D. (1971), Two studies of visual search for word targets with controlled rate of presentation, *Perception and Psychophysics*, 10, 85-89

Levine, D. (1982), Visual agnosia in monkey and man. In D. Ingle, M. Goodale, R. Mansfield (Eds.), *Analysis of visual behavior* (pp. 619-670), Cambridge, MA: MIT Press.

Levine, M. (1975), *A cognitive theory of learning: Research on hypothesis testing*, Hillsdale: Erlbaum

Levy, J. (1974), Psychobiological implications of bilateral asymmetry. In S. Dimond, S. Beaumont (Eds), *Hemispheric function in the human brain*, New York: Halstead Press.

Lissaurer, H. (1889), Ein Fall von Seelenblindheit nebst Beitrage zur Theorie derselben, *Archif fur Psychiatrie und Nervenkrankheiten*, 21, 220-270

Lucariello, J., Nelson, K. (1985), Slot-filler categories as memory organizers for young children, *Developmental Psychology*, 21, 272-282

Luria, A. (1966), *Higher cortical functions in man*, New York: Basic Books

Luria, A., Yudovich, F. (1959), *Speech and the development of mental processes in the child*, New York: Humanities

Mandler, J. (1983), Representation, in: E. Flavell, J. Markman (Eds.), Cognitive development (Vol 3 of P. Mussen (Ed.), *Carmichael's manual of child psychology*), Wiley: New York

Marcel, A., & Patterson, K. (1978), Word recognition and production: Reciprocity in clinical and normal research. In: J. Requin (Ed.), *Attention and performance* (Vol 7, pp 209-226). Hillsdale, NJ: Lawrence Erlbaum Associates.

Marr, D. (1982), *Vision*, San Francisco, Freeman

Marr, D., Poggio, T. (1976), From understanding computation understanding neural circuitry, *Neuroscience Research Progress Bulletin*, 15, 470-488

Marr, D., Nishihara, H. (1978), Representation and recognition of the movement of shapes, *Proceedings of the Royal Society of London B*, 290, 269-294

Marr, D., Nishihara, H. (1978), Visual information processing: artificial intelligence and the sensorium of sight, *Technological Review*, 81, 2-23

Marr, D., Hildreth, E. (1980), Theory of edge detection, *Proceedings of the Royal Society of London*, B, 207, 187-217

Marr, D., Vaina, L. (1982), Representation and recognition of the movement of shapes, *Proceedings of the Royal Society of London*, B, 214, 501-524

Martin, R., Caramazza, A. (1980), Classification in well-defined and ill-defined categories: Evidence for common processing strategies, *Journal of Experimental Psychology: General*, 109, 320-353

Mc Cauley, C., Weil, C., Sperber, R. (1976), The development of memory structure as reflected by semantic-priming effects, *Journal of Experimental Child Psychology*, 22, 511-518

Mc Clelland, J., Rumelhart, D. (1985), Distributed memory and the representation of general and specific information, *Journal of Experimental Psychology: General*, 114, 159-188

Mc Closkey, M. (1980), The stimulus familiarity problem in semantic memory research, *Journal of Verbal Leraning and Verbal Behavior*, 19, 485-502

Mc Closkey, M., Glucksberg, S. (1978), Natural categories: well-defined or fuzzy sets? *Memory and cognition*, 6, 462-472

Mc Closkey, M., Glucksberg, S. (1979), Decision processes in verifying category membership statements: Implications for models of semantic memory, *Cognitive Psychology*, 35, 113-138

Mc Culloch, W., Pitts, W. (1943), A logical calculus of the ideas immanent in nervous activity, *Bulletin of Mathematical Biophysics*, 5, 115-133

Mc Mullen, P., Bryden, M. (1987), The effects of word imageabiity and frequency on hemispheric asymmetry in lexical disorders, *Brain and language*, 31, 11-25.

Medin, D., Schaffer, M. (1978), Context theory of classification learning, *Psychological Review*, 85, 207-238

Medin, D. Schwanenflugel, P. (1981), Linear separability in classification learning, *Journal of Experimental psychology: Human Learning and Memory*, 7, 355-368

Medin, D., Altom, M., Edelson, S., Freko, D. (1982), Correlated symptoms and simulated medical classification, *Journal of Experimental Psychology: Learning, Memory and Cognition*, 8, 37-50

Medin, D., Dewey, G., Murphy, T. (1983), Relations between item and category learning: Evidence that abstraction is not automatic, *Journal of Experimental psychology: Learning, Memory and Cognition*, 9, 607-625

Medin, D., Altom, M., Murphy, T. (1984), Given versus induced category representations: Use of prototype and exemplar information in classification, *Journal of Experimental Psychology: Learning, Memory, and Cognition*, 10, 333-365

Medin, D., Smith, E. (1984), Concepts and concept formation, *Annual Review of Psychology*, 35, 113-138

Medin, D., Wattenmaker, W. (1986), Category cohesiveness, theories and cognitive archeology, in: U. Neisser (Ed.), *Categories reconsidered: The ecological and intellectual bases of categories* (pp. 87-124), London/New York: Cambridge University Press

Medin, D., Wattenmaker, W. (1987), Family resemblance, conceptual cohesiveness, and category construction, *Cognitive Psychology*, 19, 242-279

Molfese, D., & Molfese, V. (1979). Hemisphere and stimulus differences as reflected in the cortical responses of newborn infants to speech stimuli, *Developmental psychology*, 15, 505-511.

Molfese, D., & Molfese, V. (1980). Cortical responses of preterm infants to phonetic and non-phonetic speech stimuli, *Developmental psychology*, 16, 574-581.

Moore, K. (1896), The mental development of a child, *Psychological Review*, Monograph supplement, 1 (3)

Morton, J. (1969), Interaction of information in word recognition, *Psychological Review*, 76, 165-178

Morton, J. (1979), Facilitation in word recognition: experiments causing change in the logogen model, in: P. Kolers, M. Wrolstead, S. Bouma (Eds.), *Processing of visible language* (Vol 1), New York: Plenum Press

Murphy, G., (1982), Cue validity and levels of categorization, *Psychological Bulletin*, 91, 174-177

Murphy, G., Medin, D. (1985), The role of theories in conceptual coherence, *Psychological Review*, 92, 289-316

Navon, D. (1977), Forest before trees: The precedence of global features in visual perception, *Cognitive Psychology*, 9, 353-363

Neisser, U. (1967), *Cognitive Psychology*, New York: Appleton-Century-Crofts

Nelson, K. (1973), Some evidence of the cognitive primacy of categorization and its functional basis, *Merill-Palmer Quarterly*, 19, 21-39

Nelson, K. (1974), Concept, word and sentence: Interrelations in acquisition and development, *Psychological Review*, 81, 267-285

Nelson, K. (1977), The conceptual basis for naming, in: J. Macnamara (Ed.), *Language, learning and thought* (pp 117-136), New York: Academic Press

Nelson, K. (1983), The derivation of concepts and categories from event representations, in: Scholnick, E. (ed.), *New trends in conceptual representation* (pp. 53-69), New York: Hillsdale

Nelson, K. (1985), *Making sense: The acquisition of shared meaning*, Orlando: Academic Press

Nelson, K., Gruendel, J. (1981), Generalized event representations: Basic building blocks of cognitive development, in: Lamb, M, Brown, A. (Eds.), *Advances in developmental psychology* (Vol 1) (pp. 138-152), Hillsdale: Erlbaum

Neumann, P. (1974), An attribute frequencey model for the abstraction of prototypes, *Memory and Cognition*, 2, 241-248

Newell, A. (1980), Physical symbol systems, *Cognitive Science*, 4, 135-183

Newell, A. (1982), THe knowledge level, *Artificial intelligence*, 18, 87-127

Newport, E. (1984), Constraints on learning: studies on the study of American Sign Language, *Papers and Reports on Child Language Development*, 23, 1-22

Newport, E., Belugi, U. (1978), Linguistic expression of category levels in a visual-gestural language, in: Rosch E., Lloyd, B. (Eds.), *Cognition and categorization* (pp. 194-228), Hillsdale: Erlbaum

Ornstein, P., Corsale, K. (1979), Organizational factors in children's memory, in: C. Puff (Ed.), *Organization, structure and memory*, New York: Academic Press

Paivio, A. (1971), *Imagery and verbal processes*, New York: Holt, Rinehart and Winston

Paivio, A. (1978), Imagery, language and semantic memory, *International Journal of Psycholinguistics*, 5, 31-47

Paivio, A. (1983), The empirical case for dual coding, in: Yuille, J. (Ed.), *Imagery, memory and cognition: essays in honor of Allan Paivio* (pp. 7-34), Hillsdale: Erlbaum

Paivio, A. (1986), *Representations: a dual coding approach*, Oxford University Press

Paivio, A., Lambert, W. (1981), Dual coding and bilingual memory, *Journal of Verbal Memory and Behavior*, 20, 532-539

Patterson, K., & Besner, D. (1984), Is the right hemisphere literate? *Cognitive Neuropsychology*, 1, 315-341.

Perlmutter, M, Myers, N. (1979), Development of recall in 2- to 4-year-old children, *Developmental Psychology*, 15, 73-83

Perlmutter, M., Sophian, C., Mitchell, D., Cavanaugh, J. (1981), Semantic and contextual cuing of preschool children's recall, *Child Development*, 52, 873-881

Peterson, M., Meagher, R., Chait, H., Gillie, S. (1973), The abstraction and generalization of dot patterns, *Cognitive Psychology*, 4, 378-398

Piaget, J. (1928), *Judgement and reasoning in the child*, London: Kegan Paul

Piaget, J. (1952), *The origins of intelligence in children*, New York: International Universities Press

Piaget, J. (1954), *The construction of reality in the child*, New York: Basic Books

Piaget, J. (1962), *Play, dreams and imitation in childhood*, New York: W. Norton

Piaget, J. (1974), *The development of physical quantities in the child: conservation and atomism*, London: Routledge and Kegan

Piaget, J., Inhelder, B. (1956), *The child's conception of space*, New Jersey: Humanities Press

Pinker, S., Prince, A. (1988), On language and connectionism: analysis of a parallel distributed processing model of language acquisition, *Cognition*, 28, 73-193

Pomerantz, J., Sager, L., Stoever,R. (1977), Perception of wholes and their component parts: Some configurational superiority effects, *Journal of Experimental Psychology: Human Perception and Performance*, 3, 422-435

Posner, M., Keele, S. (1968), On the genesis of abstract ideas, *Journal of Experimental psychology*, 77, 353-363

Posner, M., Keele, S. (1970), Retention of abstract ideas, *Journal of experimental Psychology*, 83, 304-308

Postal, P. (1966), Review article: Adré Martinet, "Elements of general linguistics", *Foundations of language*, 2, 151-186

Pylyshyn, Z. (1973), What the mind's eye tells the mind's brain: a critique of mental imagery, *Psychological Bulletin*, 80, 1-24

Pylyshyn, Z. (1979), Imagery theory: not mysterious - just wrong, *The Behavioral and Brain Sciences*, 2, 561-563

Pylyshyn, Z. (1980), Computation and cognition: issues in the foundations of cognitive science, *The Behavioral and Brain Sciences*, 3, 111-169

Pylyshyn, Z. (1984), *Computation and Cognition: Toward a foundation of cognitive science*, Cambridge: Bradford Books/MIT Press

Rasmussen, V. (1922), *Et barns dagbog*, Kovenhavn, Gyldendal

Ratcliff, G., Newcombe, F. (1982), Object recognition: some deductions from the clinical evidence, in A. Ellis (Ed.), *Normality and pathology in cognitive function* (pp.314-328), New York: Academic Press

Reed, S. (1972), Pattern recognition and categorization, *Cognitive Psychology*, 3, 382-407

Reed, S. (1973), *Psychological processes in pattern recognition*, New York: Academic Press

Reitman, J., Bower, G. (1973), Storage and later recognition of exemplars of concepts, *Cognitive Psychology*, 4, 194-206

Rescola, I. (1980), Overextension in early language development, *Journal of Child Language*, 7, 321-326

Rips, L., Shoben E., Smith, E. (1973), Semantic distance and the verification of semantic relations, *Journal of Verbal Learning and Verbal Behavior*, 12, 1-20

Roberts, K. (1988), Retrieval of a basic level category in pre-linguistic infants, *Developmental Psychology*, 24, 21-27

Roberts, K., Horowitz, F. (1986), Basic level categorization in seven- and nine-month-old infants, *Journal of Child Language*, 13, 191-208

Rodel, M., & Landis, T., & Regard, M. (1989), Hemispheric dissociation in semantic relation, *Journal of clinical and experimental neuropsychology*, 11, 70.

Rosch, E. (1973), On the internal structure of perceptual and semantic cateogires, in: Moore, T. (Ed.), *Cognitive development and the acquisition of language* (pp. 111-144), New York: Academic Press

Rosch, E. (1973), Natural categories, *Cognitive Psychology*, 4, 328-350

Rosch, E. (1975), Cognitive representations of semantic categories, *Journal of Experimental Psychology: General*, 104, 192-233

Rosch, E. (1978), Principles of categorization, in: Rosch E., Lloyd, B. (Eds.), *Cognition and categorization* (pp 27-48), Hillsdale: Erlbaum

Rosch, E., Mervis,C. (1975), Family Resemblances: Studies in the internal structure of categories, *Cognitive Psychology*, 7, 573-605

Rosch, E., Mervis, C., Gray, W. Johnson, D., Boyes-Braem, P. (1976), Basic objects in natural categories, *Cognitive Psychology*, 8, 382-439

Rosch, E., Simpson, C., Miller, R. (1976), Structural bases of typicality effects, *Journal of experimental psychology: Human Perception and Performance*, 2, 491-502

Roth, E., Shoben, E. (1983), The effect of context on the structure of categories, *Cognitive Psychology*, 15, 346-378

Ross, G. (1980), Categorization in 1- to 2-years-olds, *Developmental Psychology*, 16, 293-306

Rumelhart, D., Mc Clelland, J. (Eds.), *Parallel distributed processing: Explorations in the microstructure of cognition, Volume 1: Foundations*, Cambridge: Bradford Books/MIT Press

Rumelhart, D., Mc Clelland, J. (Eds.), *Parallel distributed processing: Explorations in the microstructure of cognition, Volume 2: Psychological and biological models*, Cambridge: Bradford Books/MIT Press

Rumelhart, D., Smolensky, P., Hinton, G. (1986), Schemata and sequential thought, in: Rumelhart, D., Mc Clelland, J. (Eds.), *Parallel distributed processing: Explorations in the microstructure of cognition, Volume 2: Psychological and biological models*, Cambridge: Bradford Books/MIT Press

Ruff, H. (1978), Infant recognition of the invariant form of objects, *Child Development*, 49, 293-306

Savin, H., Bever, T. (1970), The non-perceptual reality of the phoneme, *Journal of verbal learning and verbal behavior*, 9, 295-302

Schank, R., Collins, G., Hunter, L. (1986), Transcending inductive category formation in learning, *Brain and Behavioral Sciences*, 9, 639-686

Schmit, V., & Davis, R. (1974). The role of hemispheric specialization in the analysis of Stroop stimuli, *Acta Psychologica*, 38, 149-158.

Schwartz, E., Desimone, R., Albright, T., & Gross, C. (1984). Shape recognition and inferior temporal neurons, *Proceedings of the National Academy of Science USA*, 80, 5776-5778.

Semmes, J. (1968). Hemispheric specialization, a possible clue to mechanism. *Neuropsychologia*, 6, 11-26.

Shepard, R., Metzler, J. (1971), Mental rotation of three-dimensional objects, *Science*, 171, 701-703

Shepard, R., Feng, C. (1972), A chronometric study of mental paper folding, *Cognitive Psychology*, 3, 228-243

Shepard, R., Cooper, L. (1983), *Mental images and their transformations*, Cambridge, MIT Press

Sherman, T. (1985), Categorization skills in infants, *Child Development*, 56, 1561-1573

Sidtis, J., & Gazzaniga, M. (1983), Competence versus performance after callosal section: Looks can be deceiving. In J. Hellige (Ed.), *Cerebral hemisphere asymmetry. Method, theory and application* (pp.152-176). New York: Praeger.

Sigel, I. (1953), Developmental trends in the abstraction ability of children, *Child development*, 24, 131-144.

Simon, H. (1974), How big is a chunck?, *Science*, 183, 482-488

Smiley, S., Brown, A. (1979), Conceptual preference for thematic or taxonomic relations, A nonmonotonic age trend from preschool to old age, *Journal of Experimental Child Psychology*, 28, 249-257

Smith, E., Shoben, E., Rips, L. (1974), Structure and process in semantic memory: A featural model for semantic decisions, *Psychological Review*, 81, 214-241

Smith, E., Medin, D. (1981), *Categories and concepts*, Cambridge: Harvard University Press

Smolensky, P. (1988a), On the proper treatment of connectionism, *Behavioral and Brain Sciences*, 11, 1-74

Smolensky, P. (1988b), The constituent structure of connectionist mental states: A reply to Fodor and Pylyshyn, *Southern Journal of Philosophy*, Special issue on connectionism and the foundations of cognitive science, 26, 137-163

Smolensky, P. (1990), Tensor product variable binding and the representation of symbolic structures in connectionist systems, *Artificial Intelligence*, 46, 1-2, 159-216.

Solso, R. (1988), *Cognitive psychology* (second edition), Boston: Allynand Bacon

Springer, S., & Deutsch, G. (1989), *Left brain, right brain*, New York: W.H. Freeman and Company.

Strange, W., Keeney, T., Kessel, F., Jenkins, J. (1970), Abstraction over time of prototypes from distractions of random dot patterns: A replication, *Journal of Experimental Psychology*, 83, 508-510

Strauss, M. (1979), Abstraction of prototypical information by adults and 10-month-old infants, *Journal of experimental Psychology: Human Learning and Memory*, 5, 618-632

Strauss, M., Curtis, L. (1981), Infant perception of numerosity, *Child Development*, 52, 1146-1152

Trabasso, T., Bower, G. (1968), *Attention in learning: Theory and research*, New York: Wiley

Treisman, A. (1982), Perceptual grouping and attention in visual search for features and objects, *Journal of Experimental Psychology: Human Perception and Performace*, 8, 195, 214

Treisman, A. (1988), Preattentive processing in vision, in: Pylyshyn, Z. (Ed.), *Computational processes in human vision* (pp. 341-369), Norwood: Ablex Publishing Corporation

Treisman, A., Sykes, M., Gelade, G. (1977), Selective attention and stimulus integration, in: Dornic, S. (Ed.), *Attention and perfomance*, VI (pp.333-361), Hillsdale: Erlbaum

Treisman, A., Gelade, G. (1980), A feature integration theory of attention, *Cognitive Psychology*, 12, 97-136

Treisman, A., Schmidt, H. (1982), Illusary conjunctions in the perception of objects, *Cognitive psychology*, 14, 107-141

Treisman, A. Paterson, R. (1984), Emergent features, attention and object perception, *Journal of Experimental Psychology: Human Perception and Performance*, 10, 12-31

Tsao, Y., Feustel, T., & Soseos, C. (1979). Stroop interference in the left and right visual fields, *Brain and Language*, 8, 367-371.

Tversky, B., Hemmenway, K. (1984), Objects, parts and categories, *Journal of Experimental Psychology: General*, 113, 169-193

Underwood, P., Rusted, J., & Thwaites, S. (1983), Parafoveal words are effective in both hemifields: Preattentive processing of semantic and phonological codes, *Perception*, 12, 213-221.

Vaina, L. (1983), Form shapes and movements to objects and actions, *Synthese*, 54, 3-36

Vaina, L. (1984), Towards a computational theory of semantic memory, in: Vaina, L. and Hintikka, J. (eds.), *Cognitive constraints on Communication* (pp 97-113), Dordrecht: Reidel

Vaina, L. (1987), Visual texture for recognition, in: Vaina, L. (ed.), *Matters of intelligence* (pp 89-114), Dordrecht: Reidel

Van Loocke, Ph. (1990), Neural networks and higher mental processes: providing a Boltzmann network with a meta-layer, *Cognitive systems*, 2, 238-409.

Van Loocke, Ph. (1991a), *A connectionist model for conceptual dynamics*, doctoral dissertation, University of Ghent

Van Loocke, Ph. (1991b), Study of a neural network with a meta-layer, *Connection Science*, 4, 367-379.

Van Loocke, Ph. (1991c), Properties of vote-mixtures and the construction of a two-layer neural network, *CCAI: The Journal for the Integrated Study of Artificial Intelligence, Cognitive Science and Appied Epistemology*, 8, 309-351.

Van Loocke, Ph. (1992), The right hemisphere and its contribution to semantics: a neural network perspective, in: Vandamme, F., Van Loocke, Ph. (Eds.), *New trends in neural networks*, Ghent: Communication and Cognition

Van Loocke, Ph. (1993a), A connectionist model for the conceptual database of the right hemisphere, *Cognitive Systems* (to appear in december 1993)

Van Loocke, Ph. (1993b), On the psychology of connectionism, *Cognitive Systems* (to appear in december 1993)

Vygotsky, L. (1962), *Thought and language*, New York: Wiley

Walker, E., & Ceci, S. (1985), Semantic priming effects for stimuli presented to the right and the left visual fields, *Brain and language*, 25, 144-159.

Wapner, W., Hamby, S., & Gardner, H. (1981), The role of the right hemisphere in the apprehension of complex linguistic materials, *Brain and language*, 14, 15-33.

Warrington, E., Taylor, A. (1979), Two categorical stages of object recognition, *Perception*, 7, 697-705

Warrington, E., Shallice, T. (1984), Category-specific semantic impairments, *Brain*, 107, 829-854

Wattenmaker, W., Dewey, G., Murphy, T., Medin, D. (1986), Linear separability and concept learning: Context, relational properties, and concept naturalness, *Cognitive Psychology*, 18, 158-194

Weisstein, R., Harris, C. (1974), Visual detection of line segments: an object superiority effect, *Science*, 186, 752-755

Whitaker, H., Ojemann, G. (1977), Lateralization of the higher cortical functions: a critique. In S. Dimond, D. Blizard (Eds.) Evolution and lateralization of the brain. *Annals of the New York Academy of Sciences*, 299, 459-473.

Whitney, P., Kellas, G. (1984), Processing category terms in context: instantiation and the structure of semantic categories, *Journal of experimental psychology: Learning, Memory and Cognition*, 10, 95-103

Winston, P. (1970), Learning structural descriptions from examples, AI Laboratory, MIT, Technical report no.231, Reprinted (1975) in: *The psychology of computer vision*, Winston, S. (ed.), Mc Graw Hill

Wittgenstein, L. (1953), *Philosophical investigations*, 3rd edition, Mc Millan

Woodward, S. (1988). An anatomical model of hemispheric asymmetry, *Journal of clinical and experimental neuropsychology*, 10, 68.

Younger, B. (1985), The segregation of items into categories by ten-month-old infants, *Child Development*, 56, 1574-1583

Younger, B., Cohen, L. (1983), Infant perception of correlations among attributes, *Child Development*, 54, 858-867

Zaidel, D. (1990), Long-term semantic memory in the two hemispheres. In C. Trevarthen (Ed.), *Brain circuits and functions of the mind* (pp. 266-280). Cambridge: Cambridge University Press.

Zaidel, E. (1978), Auditory language comprehension in the right hemisphere. In P. Buser, A. Rougel-Buser (Eds.), *Cerebral correlates of conscious experience* (pp. 177-197). Amsterdam: Elsevier-North Holland Biomedical Press.

Zaidel, E. (1982), Reading by the disconnected hemisphere: An aphasiological perspective. In Y. Zotterman (Ed.), *Dyslexia: Neuronal, cognitive and linguistic aspects* (pp. 67-91). Oxford: Pergamon Press.

Zaidel, E. (1983), Dysconnection syndrome as a model for laterality effects in the normal brain. In J. Hellige, (Ed.), *Cerebral hemisphere asymmetry: Method, theory and application* (pp 95-151). New York: Praeger.

Zaidel, E. (1985), Language in the right hemisphere. In D. Benson, E. Zaidel (Eds.), *The dual brain* (pp. 205-231). New York: Guilford Press.

Zaidel, E. (1986), Callosal dynamics and right hemisphere language. In F. Lepore, M. Ptito, H. Jasper (Eds.), *Two hemispheres: one brain* (pp 435-462). New York: Alan Liss.

Springer-Verlag
and the Environment

We at Springer-Verlag firmly believe that an international science publisher has a special obligation to the environment, and our corporate policies consistently reflect this conviction.

We also expect our business partners – paper mills, printers, packaging manufacturers, etc. – to commit themselves to using environmentally friendly materials and production processes.

The paper in this book is made from low- or no-chlorine pulp and is acid free, in conformance with international standards for paper permanency.

Printing: Weihert-Druck GmbH, Darmstadt
Binding: Buchbinderei Schäffer, Grünstadt

Lecture Notes in Artificial Intelligence (LNAI)

Lecture Notes in Computer Science